INTERNAL CONFLICTS
A FOUR STATE ANALYSIS

(India, Nepal, Sri Lanka and Myanmar)

INTERNAL CONFLICTS
A FOUR STATE ANALYSIS

(India, Nepal, Sri Lanka and Myanmar)

Editor

V R Raghavan

Vij Books India Pvt Ltd

New Delhi (India)

Published by

Vij Books India Pvt Ltd

2/19, Ansari Road, Darya Ganj
New Delhi - 110002
Phones: 91-11-47340674, 91-11- 43596460
Fax: 91-11-47340674
e-mail : vijbooks@rediffmail.com
web : www.vijbooks.com

© 2013, Centre for Security Analysis, Chennai, India

Centre for Security Analysis
"9-B" Ninth Floor,
Chesney Nilgiri, 71, Ethiraj Salai,
Egmore, Chennai-600008
Tamil Nadu, India
+91-44-65291889
office@csa-chennai.org
www.csa-chennai.org

The views and opinions presented in this book are of the author(s) of the chapters in the book and not necessarily that of the Centre for Security Analysis, Chennai, India.

First Published : 2013

Paperback Edition 2015

This book is meant for educational and learning purposes, the editor of the book has taken all reasonable care to ensure that the contents of the book do not violate any existing copyright or other intellectual property rights of any person in any manner whatsoever. In the event the editor has been unable to track any source and if any copyright has been inadvertently infringed, please notify the publisher in writing for the corrective action.

Contents

Acknowledgement

The Centre for Security Analysis (CSA) has undertaken a three year research project **Internal Conflicts and Transnational Consequences** supported by the John D and Catherine T MacArthur Foundation. This volume is part of the ongoing project and its publication has been possible by the project grant.

Foreword

The Centre for Security Analysis (CSA) has been engaged in analysing internal conflicts in South and Southeast Asia with special emphasis on the consequences of such conflicts. This is a new approach to conflict management and subsequent resolution. Instead of focusing on the causes of the conflicts alone, CSA explored the consequences of the protracted conflicts – Northeast of India, Jammu and Kashmir, Naxalism, Myanmar, Nepal and Sri Lanka to examine the way consequences undermine the states' efforts to bring stability, development and peace in the region. Longstanding consequences over the years have become causes for continuing the conflict. The long term consequences have been felt in all spheres of life – economy, governance, politics and the social fabric of the state, so much so that over a period of time they become drivers of the conflict. A generation or two of citizens born and grown in the conflict environment eventually become stakeholders of the conflict. Some stakeholders do not necessarily welcome a solution instead prefer to prolong the conflict as its continuation serves their interests. During the course of the conflict, some stakeholders from a section of the society and government with an entrepreneurial mind tend to develop stakes for themselves. For some, the status quo syndrome takes over, for they have not seen any other scenario and cannot visualize a more peaceful and stable society given their mental and physical experiences.

Six conflict specific studies done on four countries have established that there are three major variables that stand out in all the internal conflicts. The first being ethnic/cultural/linguistic/sub-national identity. The four countries studied are multi-ethnic, multi- lingual, multi-religious. Though ethnicity/ identity politics is seldom a sole cause for conflicts but it serves as a rallying point and many other causes tend to be seen with an ethnic prism. Ethnic groups get involved in horizontal conflicts with other groups or in vertical conflicts with the government over cultural, political self-determination or the redistribution of economic rights. Basically it has turned out to be a struggle for power based on presumed moral rights. The management of ethnicity and its related issues therefore become a critical part of conflict resolution.

The second variable is the economic cause and consequence of the conflict. A study on how and what role did the economic conditions play in aggravating the conflict, its direct and indirect consequences on the society and state at large has been examined by experts separately. The third relates to the manner, methodologies and pattern of the political management of the conflict. A popular view is that resolving conflict is a prerequisite to political stability, which in turn, is essential for implementing pro-growth policies. Internal conflict constrains the policies which the governments can implement to promote growth. While this is an ideal approach it is also often impractical. Such conflicts go on for decades. An early effort to address the consequences of socio-political-economic development during the course of the conflict offers a more realistic approach.

With this in mind, CSA has moved on to the next phase of the study to identify clusters of causes and political management practices so that policy pointers could be identified. The four countries being studied have different forms of governance, viz, India is a liberal democracy with a parliamentary system, Sri Lanka is a presidential form of system with highly centralized governance, Myanmar is managed by a military junta in civilian clothes, and Nepal was a monarchy, presently transiting into democracy in chaos. The different political measures adopted by these countries range from use of police/ armed forces to maintain law and order in conflict areas, conducting negotiations, signing peace accords and agreements, and economic & development programs. How have the four different governing systems addressed the ethnic and political dimensions of internal conflicts is a matter worth analysing through a comparative framework.

CSA engaged experts from India, Nepal, Myanmar and Sri Lanka to analyse different facets of the ethnic/identity politics and political management of the consequences. These research papers were presented at a meeting and discussed with many other experts, experienced administrators and academics. This is an edited volume of these papers. The book will be a useful tool in the hands of policy makers, scholars and students alike.

V R Raghavan
Lt Gen (Retd)
President,
Centre for Security Analysis

1

Introduction

Geeta Madhavan

The central objective of this compendium on conflict situation is the case study of internal conflict in four states viz India, Sri Lanka, Nepal and Burma. The purpose is to analyse the several factors that have given rise to a situation wherein such conflicts become inevitable. Although much literature already exists on these issues, the papers contained in this volume go beyond the obvious and immediate reasons and make an attempt to de-link the startling obvious and conspicuous from the deeper reasons. No conflict arises over minor issues; conflicts are the result of long and distressing actions on the part of one or more actors. These result in the often violent actions that translate the grievances in a manner that often results in drawing battle lines between the state machinery and the affected section of that society. The papers in this book are by those who have understood the conflict situations by going beyond the obvious and have underlined those elements that have caused the marginalities which have driven the conflict. The reasons for the resurgence of conflict in each of these cases have been described as those arising from the fact that the basic issues that created the initial conflict were not explored for their root causes; instead a superficial peace processes were initiated which left these causes simmering just below the surface waiting to erupt.

The paper on Kashmir by B G Verghese is the retelling of the historical events that have led to the current situation of turmoil in Kashmir. The entire course of events that thrust India and Pakistan into confrontational mode has been discussed in great detail. The paper examines the myths that have evolved and the historical realities of the conflict in Kashmir. Mr Verghese traces the creation of the two sovereign states – India and Pakistan in 1947 and the subsequent events that led to the creation of fear and mistrust between the two states. This paper explains how the horror of Partition, the

British conceptualization of Pakistan as a western frontline state and as an ally exacerbated the situation in the early days .The detailed narration of the political events from Partition to present date and the military actions from the 1947 raid on Kashmir by Pakistan to the Kargil war are based on documented and published papers. Verghese points out that Pakistan turned aggressor and in direct contravention of the principles of international law and with its plan to annex Jammu and Kashmir moved its forces into the territory of an independent sovereign state. The paper in detail recounts all the events thereafter: from the creation of the new state of Bangladesh from the erstwhile East Pakistan up till Pakistan's posturing with the use of the unfortunate terminology "Islamic Bomb" when it turned into a nuclear weapon state and its constant support of terrorism through the ISI and the several terrorist attacks against India. The paper deals with the apparent shift in US policy regarding Pakistan post 9/11 and USA's pressure on Pakistan to curtail terrorism within its territory. The terror connections that Pakistan's army had which were continually denied, till the shocking revelations with the US operation on May 2, 2011 against Osama Bin laden which revealed to the global community the level of complicity of the Pakistan army and the jihadists. The paper argues that the Kashmir issue is an entanglement that only the two states can unravel – but it is imperative that they seriously work towards the unravelling, for on that action depends the peace and stability of the region. Calling the Kashmir issue the *cause celebre* of the Pakistan army and the Islamic fundamental clergy, the paper states that if India is not viewed as a major threat nor Kashmir as the core issue , the two states can move closer in a manner that would prove beneficial to both the countries and lead to the economic growth across the borders for the entire region. The paper recommends joint exploration of natural resources, construction and management of hydro-electric generation projects and storages, better sharing of waters by the proper utilisation in accordance with the Indus treaty which would bind the two sides. Pakistan and India both have a stake in the stability and reconstruction of Afghanistan but instead of parrying on those grounds, peace should start with an Indo-Pak dialogue on Afghanistan which should develop cross border institutions and arrangements for cooperative developments. Projects like Iran-Pakistan-India and the Turkmenistan-Afghanistan-Pakistan-India pipelines, water resources developments and the building of many such infrastructures have been highlighted in the paper as the perfect means of moving forward a south Asia peace plan. The paper suggests two roles: usage of soft power and a new pro –active role. Revitalising the state of Jammu and Kashmir by investing in infrastructures which promotes community development, tourism, industry and economic activity and interstate and intra state connectivity viz four lane highways, power grids, optic fibre highway etc. The paper concludes with Mr Verghese pointing out that the opportunities that provide solutions to the problem are available and with the exhortation to seize the opportunities.

The paper by Rekha Chowdhary deals with the multiple and diverse identities that have socio-political impact in the conflict situation in Kashmir. The paper speaks of the several layers of identities that overlap the core issues adding to the complexity of the conflict, making composite resolution that much more difficult. The paper points out that the overlapping identities based on religion, region, caste as well as tribal identities make it clear that the lines along which "majority" or "minority " have thus far been understood are completely blurred. The problem, the paper argues , is that all stakeholders claim assets as majority and their right to it but also make claims of being the discriminated minority. The paper is divided into five sections each dealing in great detail with each complexity and the effect of each feature on the conflict.

The first section in which the diverse and multiple layers are examined states rather clearly that the several layers enmesh to create a demographic complexity that refutes the claims of majority or minority of any one section. Rather than being identified along the lines of religion as Hindus, Muslims; the identification is additionally made as those belonging to Kashmir, Jammu or Ladakh. The identity markers, therefore, are multi-layered and while some identities are parallel, others cut across the familiar lines. The other issues include the conflict between India and Pakistan, the internal dimension of the relationship of the state of Jammu and Kashmir with the Indian central government and the intra-state dimension wherein the conflict in Kashmir impacts the neighbouring Indian states.

The paper traces in the second section the Kashmir identity politics from 1953 where it is stated that the intention was to bring Kashmir on par with the other states of the Indian union. The historical developments since 1953 and each connecting event, according to the paper, led to the outcome in terms of the stages in which they evolved: the political struggle, leading to the inception of the jihadi movement and at present emerging into the form of the mass uprisings. However, with all these forms of calling for the "final resolution" and "azadi", the future of Kashmir does not seem to be clearly defined by the various organisations and their supporters. The third section of the paper underlines the connection between the conflict in Kashmir and its impact on Jammu and Ladakh. With the constant focus being on the Kashmir question and national attention trained on the issues affecting Kashmir, the other two parts are subjected to the asymmetrical Kashmir-specific infrastructure planning and growth. The other matters of concern vis-à-vis Jammu and Ladakh are issues of displacement and the question of the status of refugees. The fourth section details the plurality, political diversity and the divergences within the Kashmir and states that although there had been instances where not enough sensitivity had been shown but recent sensitivity has developed around the multiple stakeholders. The final part of the paper deals with the political future of Kashmir. The paper recommends that the politically divergent and conflicting claims require going beyond the division of the state on religious and regional lines; therefore, carving out the state on communal lines without understanding the complex layers will not solve any of the problems and recommends a process of consensus building through inclusive dialogue with all the different players.

The paper on the changing contours of armed violence in Northeast India by Nani Gopal Mahanta traces the armed rebellions in this region from the colonial days to the present. The North East region comprising of the seven states – Assam, Arunachal Pradesh, Meghalaya, Manipur, Mizoram, Nagaland and Tripura and the eighth state of Sikkim. These states are connected to mainland India by a slim stretch of land (2%) while they share 4500 km borders with other South and South East Asian countries with whom they have close historical linkages. With almost 115 armed rebel groups several active and some inactive and some secessionists operating in this region, the Indian state has had to deal with insurgency in various forms. This paper enumerates the various groups – secessionists who wish to establish independent homelands, those who seek autonomous states or separate states, groups that fight among themselves to form the dominant group and establish their tribal or caste power, the tribal groups that also seek dominance and space and entitlements under the Indian Constitution, the irredentists who demand a homeland that would require the reformation of states in a manner that would give them greater power within that territory. Their common goal is, however, defined as an attempt to ensure maximum allocation of resources and to achieve maximum benefits.

The first part of the paper deals specifically with ULFA and offers insight into the group and its transition from one demanding autonomy to its present form. The indiscriminate use of violence finally propelled the group towards Pakistan and China who provided them with training, arms and logistic support. Bhutan, Bangladesh and Nepal provided safe havens. The paper then examines the causes why these states provided such support and how pressure from the Indian government and the events within these countries and the policy changes there led to the stoppage of sympathy and support for these groups. India was able to prevail upon Myanmar and Bhutan to close down camps, withdraw all logistic support and prevent movements across the border. The extent to which Bangladesh played a role in the ULFA's activities is also set forth in great detail. The paper is a collection of documented reports and has copious notes on the working of ULFA. The paper concludes by making clear that the militant organizations that started out as organisations reflecting the grievances of the people they represented eventually metamorphosed into outfits that made substantial compromises on their autonomy. Although Mr Mahanta explains that it is not a simple transition from grievance to greed; groups like the ULFA have alienated themselves from the masses by compromising their ideals for neo terrorism.

The paper by Samir Kumar Das is a comprehensive account of the how peace was brought to vast areas of the North East India and the spin off of the process of pacification. Although, the paper explains, the pacification seems to have worked to some extent in certain areas, newer and more complex issues have evolved from the process of pacification itself. Therefore, the earlier methods of pacification appear not only out-dated but also inadequate in the given newer conflicts. The paper chooses as case study the issues in the states of Mizoram and Assam.

Taking the case of the Mizoram, the paper traces the history of Mizoram from the independence of India, when the question arose whether it should be a part of the Union of India. Famine struck the Mizoram areas in 1958, but the manner in which the Assam administration handled the issue triggered the movement for Mizo independence. The Mizo National Famine Front was formed in 1960 and soon the organisation became the MNF with demands for an independent and sovereign state of Mizoram. The paper traces the stages of growing militancy in Mizoram to the promulgation of the Armed Forces Special Powers Act (AFSPA) and the regrouping of the villages which led to forced migration and created a serious rift between the security forces and the Mizo population. All the political events that preceded the formation of the state of Mizoram have been described in detail and this portion of the paper concludes that in the case of Mizoram although a crisis like the famine was the root cause of the militancy, once formulated the insurgency easily slipped into the political role, demanding independence and redefining its charter to pursue other claims. The new areas of conflict that have emerged in Mizoram are based on the socioeconomic problems. The Mizo accord which should have brought peace and growth to the state revealed, instead the deep dissensions and discord in the Mizo society. The inflow of money from the Centre for the reconstruction of the state in terms of infrastructure and for economic growth created rifts between the various ethnic groups of the Mizo society who felt marginalized. In some cases the violence reflected distrust of the Mizos towards those smaller communities and minorities they consider as outsiders.

In the case of Assam the paper traces how an anti-foreigner movement changed into an insurgent movement. The six-year long movements against the migrant population had three objectives: identifying the foreigners, depriving them their rights and privileges of being citizens and deporting them. After an intense study of the course of the accord between the Indian government and the various factions and leaders of the movements in Assam, the paper shifts the focus to the reappearance of the conflict. The reason set out in the paper is that the problems that lead to the conflict were not resolved, instead they became marginalized. Disarming militant non state actors and peace talks do not seem to address the core issues. Military operation followed by accords and agreements and the development of the state with huge amounts of financial assistance do not solve the core issues. Instead the paper recommends that there should be public investment, tapping the natural resources of the region to benefit growth of the state under community ownership and control of the resources of the region.

The paper by Uddhab Pyakurel on the changing patterns of the ethnic movement Nepal explains in great detail the historical origins of the ethnic divisions of the people of Nepal. There are 59 identified ethnic groups in Nepal, each with their own mother tongue, customs and culture and a recent list (2010) has added more, increasing the number to 81. These ethnic groups form the crux of the problem of Nepal today as they variously fall into the categories of the privileged and advanced groups, the marginalized groups, the disadvantaged groups and the endangered groups. The paper is divided into 5 epochs and the political scenario that developed in each and its impact upon the ethnic groups of Nepal. The background history of the early kingdom of Nepal and the process of the Hinduisation of the people by the early dynastic rulers united Nepal but did so by coercion and forced assimilation of the ethnic groups. The introduction of Buddhism also had its impact on the people. The early rulers used religion and forces to unify all the outer regions and forge it into a single state. The Regime of the Ranas accelerated the growth of Hinduism and various acts of the succeeding monarchs which alienated and ignored the aspirations of the multi ethnic groups led to several revolts.

The period form 1951-60 has been identified in this paper as the pseudo democratic period where much was promised along democratic principles but very little was actually acted upon. Autocracy under the guise of democracy continued and minor concessions were made that did not address the core issues that affected the ethnic groups. During the period 1960-1990 the panchayati regime was established with absolute monarchy and the ethos of a single religion, single language and single dress. This was widely resented by all those ethnic groups who saw this as a final stroke to completely destroy their identity and their culture. Further forced internal migration under the guise of national assimilation was deeply resented and it paved the way for the Maoists to enter the socio-political chaos with the promise of hope. After 30 years of autocratic regime the need for a democratic set up to address ethnic, lingual and cultural issues led to the ethnic awakening. Since then various governments have tried to establish a government that is acceptable to all ethnic groups but have failed, as the paper concludes, due to their inability to structure a government that follows a federal structure based on ethnicity with complete autonomy for the provinces. Social inclusion of all the ethnic groups however, Pyakurel fears may lead to fragmentation into numerous provinces which in turn would lead to territorial clashes based on historical claims and claims of majority. The paper concludes that the only way out of the deep mire would be a comprehensive intense discussion with all stakeholders and not ad hoc solutions, as it seem to be happening at present, which has only led to further complicating the existing chaos.

The thrust of the paper on Nepal's armed conflict by Chiran Jung Thapa is the political mismanagement that has given rise to the current situation of uncertainty in Nepal. According to the paper, it was the mishandling by the ruling political class that started the armed confrontation which has resulted in the ensuing chaos. The paper sets out the chronological events that led to the Maoist insurrection. That armed conflict began with the launch of the People's War in 1996 but the Maoist movement began much earlier with the formation of the communist parties that opposed the autocratic rule of the monarchs. The paper refers to the palace massacre as being the turning point and the declaration of emergency as the watershed in Nepal politics.

Thapa does not consider economic grievances, marginalization and lack of governance as being the root causes that have led to armed conflict in Nepal. The paper moves beyond the social economic factors that form the background to the conflict and explores the other reasons systematically. The first cause stated is the mismanagement of the political leaders and their self-centred political agendas. Thus the resentment between the leader of the Nepali congress leader Mr Koirala and the communist forces resulted in state repression. The subsequent string of governments failed to fulfil the aspirations of the people and provided the Maoists with their support base. The monarchy's lack of understanding of the true needs of the people aided the Maoists to not only protest against the monarchy as feudal and repressive but also describe India as an expansionist and imperialist state which supported the King. The paper blames not only Koirala's personal ambition for the downfall of the government but also the lack of understanding of the government of the seriousness of the Maoist threat. Considering the armed conflict as simply a law and order problem, they underestimated the effect it would have on Nepal's political scene. The paper outlines the number of opportunities that arose which could have been used to resolve the armed conflict and how each one of them was completely misread and no genuine attempt was made for the resolution of the conflict. The peace talks thus became only half-hearted attempts to solve the problems. The next part of the paper deals with the intercession of India quoting various scholars and documents. The paper concludes with the emerging challenges for sustainable peace viz. the drafting of the Constitution, the re integration and rehabilitation of the of the Maoist combatants and the re-structuring of the state apparatus. The post conflict period also has seen proliferation of armed groups, increase in criminal activities, and the lack of effective judiciary and these are serious problems highlighted in the paper. The paper concludes with the observation that although significant changes have been made in the political scene in Nepal the tussles of the political parties with each other and within themselves has lead to a period of grave uncertainty for the people of Nepal.

The paper on the ethnicity in the post war Sri Lanka deals with the issues of prompting mutual trust among the various communities which make up the Sri Lankan society. Kalinga Tudor Silva's paper critically examines the post war concentration of the military in the Northern and Eastern provinces which has created new problems for the people of the region who have been victims of the long period of conflict. The Rajapakse regime which was very successful in militarily defeating the LTTE does not seem to be very successful in creating political and social trust in the region. The ensuing presence of the large military force, although engaged in rebuilding the physical infrastructures during the war, is unable to win the trust or confidence of the people in the region because, the paper argues, the participation of the affected minorities has not been sought. Further the policies that seem to flow from Colombo have only limited impact in these areas as the policies seem to favour particular individuals. Therefore, the Tamil politicians who have joined the mainstream politics are not trusted by the ethnic Tamil minority and the other Tamil parties that remain outside seem to be only critical of the policies without garnering any substantial benefits for the people of the war torn region. During the war, ethnic polarization took place by the displacement of people fleeing from the area as well as relocation by coercion and the post war effect of that is the mutual suspicion not only among the Sinhalese vis-à-vis the Tamils but also between the Tamils and the Muslims and the Sinhala and the Muslims. The paper cites two reasons for the fear factor in the Tamil areas – the first, the substantial military presence of the Sinhala speaking soldiers who are distrusted by the Tamil civil population and second, the demographic deficit of the male population which has led to insecurity among the Tamil civilians. Religious intolerance and suspicions of destruction of religious identity based on several actions both by the government and the majority sections of the society are also discussed with the aid of graphs. The paper underlines that outside the war zone the ethnic lines are not severe. In conclusion Silva recommends that state policies and programmes and the actions of the Tamil political parties should work relentlessly for ethnic reconciliation and not resort to actions to prevent its progress. The paper suggests that to promote trust the gradual withdrawal of the military, focus on social justice and social inclusion and the preservation of religious and cultural diversity.

The paper on Sri Lanka by Jayadeva Uyangoda deals with the role of the state in Sri Lanka's ethnic conflict. The paper argues that although the conflict in Sri Lanka has its basis in ethnic inequalities, the underpinnings of the entire conflict arises from the contest for power and this contest has emerged in the form of denial of minority rights and power sharing- in the process nation building and state building. When the ethnic conflict acquired military overtones the entire power sharing dynamics changed and led to the protracted armed conflict. The paper describes by tracing the various political actions by successive governments, how the conflict coalesced because of the the State's approaches to several important issues of citizenship and by the fact that public policies were shaped by sectional and parochial interests. The gradual escalation of the conflict in the early years was also the result of the political processes viz the Republican Constitution of 1972, which the paper sets out as the root cause for political marginalization as it established a unitary and highly centralized state that did not require the support of the ethnic parties. This forced the Tamil leaders to abandon the hope of regional autonomy and to set forth secessionist goals.The intensification of war led to the total militarization as sharing state power became unacceptable to the Sri Lankan establishment and this in turn made a political solution an impossibility. The paper refers to the various overtures for peace between the parties made by third party negotiators but offers the explanation that all the talks failed as the State was unwilling to share power and the LTTE was unwilling to settle for anything less. Therefore all the five attempts to negotiate peaceful settlement failed. Uyangoda argues that the talks resulted not in ways to explore mutually acceptable solutions but rather to measure the impossibility of any solution. Thus the conflict not only resumed but also got redefined. The 2002 peace initiative produced negative reactions from the Sri Lankan government to the proposals of the LTTE; the debate on sharing state power intensified denying possibility of devolution or minimalist power sharing. The political debate was further abandoned in favour of a military solution. The paper concludes with the argument that it was the lack of political reform and far sightedness which led to the ethnic conflict but the end of the armed conflict has resulted in a hardened stance of the State which does not permit any room for political solutions. Reasoning that economic development of the war torn areas will solve the problems, the Sri Lankan government has set the building of physical infrastructures on a fast pace but the paper argues that this will not achieve much unless there are political reforms for regional autonomy and devolution.

The paper on ethnic conflicts in Burma by Lian H. Sakhong deals with the ethnic conflict in Burma and relates the events from the Panglong Agreement of 1947 when the several ethnic groups voluntarily agreed to form a Union on the principles of association, political equality and the right to internal self-determination. However, their hope for a decentralized power structure was soon shattered when the single ethnic group called the Burmans took over the control of all the state powers and governing structures and instead of state building where all ethnic groups would share power, adopted the policy of nation building by forced assimilation of all the ethnic groups. Successive governments continued the policy by forcing and implementing the principle of "one nation, one religion, one language". Thus, Buddhism became the state religion in 1961 and by legislation and control only the

Burmese language was permitted for publications etc. Writings in any of the languages of the various ethnic groups became illegal. Continuous assault on the ethnic groups like the Arakan, Chin, Kachin, Karen, Karenni, Mon and Shan and other smaller groups who constituted almost 40 percent of the population and who occupied 60 percent of the territory led to ethnic armed conflict in the process of what the paper in detail explains as "state formation conflict". Tracing the history of how each successive Burmese governments were hostile to the ethnic multi culturalism of the country, the paper enumerates three causes as being at the core of the conflict: the national language policy, the military regime that created national integration by forced assimilation ignoring their multi ethnic fabric of the Burmese society and finally the changing of the name from Burma to Myanmar reiterating the ethnic assimilation. The Union Constitution of 1947 was revised to end the policy of pluralism and the paper describes in detail how subsequent actions by the government of U Nu and General Ne Win alienated the ethnic communities further. The Tatmadaw was used by General Ne Win to implement his "four-cut" strategy to deal with the armed insurgent groups and alienate them from the people and to cut off all contact with the local population. The 1974 Constitution of General Ne Win ended the division between the state, the army and the party and Burma became isolated from the world community creating an economic downfall that resulted in great hardship for the people. The paper explains the emergence of the National League for Democracy (NLD) and its role in the political scene in Burma. However, despite winning the election with 80 percent majority the NLD were not allowed to form a government and through several measures including house arrest of the leaders and other repressive measures the Tatmadaw ensured that the military controlled the legislature. By the promulgation of the 2008 constitution, martial hold on the country intensified. In conclusion, Sakhong states that although the military junta have declared the seven steps to democracy, and few changes seem to be on the way much more has to be done to secure rights to the people. The might of the armed insurgents fighting to secure these rights has also increased and the formation in 2011 of the United Nationalities' Federal Council indicates that the ethnic groups are not ready to give up their struggle until they can secure for themselves the right to practise and preserve their ethnic culture, religion and language.

The attempt of the various papers in this volume is to analyse each case in its own peculiar cultural and ethnic context and in that attempt some common factors emerge. It is a sociological need for all humans to be assured of their ethnic right and their capacity to determine how they should rule themselves. Internal self-determination is on the one hand claimed as a basic right by the ethnic groups; on the other hand, state machinery that pledges itself to nation building as its primary objective is not inclined to accept the diverse elements which are perceived as tearing apart the unity and integrity of its territorial might. The answer to the question, therefore, lies not in espousing the cause of one side as being more reasonable or as being the more acceptable but being able to seek solutions that are more acceptable. Hardening stances have lent themselves to prolonging the conflicts and creating newer and more complex causes as time passes. Long drawn conflicts shift focus and although the core reason for the conflict endures, the shift creates more complications for the state machinery to deal with. State building, therefore, where aspirations of the ethnic people can be addressed should be viewed as far more important than nation building, that is to say it is more apt if decentralized power sharing is seen as the core duty of the state than the continuation of a centralized all powerful unitary system.

2

Kashmir Retold: Towards
A South Asian Peace

B G Verghese

The Kashmir Question is often seen as a dangerous nuclear flash point aggravated by the Af-Pak imbroglio. It has got so tangled in myth, malice and partisanship that many perceptions can scare, be reconciled with ground realities. Uniquely, the aggressor has been placed on the same pedestal as its victim and even portrayed as the injured party. "Kashmir" is a cancer eating the vitals of Pakistan while it troubles India acutely too. Even if myth has become reality, perceptions matter and must be addressed.

The Kashmir Question is uniquely less an Indo-Pakistan problem than a Pakistan-Pakistan problem. Unless this riddle wrapped in an enigma is resolved one will continue to be locked in circular arguments.

This long standing matter is possibly nearer resolution than most imagine, as ground realities are more clearly perceived all round. But one needs to think ahead rather than rehearse the past if the opportunity is to be grasped. It is usually best to begin at the beginning and look at what in fact is the "core" problem as Pakistan likes to describe Kashmir. This is not to get locked in the past but to learn from it and move on. Both Pakistan and India need to be satisfied as well as the people of J&K as a whole. This is possible and could fulfil the hope that the two estranged brothers who separated in 1947 might thereafter live together as sovereign neighbours.

The tragedy is that the Muslim League cast Pakistan's identity in a negative mould, as India's "other". The "ideology of Pakistan" posited the new nation in opposition to a permanent "enemy", Hindu India, that official school texts teach Pakistani children to hate. This has found territorial expression in the contrived narrative of a "moth-eaten Pakistan" minus

J&K. epitomised by J&K's allegedly fraudulent severance from its rightful place as the crown of the new Islamic state. This image remains etched in ideological memory. It remains the essence of the Kashmir "dispute", rather than Pakistan's strenuous efforts to annex the state by force and subterfuge in 1947 and thereafter.

Though professedly an Islamic State, Pakistan has been unable to define Islam. The Munir Commission inquiring into the 1953 anti-Ahmediya riots lamented:

"… that the ulema (of Pakistan)…. were hopelessly disagreed among themselves…. The net result of all of this is that neither Shias nor Sunnis nor Deobandis nor Ahl-i-Hadith nor Barelvis are Muslims….".

Today, an Islamist Pakistan, radicalised with Saudi money, stands opposed to the Shias, Aga Khanis, sufis and other schools of Islam. The soft, humanistic Islam of South Asia, the largest and most advanced Muslim community in the world, is being called upon to "save" Islam from Christian, Jewish and Hindu hegemony! In the process, Pakistan has mortgaged its soul to defend Islam and reclaim "Kashmir" and fallen prey to the military-mullah-feudal combine that rules the roost.

The 1857 Uprising or Great Revolt was a turning point, marking the end of 800 years of Muslim supremacy in India. The ensuing era of modernisation and graduated democratic reform under the Raj saw Muslims retreat into a shell. An increasingly non-competitive Muslim minority feared eclipse. Hence the sense of victimhood and the demand for separate electorates and parity between the Muslim and Hindu 'nations' despite the vast disparity in relative numbers. A secular Jinnah tactically adopted the pernicious two-nation theory to leverage Pakistan and the British pandered to this sentiment through a policy of divide and rule.

Pakistan won, Jinnah was quick to realize the inherent contradictions in its founding ideology as it remained a plural state. Addressing the inaugural session of the nation's constituent assembly in Karachi on August 11, 1947, he essentially denounced the two nation theory.

Now that Pakistan was won, Jinnah told his people, "If you change your past and work together in a spirit that every one of you, no matter to what community he belongs, no matter what relations he had with you in the past, no matter what his colour, caste or creed, is first, second and last a citizen of this state with equal rights, privileges and obligations, there will be no end to the progress you will make.....

Further, "you are free to go to your temples, you are free to go to your mosques or any other place of worship in this state of Pakistan. You may belong to any religion, caste or creed – that has nothing to do with the business of the State. ....."

However, it was too late. The dragon seed of mistrust and hate, sown with Jinnah's call to "direct action" in 1946, had led to a harvest of communal horror, killing hundreds of thousands and, at final count, displacing some 20 million people both ways. The homily was repudiated by the new ruling elite of Pakistan. Jinnah later reversed gear and on January 24, 1948 told the Karachi Bar Association that the constitution would be based on the Sharia "to make Pakistan a truly great Islamic state".

By now, plans were under way clandestinely to annex Jammu and Kashmir. With official backing from the very top, tribal invaders officered, armed and logistically supported by the Pakistan Army, entered the state on October 20, 1947. Apart from irrefutable contemporary evidence, the full story was revealed by Akbar Khan, then Director, Weapons and Equipment, GHQ Pakistan, later promoted Chief of Staff in the rank of Major General, in his book "Raiders in Kashmir" (first published in Pakistan and subsequently republished by the Army Press, Delhi in 1990). The Kashmir jihad had commenced.

Britain had long back vested the Muslim League with a veto. A series of post-Second World War strategic studies undertaken in London favoured retaining influence over eastern and north-western India in order to contain communism and control over the Gulf's oil resources. This is elaborated in Narendra Singh Sarila's "The Shadow of the Great Game: The Untold Story of Partition" (2009) which details Britain's conceptualization of Pakistan as a Western "frontline" state.

Pakistan's adventure in J&K is documented from declassified British archival papers in Chandrashekhar Dasgupta's "War and Diplomacy in

Kashmir" (2001). By 1949-50, the US had written off India as a Soviet ally under cover of non-alignment and by 1953 Pakistan had formally become a formal frontline military and strategic ally in the Cold War, granting the US an air base in Peshawar and subsequently joining the Central Treaty Organisation (CENTO) and the South East Asian Treaty Organisation (SEATO).

The Security Council's consideration of the Kashmir Question was vitiated by cold war predilections. Indian appeals to principles and Pakistan's aggression went unheeded. What mattered was whose side you were on.

Sir Owen Dixon, the UN Representative for India and Pakistan, formally reported in 1950 that:

"When the frontier of the State of J&K was crossed on, I believe, October 20, 1947, by hostile elements, it was contrary to international law and when, as I believe, units of the regular Pakistan forces moved into the territory of the State, that too was inconsistent to international law....".

Howsoever politely stated, the finding was one of aggression against what had on August 15, 1947 become an independent, sovereign state. The J&K Maharaja appealed to India for military assistance. This was refused until the State acceded to India with the backing of the popular leader Sheikh Abdullah on October 26. Indian troops were flown to the Valley the next morning, just in time to repel the invaders from the gates of Srinagar. If the airport had fallen, all would have been lost.

The UN Commission for India and Pakistan (UN) constituted in January 1948 called on sides to report "any material change". The UNCIP travelled leisurely to Karachi on July 7, 1948 to be greeted with a "bombshell". Pakistan officially informed it that three of its brigades had entered J&K in May allegedly to prevent the Indian spring offensive spilling into Pakistan proper. However, the Pakistan Army was soon knocking at the doors of Leh hundreds of miles to the east, taking over a huge swathe of Baltistan in Ladakh !

A Security Council resolution on August 13, 1948 proposed a Ceasefire (Part I) that would bar any augmentation of armed forces regular or irregular; followed by a Truce (Part II), calling for a wholesale withdrawal of all

Pakistani forces and tribal invaders from J&K. The territory so evacuated was to be administered by the Local Authorities of the State under the surveillance of UNCIP with such Indian military assistance as might be considered necessary by the Commission. After this phase was satisfactorily completed, the bulk of the Indian forces would be withdrawn from the State subject to such numbers as would be required to safeguard peace, law and order. Thus India's legal right to be in J&K (and its de facto sovereignty) was not questioned. Nevertheless, after implementation of Parts I and II of the Resolution, steps would be taken under Part III to ascertain the will of the people, as subsequently elaborated in a further UN Resolution dated January 5, 1949.

Two days after J&K's accession to India, the Gilgit Scouts, under Major Brown, a serving British officer seconded to J&K, staged a coup, imprisoned the J&K Governor of Gilgit and illegally "acceded" to Pakistan. Nagar, Hunza and other feudatories followed suit. "Azad Kashmir", itself dominated by the federal government through a Kashmir Affairs Council headed by the Prime Minister of Pakistan, ceded "temporary" control over the strategic Northern Areas to the Pakistan Government which has since engineered demographic changes (to bolster the Sunni minority) and virtually ruled it with few rights or representation.

Far from implementing Parts I and II of the August 13, 1948 UN Resolution, Pakistan brazenly consolidated its administrative and military position in J&K and entered into a military alliance with the US. The conditions for a plebiscite were never fulfilled and Part III of the 1948 Resolution remained a dead letter. It was in course of time rendered effete by political and demographic changes and Pakistan's unilateral and illegal cession of Shaksgam in northern J&K to China in 1963.

At every stage, Pakistan's stance was one of denial and defiance with Britain and the US looking the other way. India's discomfiture in the border conflict with China in 1962 followed by the death of Nehru in 1964 encouraged General Ayub Khan and his ambitious lieutenant, Zulfiqar Ali Bhutto to mount Operation Gibraltar in August 1965. Five columns of Pakistani military and irregulars under Gen. Akhtar Hussain Malik were detailed to cut India's lines of communication and trigger a mass uprising as a prelude to a major military offensive, Operation Grand Slam.

Not a man rose against India. The infiltrators were decimated and Operation Grand Slam was neutralized by an Indian offensive against Lahore. The UN Military Observer Group headed by Australian General Nimmo detailed Pakistan's violations, but to no avail. Its findings were scarcely debated in the UN, which turned to peace making, once again putting the aggressor and its victim on the same footing. Soviet intervention brought about an uneasy truce at Tashkent.

Pakistan was by now simmering, with East Pakistan chafing at its colonial status. All the provinces in West Pakistan had been unnaturally amalgamated into "One Unit" to balance East Pakistan whose majority was sought to be denied at any cost even after its clear electoral victory at the 1971 polls. The Awami League's Mujeeb-ur-Rahman demanded his democratic right to form the national government. The military responded with a pogrom. Bangali refugees streamed into India, which helped arm and train the Shanti Bahini. The West backed Pakistan, unmindful of the genocide. The infamous Nixon-Kissinger "tilt" went to the length of Washington seeking to instigate China to attack India to create a diversion and save East Pakistan with a US promise to intervene to fend off any Soviet riposte, an ugly facet revealed in Kissinger's later published "Personal Papers".

The war enveloped the western theatre. Pakistan was comprehensively defeated and General Niazi, the East Pakistan Commander, surrendered unconditionally to Lt Gen J .S Aurora, the Indian Eastern Army Commander on December 16, 1971. Bangladesh, which had proclaimed its independence on March 26 that year, was now truly independent. Bangali (cultural) nationalism had triumphed over Islamic nationalism, leaving the two-nation theory in tatters.

The Simla Agreement of 1972 converted the J&K Cease Fire Line into a political Line of Control (implicitly reaffirming the 1949 CFL delineation of its northern extremity from the last grid reference NJ 9842 "thence north to the glaciers" that clearly placed 90 per cent of the Siachen glacier on the Indian side of the LOC). Bhutto promised to settle the Kashmir question bilaterally and end anti-Indian propaganda to open a new chapter of friendly cooperation.

However, Bhutto had only to return home, to renege on his assurances and launch a secret programme to build a nuclear arsenal. Enter the notorious Dr A.Q Khan. This Pakistani nuclear metallurgist had pilfered critical nuclear designs from the multinational URENCO consortium facility in the Netherlands where he had worked, and now returned home to place his services at the disposal of Bhutto to help Pakistan build what was later touted as an "Islamic" bomb. A.Q Khan's cunning and deceit in accomplishing this task and his reckless nuclear proliferation have been well documented. The programme was overseen and facilitated by the Pakistan military with the connivance of the US. The Americans got Khan off the hook in 1983 when the Dutch caught him red-handed, as later publicly disclosed by the Netherlands Prime Minister, Ruud Lubbers and, like the British, came down heavily on officials who dared probe Pakistan's Faustian bargain too diligently. Pakistan's denials reached new heights.

By the 1980s, Pakistan was more advanced in nuclear weaponry than India and more than once used nuclear blackmail to launch its new strategy of cross-border terror in Kashmir and wider afield. This was climaxed by Musharraf's brazen Kargil operation, after the Indian Premier Vajpayee had taken a Friendship Bus to Lahore to meet Nawaz Sharif and initiate a new peace process. The gambit failed. Pakistan was roundly defeated along the Kargil heights and its mala fides and dangerous adventurism exposed. Naked but unashamed, Musharraf staged a coup.

This time the US put pressure on Pakistan and post-9/11 got Musharraf to promise not to allow Pakistani soil to be used for cross-border terror against India (or Afghanistan). The promise never held – the sorry plea being that by now Pakistan itself was a victim of terror and that non-state actors, long treated as "strategic assets", were involved.

Group Captain Kaiser Tufail, then director of operations, Pakistan Air Force, later recounted that the Pakistan Army planned to sever India's crucial lifeline to the Siachen-Leh sector.

"Come October, we shall walk into Siachen – to mop up the dead bodies of hundreds of Indians left hungry and out in the cold", remarked the 10th Corps Commander, Lt Gen Mahmud Ahmad, after the operation had commenced in mid-May. He had casually sought PAF air support, if necessary, from an astonished air command that had like others been kept out of the loop.[1]

And how and when did Siachen become a bone of contention? The delineation of the CFL/LOC has already been explained. Even as Pakistan kept extending its communications eastwards after its boundary agreement with China, the US Defence Mapping Agency started redrawing the CFL in this sector from around 1967, hardening an older Air Defence Information Zone line, separating air control jurisdictions, from NJ 9842 northeast to a point just short of the Karakoram Pass. This gratuitously incorporated 250 sq kms of Indian territory, including all of Siachen, within Pakistan-held J&K. The infraction went unnoticed until Pakistan started following suit. In 1984, India got wind of Pakistani plans to occupy Siachen and present it with a fait accompli. It acted to pre-empt such an eventuality by taking control of the glacier to establish the current Actual Ground Position Line (AGPL).

It was to "correct" this "anomaly" that General Musharraf contrived his Kargil caper. The US was decades later to admit informally through its Ambassador in Delhi that it had erred in redrawing the northernmost segment of the CFL. But there was no public retraction and international atlases continue to uphold the US Defence Mapping Agency's cartographic aggression in J&K. India, strangely, never protested.

Despite Kargil, India resumed the peace process. However, the Red Fort in Delhi, the J&K Assembly in Srinagar, the Indian Parliament, the Bombay stock exchange, and carefully selected economic, scientific and communally sensitive targets elsewhere were the subject of continuing jihadi terror strikes from Pakistan, combined with unabated cross-LOC infiltration into J&K. Earlier, Indian Airlines flight IC 814 was hijacked en route from Kathmandu to Delhi and diverted to Kandahar where, after the killing of one passenger, the rest were traded for three top jihadis incarcerated in India. The hijack was believed overseen by Mullah Omar, head of the Pakistan Taliban. Latter depredations were masterminded by the Lashkar-e-Toiba (LeT) led by Hafiz Saeed. The Indian Embassy in Kabul was also

---

[1] *The Indian Express*, 12 June 2009

twice bombed by Taliban elements close to Pakistan.

No sooner was the LeT listed as a terror organisation by the UN, than it changed its name to Jamaat-ud-Dawa and declared itself a charitable body. Hafiz Saeed was arrested, nominally tried and discharged only to continue plotting against India, culminating in the horrendous 26/11 terror attack on Mumbai. Pakistan has dragged its feet in investigating this dastardly crime, starting with denials and then pleading lack of hard evidence and receipt of mere "literature" from India. Hafiz Saeed is at large and periodically leads marches in major cities spitting venom and threatening nuclear war against India for "stealing" its Indus waters and preventing "self-determination" in Kashmir.

For a time it seemed Musharraf, his options closing after 9/11, might be willing to talk peace. After initially grandstanding at Agra, he moved forward on a back channel peace plan in concert with Dr Manmohan Singh the outlines of which became public knowledge. The emerging deal envisaged the LOC as an international boundary. But the boundary was to be rendered "irrelevant" by conversion into a soft or open border to facilitate people to people and cultural exchange, trade and commerce, regular trans-LOC bus services, phased demilitarisation and so forth concurrently with a settlement of other outstanding Indo-Pakistan issues.

Mutual management of these cross-border issues could spawn joint councils and consultative bodies at various levels which could be institutionalised over a period of time. Thus, some kind of confederation of two sets of autonomous J&Ks might duly emerge binding the two sides across the current LOC within Indian and Pakistani sovereignties. Internal autonomy for its jurisdiction within J&K would be left to each side to determine. Dr Manmohan Singh hoped the two armies would face outwards and J&K restored its historic cultural and commercial relationship with Central Asia. He even hinted at joint management of further Indus water development so as to ensure optimality in terms of Article VII on "Future Cooperation" under the Indus Treaty.

The Indus Treaty has worked well but is sub-optimal as recognised in its preamble and article VII. India has been stalled in utilising its entitlement to 3.60 million acre feet of water from the three Western Rivers on account of Pakistani obduracy. Pakistan in turn is short of storage sites as the headwaters of the three Western rivers lie in the Indian part of J&K. Article VII would permit joint exploration, construction and management of further storages and hydro-electric generation as might be feasible on the basis of a mutual sharing of costs and benefits. Such an arrangement would do more to make boundaries in J&K disappear and bind the two sides together than almost any other measure.

A confederal J&K was in fact mooted by Nehru and Abdullah in 1964. The proposal was carried by the Sheikh to Islamabad and Muzaffarabad but was aborted with Nehru's passing. Such a solution would give both sides more than what they have, reunite all of J&K and open a new chapter of good neighbourly and fraternal relations between India and Pakistan that could bring SAARC to life.

SAARC-2020, envisioned by expert groups and endorsed by the Heads of State, also envisaged this body, including Afghanistan, and even Iran and Myanmar, moving towards a South Asian Economic Union or South Asian Community with a common currency. It is principally the Indo-Pakistan imbroglio that has impeded progress.

Musharraf sought a pause in the fast moving back channel discussions between India and Pakistan in 2007 on account of his own mounting political difficulties at home. The Pakistan Taliban and other radical elements accused him of selling out to India. The talks stalled and froze after the 26/11 attack on Mumbai with the PPP in office but power back in the hands of the Army Chief, Gen Kayani, and the ISI,

The new US AfPak policy and war in Afghanistan had by now spilled over into Pakistan. The US and NATO increasingly found themselves militarily and politically at loggerheads with Islamabad which was found playing both sides, securing vast amounts of US military and civil aid but using much of this to frustrate the war on terror, while assisting it at other times, making plain that its military-strategic posture was India-centric. The busting of the Osama bin Laden hideout in the garrison town of Abottabad, on May 2, 2011, finally brought out the ugly truth of Pakistan's complicity with terror, its incredible and contradictory denials notwithstanding. The terror attack on the Mehran naval-air base near Karachi later that same month gives cause for concern regarding the safety of Pakistan's nuclear assets.

Where do we go from here? The US sees itself as part of the solution in Afghanistan and Pakistan but is in fact part of the problem. Over the years it has propped up Pakistan's unreasoning malice towards India – a sentiment not shared by its hapless people who have become the victims of savage jihadi killings, the medieval barbarism of jihadi Islamism, and military-mullah-feudal overlordship. Democracy has not been given a chance and civil society remains fragmented, with even the judiciary lauding the appalling public murders of the Punjab Governor and Minister for Minorities for speaking against the brutal tyranny of blasphemy laws.

Few know that the Pakistan military controls a significant slice of the Pakistan economy and large chunks of the best agricultural land through various Foundations manned by serving and retired military personnel and land grants to them. This constitutes a huge vested interest which would be jeopardized if the military lost its raison d'etre without a make-believe Kashmir "dispute" and an ever-present enemy - India. The military-mullah nexus is also mutually self-serving. Most Pakistanis are secular liberals who wonder what the "ideology of Pakistan" is about and for whose benefit, when all they want is to get on with their lives rather than flounder in a failing state.

Pakistan's democratic roots have not altogether withered. But despite its knowledge of Islamabad's perfidy, the US believes that any loosening of ties could destabilize Pakistan and jeopardize the safety of its nuclear facilities, hence the continuing alliance and aid and cultivation of the military to keep the war on terror in Afghanistan going. The real answer would be to curtail both civil and military aid to compel Pakistan to abandon terror as an instrument of state policy. The fear that China will immediately fill the breach is exaggerated. The Pakistan economy is on drip and Western/UN pressure could encourage a transfer of power from the military to the people.

The US launched its war on terror in Afghanistan after 9/11 in order to destroy al Qaeda and get Osama dead or alive. Osama is dead and a splintered al Qaeda has been reincarnated in related radical Islamist formations such as the Taliban and Lashkar-e-Toiba, and Harkat-ul-Jihad al-Islami (HuJI).The US and NATO now have good reason to have commenced troop withdrawals from Afghanistan from July 2011, well before the 2012 November US presidential polls.

The war is not won but, rather, appears to have reached an uneasy stalemate. All sides, India included, now seem committed in one way or another to Karzai's policy of "reintegration and reconciliation". This in turn implicitly distinguishes between moderate and extreme Taliban elements. India's endorsement of this view was reflected in Dr Manmohan Singh's remarks during his recent visit to Afghanistan. He expressed India's long standing historical and cultural ties with Afghanistan, said India was there for the long haul and announced an enhancement of Indian assistance to Afghanistan by a further $ 500 million to $ 2 bn.

Recent Track-II interlocutors from Pakistan, though still in denial, admit to shock, shame, despair, fear and frustration over what is happening back home. Yet they discern signs of resilience among the people and growing recognition that civil supremacy must be restored. There is a dawning realisation that India is not the major threat nor Kashmir the "core issue" and that non-state actors and rouge elements within the establishment must be curbed. Heart is taken from the fact that the national assembly grilled the military for almost 12 hours after the Abottabad and Mehran incidents. Yet, no one is in any doubt that the military is still in charge.

Though the US is hugely unpopular in Pakistan and much of the Islamic world, sober Pakistanis know that China cannot yet substitute it as an overall strategic partner. Nevertheless, recognising America as part of the problem even if part of the solution in Afghanistan and the region generally, it is necessary to search for other options.

Pakistan obviously has a close and legitimate interest in Afghanistan. It is concerned that India is somehow using its presence there to destabilise it via Balochistan and undermine its critical Pakhtun interest by buttressing the remnants of the Northern Alliance or Tadjik influence. It dare not take on the Taliban full scale in FATA for fear of the perceived threat from India in the east! These are fanciful notions; but hardened perceptions matter.

What then can be done? Perhaps the time has come for a frank Indo-Pakistan dialogue on Afghanistan when both sides can set out their interests and concerns. India can then use its good offices to bridge the Pakhtun-

Tadjik/non-Pukhtun divide and also bring President Karzai on board. India could also try and broker a make-boundaries-irrelevant formula for the Durand Line on the proposed J&K LOC model. The Durand Line is 120 years old and cannot be redrawn. But it can be made an even more porous border than it is at present by building cross-border institutions and arrangements for cooperative development and local governance without impairment of Afghan or Pakistani sovereignty.

In preparation for a progressive and accelerated, US-NATO troop withdrawal, an international conference on Afghanistan should be held under UN auspices to encourage regional powers, including Pakistan, Iran, India, China, Tajikistan, Russia and some others to play the leading role in building peace and reconciliation in that troubled country.

The very ending of US-NATO military intervention and drone attacks will have a calming effect. The US and NATO should however be part of a UN-led Reconstruction Plan for Afghanistan with World Bank and ADB backing aimed at rebuilding and modernising its economy, infrastructure and institutions of governance. Such a reconstruction plan should logically include Pakistan's FATA region, a wild, undeveloped, ungoverned area that has become home to the Pakistan Taliban. India should not hesitate to contribute maybe up to $ 1 billion to a FATA fund in lieu of transit through Pakistan to Afghanistan, which is a member of SAARC.

Wider regional cooperation and infrastructure building could be promoted by undertaking projects like the Iran-Pakistan-India and Turkmenistan-Afghanistan-Pakistan-India (TAPI) pipelines, the building of a Central Asian-SAARC power grid based on Central Asian hydro-electric generation, water resource development of the Kabul and Helmand basins with Indian participation, and exploitation of Afghanistan's iron ore and other mineral reserves for regional benefit. The growing Indian market could underpin such developments of which Pakistan could be a major beneficiary.

For this to happen, Afghan neutrality must be respected by all and the country restored to its position as a crossroads and a bridge to many worlds. Afghans of all hues should welcome such a plan that would isolate extremist and radical elements, the drug mafia and sundry warlords. None of this should threaten legitimate US and other Western interests.

American intervention in Libya, Iran and elsewhere in West Asia has also proved disastrous. Regime change and propping up pliant dictatorships will not work much longer. The "Arab spring" marks a process of awakening and an urge for democracy. Al Jazeera possibly played a bigger role than anything else in promoting the movement for change. The Saudis and other monarchies are literally bribing their people to win momentary support. This too will not work.

How is India positioning itself in this new situation? Our very considerable interest in the region and the presence of a 4.5 m diaspora dictate a more pro-active role. Two policy strands suggest themselves. India, Pakistan and Bangladesh represent not merely by far the largest but the most advanced, progressive and liberal Islamic community worldwide. Their tragedy has been to allow their soft, humanistic, sufi Islam to be radicalised by more fundamentalist Wahabi teachings largely imported from Saudi Arabia and funded by it. This process of 'conversion" has spawned ideas of victimhood, lost glory, false piety, religious nationalism and revenge as part of a new crusade. This is paralleled by other forms of fundamentalism that have vainly tried to take over India.

The Muslims of South Asia have begun to see through the underlying fallacy of this approach. Situated as it is by and large within a liberal democratic framework, South Asia can play a part in redeeming world Islam by its example and through imaginative Indian diplomacy and use of its considerable soft power.

The other leg of this policy has to be a new, pro-active approach to the tragic Palestine-Israel divide. India has good relations with both sides – Arab and Jewish – since ancient times. Netenyahu's recent address to the US Congress had many positives but for his inability to bridge the crucial last mile, which rendered it almost totally negative. Can India not lend its good offices here to help close the gap. It has no axe to grind and could truly be an honest broker.

A regional settlement in Afghanistan through a policy of reconciliation and development as a stable and neutral member of SAARC could get America off the hook and bring reassurance all around. Once Pakistan begins to shed its permanent enmity to India it will discover its own inherently rich personality and place in the sun and regain its soul.

Pakistan has a plethora of emotional arguments for its case on J&K but they simply do not wash. Its plea of contiguity and a Muslim majority do not square with its seeking to take over Hyderabad and several other princely Indian states. The Muslim League's pre-1947 insistence that the ruler's decision on accession must be final does not square with its now echoing India's consistent plea that the popular will must be taken into account in some form. Its clamour for "self-determination" in that part of J&K with India is contradicted by its absolute control over PAK and the Gilgit-Baltistan Area which have little or no autonomy and very limited democratic freedoms. Its prolonged resort to military seizure and cross-border terror are totally inconsistent with international law and solemn commitments to India.

India's handling of the internal situation in J&K too has not been altogether satisfactory - Sheikh Abdullah's dismissal – though there was an ultimate reconciliation, rigged elections in the early phase, highhanded law and order measures and so forth. But these are internal affairs and give no right to Pakistan to intervene.

However, things have moved on and there is now people to people exchange and some trade across the LOC. More CBMs are possible and the Manmohan-Musharraf package holds out that promise and much beyond. Unfortunately, the present PPP Government in Islamabad has to find the will to endorse a proposal advocated by its arch-enemy, Musharraf but hopefully it will find a way of doing so by incorporating minor amendments in the scheme and presenting it anew as its own formula.

The Hurriyat, a squabbling body with little credibility and widely seen as Pakistan's cats-paw, like Ghulam Nabi Fai's now-exposed Kashmir Affairs Council in Washington, is welcome to play a more constructive role and participate in talks. But grandstanding, making outlandish demands and constantly trying to throw a spanner in the works will get it nowhere and reduce it to total irrelevance.

The July 2011 visit to India of the new and youthful Pakistani Foreign Minister, Hina Rabbani Khar for talks with her counterpart were by and large constructive and indicated a desire to move on India's cross-border terrorist concerns while moving on building CBMs in J&K and taking other measures. Pakistan will continue to air past rhetoric to mollify hard liners at home and talk of UN resolutions and self-determination in J&K until it is confident that it has a saleable settlement. It may raise the pitch on water meanwhile to balance the seeming softening of its stance on J&K. Allowance must be made for such tactics unless it remains the staple diet. Pakistan cannot expect India to bail it out every time or try playing both sides. Quiet diplomacy is called for through the back channel or continuing "Warsaw-type" talks between the US and the Soviet Union during the latter stages of the cold war.

This will require more than a bipartisan effort. Right wing terror in India is only the most recent manifestation of nationalist radicalisation in India that has brought grief in the past. The Oslo killer's rantings show how international linkages could complicate the problem. India cannot realise its full potential with a Hindu-Muslim divide that is exacerbated by Indo-Pakistan tensions and mistrust. Hence the need for the government of the day to keep the opposition and relevant border states in the loop.

J&K's autonomy has been eroded substantively and symbolically since 1953. This rankles deeply. Hence issues of restoring fuller autonomy to J&K, regional autonomy within it, and human rights issues arising out of years of internal conflict must be addressed and call for resolution. This is happening. An internal resolution in J&K will greatly reduce Pakistan's leverage to legitimise its cross-border interference or international campaign. The UN Resolutions are dead and rather than look back at the past, both sides need to look ahead towards a new future in J&K and between India and Pakistan.

A consensus will have to be built both within J&K and in India so that hard-liners cannot wreck progress. Nor should they be given a veto. The background given in this paper is not intended to score points but to generate a better understanding of what the J&K issue is about. India has a very strong legal and moral case and if this is understood, any seeming concessions made in the interest of a wider Indo-Pakistan settlement and regional harmony will be seen not as sign of weakness but based on a genuine desire to ensure that Pakistan does not feel humiliated and comes to realise that India is not a permanent enemy. J&K can be shared and bind the two sides in friendship and cooperation.

The fugitive hope surrounding Partition was that India and Pakistan would separate to come together in time as fraternal friends and partners in a larger South Asian Union without derogation of their sovereignty. That time has come. Kashmir is not the "core problem". It can be shared. This will not undo Pakistan; reconciliation with India could make it whole.

J&K 2012-15 And Beyond

It has been a good year for J&K with less internal turmoil, jihadis and separatists on the retreat and buoyant tourism. In contrast, Pakistan faces a near-implosion, essentially the backlash of a mistaken foundational ideology of permanent enmity towards India that has engendered radical Islam and militarisation. How things pan out remains to be seen as civil authority struggles to assert itself, but the people of J&K realise that Pakistan has brought them grief. Any viable inter-country settlement must relate to the Manmohan-Musharraf formula of making boundaries (read LOC) "irrelevant" through cross-border movement and exchanges leading to the two parts of J&K, each internally autonomous, evolving into a partial "condominium" within twin but separate sovereignties.

The Home Minister plans shortly to unveil the J&K Interlocutors' report for discussion. This internal dimension is best addressed along with the PM's Five Task Force reports submitted earlier. Starting with a parliamentary debate, this is best followed up by and through a steering group with major political party representatives drawn from both the Centre and States and a few Wise Men so that consensus can be built at all stages and levels. The separatists will huff and puff, but none should be allowed a veto. A time line of one year should help concentrate the mind.

Simultaneously, Omar Abdullah, halfway through his term of office, should now focus on an "Agenda for 2013-15 and Beyond" in anticipation of on-going developments that are going to open up huge opportunities for investment, employment, commerce and income-generation through improved connectivity, greater availability of power and the opening up of new tourist circuits.

The Banihal rail tunnel is through. This should speed work to connect with the Baramulla-Srinagar-Qazigund sector by 2013 and the more difficult Banihal-Katra sector, and Chenab bridge en route, two years thereafter. The shorter, all-weather four-laned national highway from Jammu to Srinagar should also be commissioned by that time. The consequent reduction in the physical and psychological distance between the various regions of J&K and the State and the rest of India will be transforming. An extension from Baramulla to Uri (and beyond to Muzaffarabad) merits consideration.

In the interim, Rail-medicars and Rail-banks can be provided along the existing Baramulla-Qazigund route on fixed days, extending much-needed facilities to underserved areas.

The existing optic fibre highway, better insulated from the elements, could be extended and upgraded. The international airport at Srinagar too will soon be fully operational. Pakistan has barred Air India over-flights from Srinagar to Dubai but could be challenged to allow flights from Srinagar to Lahore and Karachi and beyond to the Gulf while China might be willing to consider services to or over Xinjiang to Central Asian destinations and Russia to restore connectivity along the old Silk Route across the Karakoram pass to Leh and Srinagar. There is tourist and commercial potential to be exploited, not least by charter flights geared to particular seasons, events and specially packaged tours.

The power situation should greatly improve within the next few years with the completion of on-going projects and improved transmission facilities. J&K plans to repatriate build-operate-own projects like Sallal from the NHPC over the next few years. Further, the State government intends to cure the problem of power theft and high Transmission & Distribution losses by selling electricity in bulk to local communities from designated transformers, making them responsible for distribution, maintenance and billing. Such "communitisation" of elementary education and primary health in rural areas and electricity supply in urban *mohallas* has yielded extraordinary results in Nagaland and can be an effective instrument for local participation and accountability in J&K.

A programme of this nature would mesh very well with the promise and need further to empower and upgrade panchayati raj and municipal bodies in J&K. The 80 per cent turnout in last year's panchayat poll shows that ordinary people want development and good governance. Such multi-tiered self-determination would probably meet regional and community aspirations for local autonomy and provide a salve to embittered intra-regional relations.

Given better connectivity and power availability, the State Government should think in terms of setting up a series of well planned townships with good educational and medical facilities and other social infrastructure. There is a model for such economic opportunity hubs along the Baramulla-Srinagar-Jammu rail and road corridor in the Delhi-Mumbai Rail Corridor project. This could attract investments, especially in the IT and IT-enabled services as well as in the food processing industry which is going to expand greatly in the years to come. IT-related industries would be weather proof and J&K could well become another IT and electronic hub. With its rich bio-diversity covering fruit, vegetables, herbs and flowers, J&K has a huge processed food and pharma potential awaiting exploitation. Small units could be cooperativised on the Amul pattern apart from promoting contractual partnerships between corporate houses and small produces or suppliers with a variety of backward and forward linkages to serve the national and international market.

Security is often cited as a negative factor. But peace and development go hand in hand and economic opportunity with suitable training could wean away angry youth from stone-throwing or the gun. The Centre could also offer counter-guarantees for a period of five years against security risks for projects above a certain value. All this could make J&K a major food processing training and R&D centre. Among those attracted back to work and/or invest would be Pandits, émigré Muslims who fled the Valley and the larger J&K diaspora around the world.

Power generation too could be enhanced were Article VII of the Indus Water Treaty on "Future Cooperation" to be activated. India has been unable to harness its limited entitlement to the waters of the Indus, Jhelum and Chenab, otherwise fully allotted to Pakistan, because of Islamabad's obduracy. The latter, in turn, cannot build storages in the upper reaches of these same rivers, as they lie in India. Article VII would permit the two sides jointly to construct and manage engineering works on either side of the LOC for optimal benefit on agreed terms of cost and benefit sharing. Nothing would make boundaries more "irrelevant" than such an arrangement.

The best way to exploit upcoming connectivity and enhanced power gains would be to think and plan concurrently, not sequentially, so that no time is lost in encashing the multiplier effect. To this end, the State government should convene a high level "J&K 2013-15 and Beyond" convention with local, national and international participation. Thereafter a special planning group should refine the programme, breaking it down into discrete projects with necessary land-clearances, a major obstacle to industrial development by non-state subjects at present, and develop a phased master plan.

The opportunity is there. Seize it.

3

Multiple Identity Politics in J & K

Rekha Chowdhary

The politics of Jammu and Kashmir is characterised by multiplicity of identities and multiple claims and assertions. Though the conflict situation of the state has its specificity in the Kashmiri identity politics, however, it does not exhaust the range of identity politics of the state. Besides the politics of Kashmiri identity, there are many other competing identities which not only bring about a context of complexity in the conflict situation but also make the process of conflict resolution a difficult one. This paper is focusing on the implications of the multiple identity politics of J&K on the conflict situation and conflict resolution. It is divided into four sections. The first section reflects on the issues of diversity and multiple and layered identity politics. The second section explores the Kashmiri identity politics and the third section seeks to locate the identities beyond the Kashmiri identity and their politics. The fourth section deals with the impact of multiple identity politics on the conflict situation and the fifth section deals with the response of the state vis-à-vis the identity politics. The last section focuses on the prospects of the consensus building in the context of multiplicity of identity politics and divergent political positions.

Diversity and Multiple & Layered Identity politics

Jammu and Kashmir is highly diverse society that reflects a multi-layered identity politics. Its diversity ranging from religious to cultural- regional markers operates in such a manner that it generates a picture of complexity. Though a Muslim-majority state, it is only in the region of Kashmir that Muslims have a predominant presence. While Jammu is a Hindu-dominant region, Ladakh has larger number of Buddhists. However, it is only Kashmir region which has a homogenous demographic character, both Jammu and Ladakh represent a mixed society. The Muslims form a substantial minority in both these regions. One of the two districts of Ladakh and four of the ten districts of Jammu are Muslim majority districts.

However, the demographic complexity of the state does not exhaust with the religious plurality, the regional identity introduces further intricacy in it. Thus rather than being identified as Hindus or Muslims or Buddhists, people here are identified as those belonging to Kashmir or Jammu or Ladakh. It is the regional identification that differentiates the Kashmiri Pundit from the Hindus of Jammu; the Kashmiri Muslims from Jammu Muslims; and Ladakhi Muslims from both Kashmiri and Jammu Muslims.

Beyond these, there are other identity markers that overlap with the religious and regional markers. The caste identity, for instance is very crucial not only for the Hindus but also Muslims, especially of Jammu region. The dominant 'Rajput' identity cuts across the religious lines and provides a very strong sense of belonging to a large number of Hindus and Muslims of Jammu region. The tribal identity similarly operates in a crucial manner not only for the Ladakhis, but all-Muslim group of Gujjars who distinguish themselves from other Muslims on the basis of this identity. Competing with them are Hindu-Muslim combine of Paharis who have been demanding the Scheduled Tribe status on the line of Gujjars.

In a diverse society like Jammu and Kashmir where each identity marker is internally differentiated and overlaps with other identity markers, the identity politics assumes a complex character. This complexity is provided firstly by the fact that there is no clear cut context of 'majority' or 'minority'. Each of the identity while asserting its collective numerical strength also simultaneously voices its victimisation as a minority. Thus the Kashmiri identity politics while asserting the numerical dominance within the state, bemoans the marginalisation of 'Kashmiris' and 'Muslims' in the larger context of Indian state. Those asserting the regional identity of Jammu claim that this region is larger in territorial terms in comparison to Kashmir but complain about its political marginalisation vis-à-vis Kashmir region. Gujjars claim to be the third largest demographic grouping after 'Muslims' and 'Hindus' but again lament their backwardness vis-à-vis other people of the state.

The multiple identities that operate within the state engage with each other in a variety of ways. While some identities operate parallel to each other, there are others which cut across each other – claiming to represent the same political constituency. These later identities are located in a mutually exclusive and contradictory relationship with each other.

Conflict Situation and Multiple identity Politics

The conflict situation in which the state of Jammu and Kashmir is involved for more than six decades now, has both external as well as internal dimensions.[1] The contestation between India and Pakistan over their respective claims leading to a number of wars and prolonged hostility between the two countries forms the external dimension of conflict. The internal dimension of conflict, however, is defined by Kashmir's relationship with India, specifically the context of political alienation in Kashmir and the consequent political situation. Seen from this perspective, the internal context of conflict has evolved around the Kashmiri identity politics. However, this identity politics does not exhaust the whole range of political claims and assertions. Political divergence is the reality of the state and provides a complexity both to the nature of conflict as well as its resolution. [2]

The conflict is specifically located in the identity politics of Kashmir. However, the implications of conflict reach far beyond the valley of Kashmir. The political uncertainty and instability that has been caused by Kashmir-specificity of conflict has its spill over effect on the rest of the state. It also generates its own kinds of political dynamism that goes a long way in redefining the very context of conflict. To begin with, there remains a huge gap between claims and representation. Despite its specificity, the claims within the Kashmiri identity politics are made on behalf of 'all the people of the state'. Apart from the question of legitimacy of representation of those who are not located within this politics, there is the other situation of contestation both of these claims as well as representations. It is this context of internal contestations that takes the conflict to a third level – the intra-state level (besides the oft cited 'external' and 'internal' levels).

---

[1] Sumantra Bose, *The Challenge in Kashmir: Democracy, Self Determination and a Just Peace*, (New Delhi: Sage Publications, 1996)

[2] Rekha Chowdhary, *Identity Politics in Jammu and Kashmir*, (New Delhi: Vitasta, 2010)

What is involved in the third level of conflict is the issue of political divergence in the context of its specificity. Apart from the Kashmiri identity politics, there are host of other identity assertions which have provided a sense of vibrancy to the internal politics of the state. While some of these identities operate parallel to the Kashmiri identity politics, there are others which are located in a mutually exclusive and contradictory relationship to it.

The very Kashmir-specific context of conflict itself has generated a number of political demands and assertions. These assertions either aim at contesting the claims made from the Kashmir-specificity and laying down counter-claims or alternatively seek to broaden the very contours of conflict so as to incorporate the interests of those unrepresented in the Kashmiri identity politics.

In order to further clarify the above points, it may be pertinent to preview the multiple identity politics of the state.

Kashmiri Identity Politics

Kashmiri political identity has evolved since the decades of 1920s and has taken various forms since then. To begin with, this identity had taken a shape in response to the feudal and monarchical order that had resulted in the impoverishment of the mass of Kashmiris, mostly the landless peasantry and the artisans. The process of modernisation had created a small class of educated elite which was exposed to the anti-colonial struggles in the sub-continent. However, the first manifestation of Kashmiri identity politics had 'religious' identity of Kashmiris as its central point and Muslim Conference was first political organisation that was formed in Kashmir to struggle for the educational, employment and religious rights of Muslims of the state. These political goals were redefined later to incorporate the more progressive agenda of land reforms and popular control over power.[3] The rechristening of the Muslim Conference as National Conference reflected the change in

---

[3] The linkage of the peasantry with the National Conference is very important for understanding the process of scularisation of political identity in Kashmir. Land being one of the major issues for the mass of economically oppressed and exploited peasantry, politics of land reform had a definite impact on the political psyche of people.

the nature of identity politics of Kashmir. It acquired regional character in 1940s. With the internal difference within the Muslim leadership of the state widening and the Muslim leadership of Jammu deciding to revive the 'Muslim Conference', the regional context of Kashmiri identity assumed precedence over the 'religious' content of identity.[4]

It was because of the regional marker of identity that had assumed pre-eminence over the religious affiliation of Kashmiris, that there was a lack of enthusiasm among the Kashmiri leaders towards the idea of Pakistan. Despite the fact that the state was a predominantly a Muslim state and fitted in the scheme of 'Muslim Homeland', the leaders felt its ideology antithetical to the progressive agenda of Kashmiri movement. The major concern of the movement at the time revolved around the dismantling of the feudal structure and initiation of radical land reforms. Sheikh Abdullah, the charismatic leader of the movement, did not have any hope of pursuing this agenda in 'feudal Pakistan'. Apart from that there was the apprehension that the 'Kashmiri identity' may submerge in the larger Muslim identity of Pakistan.

Though the accession of the state of J&K with India took place under extraordinary circumstances created by the tribal attack, the Kashmiri leadership was quite positively inclined towards India and saw better prospects of negotiating constitutional autonomy in a plural, secular and democratic India. By committing a special constitutional status for the J&K, the national leaders succeeded in harmonising the Kashmiri nationalist aspirations within the larger Indian nationalist mould. Apart from Article 370 that guaranteed special constitutional status of the state, the state went ahead with the framing of its own constitution and adopting radical land reform legislations. It was the satisfaction of being provided the desired

---

[4] The political response of the two regions started facing divergence by the time the Muslim Conference was converted into the National Conference in 1939. The Muslim leadership of Jammu was not quite supportive of the idea of changing the character of the organisation and opening it for the non-Muslims and radicalising its goals. That is the reason that they chose to revive the Muslim Conference a few months after it was dissolved. Since 1940 the Muslim politics of Jammu region took an altogather a different path from that of National Conference. While National Conference during this period came closer to the Nationalist politics, particularly the Congress Party and the Left movement, the Muslim Conference affiliated itself with the Muslim League politics.

political space that Kashmiri leadership welcomed Kashmir's association with India. That is why despite Pakistan's contestation of this accession, the most vociferous defence of Accession of the state with India came from Sheikh Abdullah.[5]

However, the situation reversed in 1953 when Sheikh Abdullah was removed from power and kept in detention for a number of years. The sense of 'political autonomy' that the Kashmiri leaders were celebrating in the post-Accession period was lost. This was due to three major factors.

First, the post 1953 saw a reversal of logic of Article 370. Till 1953, the Centre-State relations were determined by the logic of 'autonomy' and hence all constitutional developments including the incorporation of Article 370 in Indian Constitution; the convening of the Constituent Assembly of the State; the Delhi Agreement of 1952 to negotiate the future constitutional relationship between the Centre and the state – were aimed at promoting maximum autonomy for the state vis-à-vis the Centre. However, after 1953, the logic of 'integration' assumed importance and all constitutional and legal developments were aimed at removing the constitutional gap between Centre and the state. Starting with the Presidential Order of 1954, a total of 42 Presidential Orders were passed in post 1953 period to bring the state at par with the rest of Indian states.[6]

Second, the post-1953 period witnessed bigger involvement of the Centre in the politics of the state. Not only the removal of Sheikh Abdullah from power was at the behest of the Central government, the political

---

[5] Following is one of the examples of the way Sheikh Abdullah generally addressed Kashmiris about State's association with India in the immediate post-Accession period: 'The position today, as heretofore, is that our State is a constituent unit of the Indian Union and the relationship is based on the same terms as were laid down in the Instrument of Accession. The State has transferred three subjects of defence, Foreign Affairs and Communications and for the residuary powers inherent in it, it has complete freedom to exercise an autonomous position. I am fully convinced that this position, consistent with the principles of democracy, could be secured for the State only through a continued association with India, where the large majority of the people are striving to democratize their mode of economic and political development. The support given to our decisions by the Indian people is an effective guarantee that we shall have the fullest opportunities of adopting progressive policies for the benefit of the masses.' ('Sheikh Abdullah's Broadcast', *Statesman*, September 2, 1952)

[6] Government of Jammu and Kashmir, State Autonomy Committee Report, 1999.

arrangements after his removal also reflected the active intervention of the Centre. The political leaders who succeeded the Sheikh lack lacked popular support and legitimacy and remained in power with the support of the Centre. The Central intervention also extended to the party politics and the National Conference which had the reputation of being the most indigenous and popular party, came to be encroached by the Congress and after a decade of heavy 'congressisation' of this party, it was formally merged into the Congress.[7]

Third, the most important development in the post-1953 period was the sense of loss of partnership that the Kashmiri leadership had evolved vis-à-vis the Centre. The political leadership at the helm of power politics in the post-1953 period did not enjoy either the credibility or the popular support basis to feel at par with the national leadership and negotiate relationship accordingly.

The contours of Kashmiri identity politics therefore were defined by the contestation of the Indian claim on Kashmir and the demand for 'plebiscite' in the post-1953 period. However, in 1975, with Sheikh Abdullah joining the power politics, the issue of 'autonomy' and the demand for reorganisation of Centre-state relations assumed centrality. The recovery of democratic space, as well as political autonomy of the local politics vis-à-vis the Central government, helped redefine the political discourse in the period from 1975 to 1983. However, the increasing central intrusion in the post-1983 period, especially the removal of a popular elected government through Centrally-engineered defections and later on the unpopular alliance of Congress with the National Conference created the space for a more aggressive phase of Kashmiri identity politics. This phase saw the onset of armed militancy on the one hand and a popular separatist movement on the other. [8]

The separatist movement that characterises the identity politics of Kashmir since 1989 had undergone various changes in last two decades. From a stage of indigenous political struggle led by Kashmiri militants to

---

[7] Balraj Puri, *Towards Insrugency*, (New Delhi: Orient Longman, 1993)

[8] Victoria Schofield, *Kashmir in Conflict: India, Pakistan and the Unending War*, (London: I B Tauris, 2003)

begin with, it incorporated the *Jehadi* elements with foreign mercenaries joining the insurgency in large numbers. This had the impact of bringing religion to the centre of identity politics. However, strong internal critique both of the *Jehadi* elements as well as the role of religion as the defining factor of identity politics, resulted in assertion of 'indigenous' character of identity politics. By the end of the decade of 1990s, the political movement had turned its back on the *Jehadi* elements.

With the armed militancy declining in the later years, another shift came in the separatist politics. This shift characterised by spontaneous mass protests, was clearly visible in Kashmir in post-2006 period. The massive political upsurge during the summers of 2008, 2009 and 2010 clearly reflected this shift. While 2008 witnessed massive protests lasting for five months around the Amarnath land row; 2009 recorded huge protests all over the year around the issue of rape and killing of two women in Shopian; in 2010 again there was massive upsurge that lasted for five months in continuity.[9]

The Kashmiri identity politics in its present phase is characterised by the demand for 'final resolution of conflict' in accordance to the aspirations of people. Thought the slogan of 'azadi' symbolises this demand, the vision for the future of Kashmis is not that clearly drawn. What is clearly identifiable element in this identity politics is the sense of popular alienation and trust-deficit vis-à-vis the Indian state. There is a general consensus regarding the need for reorganising and renegotiating the relationship of the state with India. However, there is no consensus around the scope of this reorganisation and the actual route through which this is to be done. While there is a section that emphasises the role of UN resolutions and the demand for self-determination; most of the leaders are in favour of a dialogue and finding a resolution in the process of dialogue that involves India, Pakistan and the people of Kashmir.

It is the separatist politics that is the mainstay of the identity politics of Kashmir. The All Party Hurriyat Conference that was established in 1993 with the aim of providing a political face to the armed militancy and popular discontent has itself undergone various phases of evolution. These phases

---

[9] Rekha Chowdhary, "The Second Uprising", *Economic and Political Weekly*, Vol. XLV No 39, (September 25, 2010), 10-13

reflect the internal dynamics of the identity politics and political movement in last two and half decades. One of the major issues that confronted the Hurriyat Conference from the very beginning was the ideological difference, especially between those who upheld the religious basis of the movement and desired the merger of the state of J&K with Pakistan and those who desired the independence of the state both from India and Pakisan. These differences were sharpened in the mid nineties when the foreign mercenaries entered the rank of militants in a big way. It was in late nineties that Abdul Gani Lone openly contested the religious basis of the movement and critiqued the position taken by Syed Ali Shah Geelani that the ongoing movement of Kashmir was a part of the Global Jehad. Though Lone was assassinated soon after, the ideological differences led to a major split of Hurriyat Conference with Hurriyat led by Mirwaiz forming one faction and the Hurriyat led by Geelani forming the other faction. There were other prominent separatists like Yasin Malik of JKLF and Sajjad Gani Lone who remained out of these two factions.[10]

Though much of the identity politics of Kashmir is manifested in the separatist political space, the mainstream politics also privileges the issues of Kashmiri identity. Two major political parties, the National Conference and the PDP both acknowledge the reality of conflict and have their own preferred solutions for it. While National Conference refers to its agenda of 'Autonomy' or reversal of the constitutional relationship to the pre-1953 situation, the PDP talks about the 'Self Rule' that goes beyond reorganising the centre-State relations to developing linkages across the LoC.

What remains peculiar about the Kashmiri identity politics is that though it is has element of specificity in the ethno-nationalist politics of Kashmir, it makes claim for the whole of Jammu and Kashmir. The reference point is not the state of J&K as it exists now within India, but the undivided state as it existed prior to 1947.

Beyond the Kashmiri Identity

Though Kashmiri identity is the most visible one in Jammu and Kashmir, there are other variants of identity politics within the state. Both Jammu as

---

[10] Rekha Chowdhary, *Identity Politics in Jammu and Kashmir*, (New Delhi: Vitasta, 2010)

well as Ladakh, the two other regions of the state, are politically vibrant and reflect multiple identity politics. The contours of the identity of politics of both the regions, however are quite different from those of the Kashmiri identity politics. While for Kashmiri identity politics 'India' remains the major reference point, for the identity politics of Jammu and Ladakh 'Kashmir' remains the reference point.

The regional politics of Jammu as well as Ladakh is defined by a sense of marginalisation within the power politics of the state. With Kashmir being seen as the dominant regional partner, there is a deep-rooted political psyche of 'regional deprivation' in both these regions. This political psyche, with regard to Jammu region, is as much a consequence of the particular historical context of the power politics as the 'structure' of power.

The roots of the 'regional tensions' can be traced to the very nature of political developments in the decades of 1930s and 1940s when the resistance politics of Kashmir was taking shape. Though the resistance movement in Kashmir was targeted against the feudal regime of the Dogra ruler, the entrenched elites of Jammu projected it as 'anti-Jammu' movement. Being the beneficiaries of the Dogra rule, they were quite apprehensive of the economic agenda of the movement. Soon after the Accession, when the National Conference government went ahead with the most radical land reforms, these elites felt the pinch of the shift in the power structure of the state. Being beneficiaries of the feudal regime, they were the ones to lose the most, not only in terms of the land in access to the ceiling limit provided by the land reform legislations, but also in terms of state employment and other privileges emanating from their close association with the monarch. This is not to say that there were no beneficiaries of the land reform legislations in Jammu region. In fact a large number of tillers, many of whom belonged to the lower castes, especially the dalits, overnight became the owners of land. However, they were neither politicised nor had a political voice. Unlike Kashmir where the mass interest was represented in the dominant politics, in Jammu, the dominant politics represented the upper caste-upper class interests. This class became quite resentful of the post-Accession political developments in the state, not only in the context of relocation of political power from 'Jammu-based' Dogra ruler to 'Kashmir-based' National Conference, but also in the context of de-linking of the state policies from the Indian Constitution. With the protection of Article 370, the National Conference could free itself of the constitutional obligation of providing 'compensation' to the landowners whose land was appropriated by the state. With a large number of landowners located in Jammu region and the larger number of beneficiaries of land reforms being located in Kashmir region, the land reform policy of National Conference could easily be projected as 'anti-Jammu' policy of the 'Kashmir-based' government.[11]

The fact that the National Conference which formed the government after the Accession was confined in its politics to Kashmir region and did not either have a popular base in Jammu region nor a cadre or leadership that could win the confidence of people of this region, the distance between the two regions kept on increasing in the post-Accession period. The strong regional component of Kashmiri identity politics hampered the process of broadening its political constituency and extending it beyond the valley of Kashmir. There was no other local political organisation in Jammu which could take up the challenge of politicising the impoverished Dogra masses. It was in this situation that Praja Parishad, a Rightist organisation representing the feudal and entrenched classes, filled the political vacuum. Supported by the Bharatiya Jana Sangh, this organisation raised the pitch of anti-Kashmir politics. In 1952, it led a massive agitation in Jammu demanding abolition of Article 370 of Indian constitution and full constitutional integration of the state with India. This agitation was to set the direction of the 'regional politics of Jammu' in the binary opposition to Kashmir, for the decades to

---

[11] The decision of the state government to go ahead with land acquisition without paying the compensation inevitably led to the acute hostility of the landed class against the National Conference led Kashmir government. Since the issue was linked with the constitutional autonomy of the state because of which the fundamental rights which ensured compensation for the land acquisition were not applied to this state, the hostility was extended to the very constitutional arrangement as well. This also had the implication of seeing the very nature of the land-reforms rather than in the context of the anti-feudal principles but in terms of its regional and communal implications. Since the majority of the beneficiaries of the land reforms were the Kashmiri Muslims and since most of the dispossessed were Dogra Hindus (apart from the Kashmiri pundits) the issue tended to be seen in regional-communal terms – as measures taken to benefit the Muslims of Kashmir and to harm the Hindus of Jammu. The political vacuum of Jammu and the lack of mobilisation of the marginalised sections of society in the progressive direction further contributed to this. With no tradition of anti-feudal struggle (unlike a very active one in Kashmir) it was easy to assign meanings of the reforms purely in regional-communal manners.

come. As this agitation articulated the regional identity politics of Jammu, it not only sought to represent Jammu's political aspirations different from those of Kashmir, but also in conflict with it.

What has sustained the 'Jammu versus Kashmir' discourse in this region is a deep-rooted feeling of 'political neglect'. This feeling is generated both in the context of the power politics as well as the context of conflict situation. The power politics emanating out of the model of single party dominance till very recently, has reflected a bias in favour of the Kashmir-based political elite. For a long time (from 1947 to 1965 and later on from 1975 to 2002) the power politics has been dominated by the National Conference which has been able to give at best a token representation to Jammu's political elite, in the positions of power. With most of the Jammu-based political parties having no scope of being represented in power, the only role for the political elite of Jammu has been in the oppositional space. It is in this space that the 'Jammu versus Kashmir' discourse assumes a strident form. However, since 2002, the coalition politics has broadened the scope for representation of Jammu's political elite in power structure. The emergence of PDP as another Kashmir-based party in 1998 resulted in fragmentation of regional politics of Kashmir and consequently opening the space for Jammu-based Congress party to be a major coalition partner either with the National Conference or the PDP. However, the newfound political space for the political elite of Jammu has not as yet addressed the deeprooted psyche of political deprivation in this region.

Besides the power politics, it is the context of conflict which has aggravated a sense of political neglect in Jammu region. Since the conflict is Kashmir-specific, Kashmir not only remains the centre of political attention at the national and international level, but also in the political arrangements between the Centre and the State. It is a different matter that such political arrangements have not assuaged the feeling of discontent in Kashmir, but these have generated a feeling of political deprivation in other regions. There is a general feeling that all post-1947 occurrences, including the asymmetrical federal relation between the Centre and the state; various political accords and other political developments have mainly followed the logic of Kashmir's politics and Jammu has been either bypassed or taken for granted. Neither the consent of the people or the leaders of the region has been sought nor the local sensibilities taken into account.

Like the identity politics of Jammu, the identity politics of Ladakh also has 'Kashmir' as its reference point. The central focus of the politics of Ladakh Buddhist Association (LBA) has been around the 'Kashmir-centric' power as well as Conflict politics. It has been raising the demand for Union Territory Status of Ladakh due to 'political deprivation' and 'political neglect' of the region in the existing structure of the state. In the similar vein to the dominant politics of Jammu region, this organisation has been referring to concentration of power in 'Kashmir' and maginalisation of Ladakh in the power politics of the state. Though in response to this politics, two autonomous Hill Development Councils for the district of Leh and the other for the district of Kargil, have been constituted, the political discontent in Ladakh against existing power arrangement continues.

However, the regional context of the identity politics is not exhausted at the level of inter-regional relations. There is another dimension to this politics which operates at the sub-regional levels. In both the regions of Jammu and Ladakh, the people of the peripheral areas feel alienated by the dominant politics of the region and therefore demand political attention. Within Jammu region, there is a vibrant politics in favour of demand of 'Chenab Valley Hill Council' for the peripheral Doda belt and the 'Pir Panchal Hill Council' for the twin border districts of Rajouri and Poonch. In both these areas there is a strong feeling that the people here are neglected both in the political discourse of Kashmir as well as of Jammu. In the region of Ladakh also, there is internal differentiation. The relatively more backward district of Kargil feels alienated by the dominant politics of Ladakh which is Leh-centric.

Identity Politics and Conflict Situation

The interplay of the competing identity politics, especially during the last two decades, has made it amply clear that the conflict resolution is not a simple process of involving a formula or delivering a package. It is also not a process that ends with a dialogue between the state and the disgruntled elements in one part of the state. It is also a long term process of building a consensus among the stakeholders. However, before any consensus can be evolved, it may be important to delineate the basic issues emerging out of the multiple identity politics vis-à-vis the conflict situation.

The first issue relates to the question of claims and representation. Not only there is multiplicity of claims within the state but there is also a competitive context of claims. The political leaders in Kashmir tend to make claims for 'all the people of Jammu and Kashmir'. Whether referring to the demand for self-determination or Azadi, or even the demand for 'Autonomy', these leaders seek to represent all the regions and all the people of the state. However, due to the specificity of the movement politics to Kashmir, there remains a gap between the claim and representation. The claim is contested not merely by the very limited influence of the separatist politics in areas beyond Kashmir but by the explicit claims being made by various organisations. Thus the BJP has been making claims on behalf of people of Jammu demanding 'full integration of the state with India' and abrogation of Article 370 of Indian constitution; various Hindu Rightist organisations including the RSS, Shiv Sena and Jammu Mukti Morcha, similarly seeking to represent the people of Jammu make demands for separation of Jammu from Kashmir; LBA making claims on behalf of people of Ladakh demands the UT status, and the Panun Kashmir makes demand for 'Homeland' for Kashmiri Pundits. Interestingly, each of these demands is equally exclusive in nature and seeks to make claims on behalf of a community that is supposedly 'homogenised'. Thus it is not only the 'homogenised' representation of J&K that is reflected in the separatist demand, but also homogenised representation of Jammu and Ladakh. The internal differentiations and divergences within are equally ignored. These differentiations and divergences, however, act as the limits on the politics of representation. All these claims therefore remain internally contested.

The second issue relates to the very nature of conflict. Despite the general perception that there is a singular context of conflict, there are multiple layers at which the conflict actually manifests itself. These layers are linked with each other in such a manner that none of the layers can be treated in an autonomous manner without having some impact on the other layers. While the Kashmir-specific nature of conflict remains central, there are other aspects of conflict which either go beyond Kashmir or are generated in response to the issues raised by the Kashmir-specificity of conflict. There is for instance, the whole context of border-related problems that range from the day-to-day hardships for the people living near the border to the issue of displacement of various kinds.[12] Then there is the unsettled problem of refugees. The division of the state in 1947 created a situation in which there were large number of refugees who came to settle in various parts of Jammu region. Mainly belonging to two categories – those who came from Pakistan administered Kashmir and those who came from Pakistan, these refugees have lot of grievances. In the case of the first category of refugees who were the permanent residents of the undivided Jammu and Kashmir, their problems are linked with the unresolved status of the state. With official claim being made that the area under Pakistan's control as part of India, these displaced people have not been treated at par with similarly displaced refugees in other parts of India. Due to the unsettled nature of conflict, their problems of rehabilitation and resettlement also continue to remain unresolved. In the case of the second category of displaced, the basic issue remains linked with their citizenship status. Despite being settled in Jammu since 1947, these people have not been granted the status of Permanent Residents of the state and hence they are deprived of various rights emanating from this status.

It is the complexity underlying the context of conflict that has made it very much intractable. Such a complexity to begin with, is provided by the way the external and internal dimensions have been fused with each other and thereafter add to this are the internal intricacies. These internal intricacies introduce a third dimension to the conflict situation which is defined by the inter-regional relations. Identifying this third dimension of conflict, Balraj Puri, with reference to Jammu's relationship of Kashmir has been arguing that without resolving the tension between Jammu and Kashmir, it may not be possible to resolve the context of conflict.[13]

Multiple Identity Politics and the Response of the State

The State's response vis-à-vis the identity politics in J&K has been changing over the period. It is in the last few years of the peace process, that there

---

[12] With the border remaining very volatile even during the peace time, the life of the people in the villages near the border has been quite difficult. Apart from Intermittent shelling and bombing and mining they have been faced with the problem of often losing the control over their agricultural land.

[13] Balraj Puri, *Jammu: A Clue to Kashmir Tangle*, (Delhi, 1966)

has developed a bit more nuanced approach to acknowledge and respond to the complexity underlying the identity politics. For quite some time, the complexity remained either unacknowledged or unaddressed, adding to the gravity of problems within the state. Many of the issues that became politically sensitive resulted from the failure of the political regimes, both at the level of the Centre as well as at the level of the states, to respond to the plurality, political diversity and divergence within the state. Much of the popular alienation that manifested through the armed militancy, separatist politics and popular upsurge in Kashmir in 1989 was in fact, a reflection of the deep-rooted sense of disenchantment with the Indian state. This sense of alienation was reflected in the Kashmiri identity politics in the period following the dismissal and detention of Sheikh Abdullah in 1953. Refusal of the state to acknowledge this sense of alienation for a prolonged period resulted in a political psyche of Kashmir that manifests not only a sense of political isolation vis-à-vis the nationalist politics but also a deep-seated distrust of the Indian state. The separatist politics that has been operating in Kashmir during last two decades, is based on these feelings.

However, it is not only the political sensitivities of Kashmir that have remained unaddressed but also the other kinds of sensitivities. More importantly, what has remained unaddressed is the fact of political divergence and multiple identity politics. As a result of the lop-sided response of the State, these multiple identities have tended to be not only mutually exclusive but also at odds with each other. The inter-regional context of conflict actually emanates from the lack of sensitivity towards the political divergence within. Right from the very beginning, the response of the governments, whether the Central or the State, towards the political issues within J&K, has been to see these as emanating from one homogenised political unit and thereby responding to these in that manner only. As a consequence, there emerged one or the other source of discontent. The political arrangements made in response to Kashmiri identity politics in the pre-1953 period, for instance, did not take into account the political response of the dominant elite in Jammu. The sharpening of regional identity politics of Jammu and its leaning towards the Rightist organisations was a result of the acute feeling of neglect in the 'negotiated' relationship that had evolved between the Centre and the state in the form of Article 370 of Indian constitution. That explains the aggressive opposition to this arrangement in Jammu, as reflected in the 1952 Praja Parishad agitation. Similarly, the post-1953 political arrangement, that emanated from a response of the Indian state to constitutionally 'integrate' the state of J&K with India, did not take into account the political aspirations of Kashmir region. Though satisfying to the dominant political elite of Jammu, these arrangements generated a very strong sense of discontent in Kashmir region. One can give similar examples about the later period. The 1975 Indira-Sheikh Accord aimed at addressing the alienation of people of Kashmir, again assumed 'Kashmiris' to be the major stakeholders in the politics of Kashmir, without considering the implication of a new arrangement on the people of Jammu and Ladakh. That the ruling Congress that had made a way for the newly revived National Conference under the leadership of Sheikh Abdullah to take on power, had a base in Jammu and represented the political voice of the region, was totally undermined and the new political arrangement was seen as 'Kashmir-centric' by the vocal elite of Jammu region. The later political developments, especially those linked with the political ambitions of the Indian National Congress as the ruling party in the Centre in the decade of eighties, alienated the people of Kashmir.

The lopsided response of the state towards the divergent political aspirations within the state continued through the decade of nineties. The most illustrious case in the context of the slackness on the part of the Centre (as well as the State government) in dealing with the multiple identity politics of the state is that of the issue of state and regional autonomy. The appointment of the State Autonomy Committee and the Regional Autonomy Committee by the NC-led state government in 1997 was first initiative of its kind to address the conflicting regional response to the issue of autonomy by acknowledging the divergence around this issue on the regional basis. The State Autonomy Committee which was to address the issue of 'restoration' of the 'pristine' form of the Centre-State relations as these were available in the pre-1953 period, was aimed to address the sense of alienation of the people of Kashmir. Meanwhile, the Regional Autonomy Committee was appointed to address the regional discontent arising from the feeling of 'political neglect' arising out of 'Kashmir-Centric' political arrangements. The presumption underlying the appointment of these two committees was that by addressing the demand for regional autonomy along with the State autonomy, the grievance of people of both the regions would be addressed. However, this could not be possible due to the tactless approach both of the Central and State governments. While the Central government totally dismissed the recommendations of the State Autonomy Committee, the state government botched up the very basis of demand of regional autonomy. Subsequent to the submission of the report of the State Autonomy Committee, the state Legislature passed a resolution endorsing the demand of restoration of pre-1953 constitutional position of the state. The resolution that was sent to the Centre was not put for debate in any forum. On the contrary, when placed before the cabinet, it was summarily dismissed, generating a further sense of despondency in Kashmir. As regards the regional autonomy, the state government after dismissing and replacing the chairperson of the committee endorsed a report that questioned the very existence of Jammu and Ladakh as regions.

It was during the initiation of comprehensive peace process that was initiated by Atal Bihari Vajpayee that greater sensitivity developed around the multiple stakeholders in the state and divergent political aspirations and responses. Hence, the idea of extending the definition of conflict from external and internal to the intra-state level was mooted in various conferences and processes of dialogue. Of these, the Round Table Conferences (RTCs) that were held under this leadership are the most important ones. The five working groups that were constituted through these RTCs came up with elaborate report that took into consideration the political aspirations not only at the state, regional and sub-regional levels but also those of the marginal and backward groups including the internally displaced people of various kinds and the tribal Gujjars. More recently, the interlocutors appointed by the government of India have also shown sensitivity towards the multiple identity issues and have recommended the resolution of the conflict by taking into consideration the complexity arising out of the political divergence within the state. However, the reports of these groups remain mostly on papers.

Towards the political Future: Need for consensus building

The complexity that has been generated by the multiple identity politics of the state has made the conflict-resolution a challenging task. More particularly, it is the context of mutually exclusive and conflicting claims that makes it difficult to make progress in the peace process. Politically divergent positions have already led many to think of simplified solutions like the division of the state. This idea has been floated in different forms, off and on, from different quarters at different times. Of the early formulations that have been proposed to deal with the intricacies of the state include the 'Dixon' formula or the 'Chenab-based' division. As per this formulation, the division of the state around the river Chenab is suggested. Since this divide is regional-cum-religious divide (in the sense that it not only divides Kashmir region from Jammu but also places the Muslim-dominated districts of Jammu along with Kashmir), it has met with fierce criticism on the ground that it is purely communal in nature. However, despite its dangerous communal implications, it has continued to attract many academicians, intellectuals and organisations. The Kashmir Study Group, a think tank based in USA, came up with a report in late nineties which suggested the division of the state on regional/religious lines and adoption of different approaches to deal with each part of the state. Later on, General Musharraf also suggested the 'regional' solution to Kashmir problem, defining J&K on the basis of five regions, two on the sides of Pakistan and three on Indian side (Jammu, Kashmir and Ladakh). The idea of division of the state has also been floated by the Hindu Rightist groups as well. The RSS actually passed a formal resolution about the division of the state. Nearer home, the demand for separation of Jammu from Kashmir and its reorganisation as a separate state; the separation of Ladakh and its recognition as a Union Territory; and the demand for 'Homeland' for Kashmiri Pundits (carved out of few districts in Kashmir) has been made by organisations like Jammu Mukti Morcha/Jammu State Morcha; Ladakh Buddhist Association and the Panun Kashmir respectively.

This simplified resolution of complex nature of conflict has been rejected by many on the grounds of its being communal in nature. The religious carving of new units or reorganisation of the state on religious principles, does not cater to context of identity politics of the state. The identity politics of the state is not simply based on the factor of religion and religious identities not only overlap with other kinds of identities but are also internally differentiated. Hence, the religious basis of division of the state, cannot succeed beyond a point. At the most it can generate communalised politics, but not actually resolve the conflict.

The only way the conflict situation in the context of multiple identities and divergent political positions can be resolved, is through the process of consensus building. Though consensus may seem to be a far-reaching idea in the State, however, it can be stated that during the last two decades, some minimum consensus has been evolved within the state. Most of the stakeholders within the state are insistent on maintaining the integrity of the state and sustaining its plural character. This in itself is a very good starting point for building further consensus on more intricate issues. There is also a consensus that the communal and divisive politics is no solution to the problems in the state.

It is on the basis of these minimums, that a process of consensus building has to be attained. However, this process has to be a very intricate one, not merely involving multi-layered dialogues and negotiations but also generating a sense of partnership among the various kinds of stakeholders. Beginning therefore has to be made through a really inclusive process of dialogue, giving a sense of ownership to all the stakeholders,

4

Changing Contours of Armed Violence in Northeast India

Nani Gopal Mahanta

Terror attack, Civil wars, struggles over Right to Self Determination in the post 1990 period have redefined our perceptions about war, religion, ethnicity and the role of the State as the sole custodian over violence and authority. Although the whole world is facing acute crisis of terrorism and insurgency from 1990s, it is only after the 9-11 that the subject has gained global significance –thanks to the reaction of the American media! From 1990s various insurgents have arisen and gained momentum across the globe. Most wars in the 21st century are intra-state and they are incredibly resistant and tend to defy easy solutions. These contemporary conflicts have been defined in various manners— These wars have been described as 'New Wars'(Kaldor), 'internal conflicts'(Brown), 'Small wars' (Harding), 'Conflict in post colonial states' (Van de Goor), "protracted social conflicts' (Edward E. Azar) , 'deep-rooted conflicts' (John W. Burton) and so on.[1] Preferring the term "intractable conflicts", Benjamin Gidron, Stanley N. Katz and Yaheskel Hasenfeld argue that characteristics of these conflicts include being protracted, continual, violent, perceived as irreconcilable, zero sum, central to the lives of the identity group involved.[2]

---

[1] Mary kaldor, New and Old Wars :: Organised Violence in a Global Era , Palo Alto, CA : Standford University Press, 1999; Edward E. Azar, " The Analysis and Management of Protracted Conflicts," in *the Psychodynamics o international Relationships*, Vol II : Unofficial Diplomacy at work, eds Vamik D. Volkan, Joseph Montville etc (Lexington, MA: Lexington Books, pp-1993-120 ; John W. Burton, resolving deep rooted Conflict : A Handbook , Lanham, MD,University Press of America, 1987

[2] Benjamin Gidron, Stanley N. Katz and Yeheskel Hasenfeld, Introduction : "Introduction, Theoretical Approach and Methodology," in Mobilizing for Peace : Conflict resolution ....., eds Benjamin Gidron, Stanley N. Katz and Yeheskel Hasenfeld, New York, OUP, 2002, pp3-35.

Northeast India: Militarization – a way of life

Northeast India is one such conflict zones where some armed rebellions go back to the days of colonial period. In the post-independence period the first major challenge to the Indian State as one unified nation had come from the Northeast (NE) India – a region, which is a conglomerate of seven (now eight with the inclusion of Sikkim) predominantly tribal states. The NE, comprising the states of Assam, Meghalaya, Manipur, Nagaland, Tripura, Arunachal Pradesh and Meghalaya is perhaps the most heterogeneous region of India with 250 social groups and more than 150 languages. Only 2 percent of the landmass is connected with India and the rest of the boundaries which is more than 4500 KM international border is shared with South and South East Asian countries like Bangladesh, Nepal, Bhutan, China and Myanmar. The whole region is connected with the rest of the county by a tenuous 22 kilometer land corridor through Siliguri in the eastern state of West Bengal—a link that come to be referred to as the 'chicken's neck'.

The Naga rebellion—sometimes called the mother of the region's insurgencies—began in the 1950s. Though dormant since a ceasefire in 1997, it is one of the world's oldest unresolved armed conflicts.[3] A recent World Bank report describes the region as a victim of a low level equilibrium where poverty and lack of development (compared with the remainder of India and other Southeast Asian nations), lead to civil conflict, lack of belief in political leadership and government, and, therefore, to a politically unstable situation.

The sheer number of armed rebel groups in the region is extraordinary. According to one recent count, there are as many as 115 armed rebel groups. Manipur State tops the list with forty such organizations, six of which are banned, and in addition there are nine "active" and twenty five "inactive" rebel groups. Assam is next on the list with thirty-nine rebel groups – two of which are banned, with six active and twenty six inactive armed groups. Meghalaya has armed rebel groups, of which three are active and one

---

[3] Sanjiv Baruah 'Confronting Constructionism : Ending the Naga war' in *Ethnonationalism in India –A Reader* ed by Sanjib Baruah, (New Delhi: Oxford University Press, 2010), p.239

inactive. Mizoram has two rebel organizations and both are listed as active. Nagaland has two active and two inactive groups of rebels. Tripura has two rebel groups that are banned, in addition to one active and twenty-two inactive groups. Only Arunachal, according to this count, has no armed rebel organizations.[4]

A typological analysis of the conflicts in NE India can be made in the following manner:-

1. First category is secessionist or exclusivist type. These type of movements, which are essentially violent in nature such as United Liberation Front of Assam (ULFA), National Democratic Front of Bodoland (NDFB), NSCN (I-M) etc. want to establish independent homeland.

2. The second type is autonomist in character. Assam movement from 1979-1984 was a non violent way of redefining the relationship between the centre and the periphery. In addition, there are many insurgent groups who want to redefine their relationship within Indian union as an autonomous state or as a separate state or demanding district council within the existing system. The Bodoland, the tribal movements in Tripura and in Karbi Anglong etc. are some of the examples of this type.

3. There are struggles which fight against the dominance by the dominant group within the state. The Bodos fight against the Assamese, the fight between the Nagas and Kukis and Nagas and the Meiteis, the Karbis and the Dimasas, Karbis and Kukis are some of the examples of this type. In many of such inter tribal clashes it leads to massive killing and displacement.

4. There are intra-tribal clashes which also lead to violence in the region. The Nagas for example are fighting not only against the Indian State but also against themselves for dominance and power. The Bodos have significant differences that led to the killing of many Bodos from 1996-2000.

---

[4] Compiled by the figure given by Institute of Conflict Management, see http://www.satp.org/ accessed on 15th August, 2010

5. There could be another category – those who are fighting for an autonomous state within constitution of India under article 244 A. The Karbis and the Bodos are demanding this status from time to time.

6. There are some movements which seek to gain some benefits within the Indian constitution such as recognition as the SC and ST. In recent times groups like Chutia, Koch-Rajbangshi, The Adivasis, the Ahoms and the Motok and Moran are demanding ST recognition.

7. There are some movements which are irredentist in its character. The demand for "Nagalim" encompassing the territories of Assam, Manipur and Arunachal Pradesh is the best example of this type. The Bodos in Assam are also encroaching reserved forest land and forcing people to leave in the Bodoland area so that they can form one homogenous homeland in the area.

8. However these movements are not mutually exclusive in their character. Many of violent movements are successfully co-opted and settled within Indian union like that of the Mizo movement. Even groups like NSCN are now negotiating for a "special Federal relations" with India. Many of the groups referred above are having "suspension of operations" with the Ministry of Home Affairs, GOI.

Needless to say, the common referent point for all the movements is the Indian State from whom they want to derive maximum allocation of resources and benefit. All these movements have made serious repercussions leading to profound human insecurity in the region. The Indian federal government and those governing the states in the Northeast have deployed large formations of regular army, federal paramilitary forces. The inevitable militarization of the region and the murky "covert operations" has been accompanied by rampant human rights violations due to the unrestrained use of terror by both state forces and rebel factions. Extra-judicial killing, ethnic cleansing and large-scale massacres followed by substantial internal displacement—India's northeast has witnessed it all. The growth of the civil society in the strife torn region has been impeded by the lack of democratic space, because special laws, all very draconian and very unpopular with local communities, have remained in effect in the Northeast to fight the insurgencies. The high level of legislative instability in some of the northeastern states have been compounded by the growing linkages between legitimate political parties and the underground rebel factions or those who have gained state patronage after surrender. Forming a complex matrix, no other region of India, South Asia, or the world for that matter, have seen the existence of the numerous ethnic based insurgent outfits nor the proliferation and mushrooming of militant outfits as in North East India. A small glimpse of active insurgent groups in the region is given here —

State wise List of Major Militant/Insurgent Groups Active in the North Eastern States[5]

Assam

    (i)   United Liberation Front of Assam (ULFA).

    (ii) National Democratic Front of Bodoland (NDFB).

    (iii) Dima Halam Daogah (Joel Garlosa) – DHD (J).

Manipur

    (i)   People's Liberation army (PLA).

    (ii) United National Liberation Front (UNLF).

    (iii) People's Revolutionary Party of Kangleipak (PREPAK).

    (iv) Kangleipak Communist Party (KCP).

    (v) Kanglei Yaol Kanba Lup (KYKL).

    (vi) Manipur People's Liberation Front (MPLF).

    (vii) Revolutionary People's Front (RPF).

Meghalaya

    (i) Hynniewtrep National Liberation Council (HNLC).

---

[5] Government of India, Ministry of Home Affairs, Annual Report 2011.

Tripura

(i) All Tripura Tiger Force (ATTF).

(ii) National Liberation Front of Tripura (NLFT).

Nagaland

(i) The National Socialist Council of Nagaland (Isak Muivah). [NSCN (1/M)]

(ii) The National Socialist Council of Nagaland (Khaplang). [NSCN (K)]

All the militant outfits mentioned above except the two factions of National Socialist Council of Nagaland, have been declared 'Unlawful Associations' under the Unlawful Activities (Prevention) Act, 1967 (3) of 1967). In addition, the outfits named above in respect of Assam, Manipur and Tripura have also been listed as 'terrorist organizations' in the schedule of the above Act. In addition, other militant groups like the Dima Halam Daogah (DHD) and United Peoples Democratic Solidarity (UPDS); Karbi Longri N.C. Hills Liberation Front (KLNLF), Kuki National Army (KNA) and Zomi Revolutionary Army (ZRA); Naga National Council (NNC) etc. are also active in the North East.

Current Status of Militancy in the Northeast

Head	2001	2002	2003	2004	2005	2006	2007	2008	2009	2010
Incidents	1335	1312	1332	1234	1332	1366	1489	1561	1297	773
Extremists Killed	572	571	523	404	405	3231	2609	4318	3842	3306
Security Forces Killed	175	147	90	110	70	76	79	46	42	20
Civilians Killed	600	454	494	414	393	309	498	469	264	94

Source: Computed from Annual Report, 2011.Ministry of Home Affairs, Government of India

- It would be wrong to say the Indian State resolves the identity and ethnicity issues only through coercive means. Many such violent and nonviolent movements are co-opted within the Indian political system.

This paper is organized in the following manner:-

1. It makes attempt to look at the transformation of insurgency in the Northeast with a case study of United Liberation Front of Asom (ULFA). It tries to decipher the transformation process of insurgency in the region.

2. The paper tries to argue that the use of violence by the insurgent groups become indiscriminate as they grope for support base from place to place. In the process they become hostage to the international terror network.

3. The paper also tries to look at the nature of international terror network that provide infrastructural and other logistic support to insurgent groups in the region. The paper looks into the nature of sanctuary provided by Bhutan and Bangladesh.

4. The paper argues that an insurgency movement like ULFA can't be exclusively looked from the binary prism of 'Greed and Grievances'. The paper urges for a more pro-active role of the Indian State in resolving protracted conflicts in the region.

Essentially there are two approaches to look at the causes of civil conflict or violent conflict in the society—the Greed or the supply side of violence model vis-à-vis Grievances model. The supply side of violence model or greed theories has concentrated on economic opportunities in war. It argues that much of the post-cold war civil conflicts have been driven by not purely for political reasons but rather by powerful economic motives and agenda to grab booty. The Greed theorists concluded that conflict could be seen instead as the continuation of economics by other means. Warfare was to be better understood as 'an instrument of enterprise and violence as a mode of accumulation'.[6] Paul Collier's empirical research into the cause

---

[6] Paul Collier, 'Doing Well Out of War' in M Berdal and D. Malone, ed *Greed and Grievances : Economic Agendas in Civil Wars*, (Boulder, CO, Lynne Rienner, 2000).

of large scale civil conflicts from 1965 to the present for World Bank concluded that the best predictors of conflict, all other things being equal, were low average income and the availability of a high proportion of young men with inadequate access to educational opportunities, low growth and high dependence on primary products such as oil, diamond etc.

The Grievance model is based on the more traditional perceptions of the reasons for conflict ; the theorists focus on the failures of the social contract between the states and citizens like inequalities, weak institutions, poverty and lack of social services as root cause of the conflict. They noted that while wars were essentially group activities, individual motivations could prolong conflict. In studying the economic and social causes of war and Development, they categorized group formations around religions, class, clan and regional interest. Power inequalities and asymmetries can include sources of long term as well as short term grievances. It's not merely the existence of these inequalities, but a collective feeling of 'unfairness' stemming from a skewed distribution of development gains and power sharing. The failure of political structures to address inequalities and curb the dominance of particular group leads to dissatisfactions that ignite conflicts.[7]

Most of the academic writings on ULFA have underestimated the role of exogenous factors in the sustenance of insurgency. The role of internal dynamics in the rise and sustenance of ULFA can hardly be overlooked. In fact we have shown in the previous chapters how the Assamese middle class led the identity issues against New Delhi. But to say that the Assamese middle class is still the support base of ULFA will be too a simplistic argument without taking into account some other factors. Initially Assamese middle class provided qualified support to ULFA for being able to draw the attention of New Delhi in the form of more money; more business means more money for the middle class. There are indications to show that the Assamese middle class is extremely critical of ULFA's view on certain issues of Assam, like the illegal migration issue, ULFA's support to Pakisatn over Kargil war, it's shelter at Bangladesh, some thoughtless killing the recent being in Dhemaji and so on.

---

[7] For details see G Ostby, ' Horizontal inequalities and Civil war.' Centre for the Study of Civil War, Oslo, International Peace Research Institute (PRIO), Norway 2003.

In this age of 'new terrorism'[8], an organization can't survive on basis of the internal source only—particularly when that source is fast depleting. Globalization of terrorism has brought insurgent groups, smugglers, weapon merchants and other non-State actors together in one platform. More than 98 percent open border, thick jungles, a cooperative hand at the neighboring countries, inability of some countries to take strong actions against the insurgent groups , accessibility of a vast arms market in the golden triangle etc. are some of the factors responsible for a south Asian terrorist network. All the major insurgent groups have a mutually interdependent relationship and ULFA is not an exception to it.

ULFA , NDFB and KLO in Bhutan :

Thus insurgent groups of Assam and the Northeast have received support from neighbouring countries, including Pakistan and China.[9] In addition, Myanmarese fringe outfits (primarily the Kachins) have deepened existing historical-cultural ties further by supporting local movements by offering training, safe havens and outward routes. As a matter of detail, the Myanmarese connection in the separatist campaigns of the region predates almost all other such external aid.[10]

The roles of Bhutan and Nepal in 'the little wars' have largely been those of accessories. The two Himalayan nations have provided safe havens to separatist groups from the Northeast, as also transit facilities. The United Liberation Front of Asom (ULFA) and the National Democratic Front of Bodoland (NDFB) had their headquarters in Bhutan until the Bhutan Government clamped its military power on ULFA and NDFA. Perhaps the most fruitful support that ULFA receives are the Islamic militancy in Bangladesh and from ISI and DGFI of Bangladesh.

---

[8] Ian o. Lesser, "Countering New Terrorism: Implications for Strategy" in Ian O. Lesser etc. ed, *Countering New Terrorism* (Rand, April, 2003).

[9] See for detail , Nirmal Nibedon, *Nagaland : The night of the Guerillas*, New Delhi: Lancer, 1983, second edition and also see Subir Bhaumiik, *Insurgent Crossfire*, New Delhi: Lancer, 1996.

[10] See for details, Dipankar Banerjee, *Myanmar and Northeast India*, New Delhi, Delhi Policy Group, 1997 and also Bhaumik, *Insurgent Crossfire*, p-32.

Writers like Jaideep Saikia and Wasbir Hussain have provided security oriented analysis of such sanctuaries in Bhutan and Bangladesh.[11] However it is also essential to look at the political dynamics why Bhutan and Bangladesh have provided political sanctuary to ULFA at a certain point of time and what is the nature of assistance and why have denied such patronage at a particular point of time ?

The most important treaty that guides Bhutan –India relationship is 1949 treaty of Friendship and Cooperation. The treaty has three main characteristics-[12]

1. By this treaty, India recognizes the independence of Bhutan.

2. India will not interfere in the internal matters of Bhutan

3. Bhutan accepts India's guidance on foreign policy.

ULFA and later on host of other insurgent groups like NDFB and KLO preferred to take shelter in Bhutan after the first organized military offensive in Assam named as 'operation Bajrang' took place on November 27-28 ,1990. The process of taking shelter in Bhutan increased as the pro India Awami League came to power in Dhaka in 1996 and crackdown on the rebels were intensified. Stefan Preisner has said the Bhutanese Government initially used to ignore them mainly in the Sandrup Jangkhar district of southern Bhutan along the Indo-Bhutan border.[13] The Foreign Ministry has said that the rebels were operating from 30 camps which include 13 for ULFA, 12 for NDFB and 5 for KLO. The ULFA camps were located in Sandrup Jongkhar district, Sarpang district and the lower Zhemgang , the NDFB camps were located in Sandrup Jongkhar district, Sarpang district and the

---

[11] See Jaideep Saikia, *Terror Sans Frontiers*, Vision Books, New Delhi, 2004 ,'Asom : Quest For Peace' in Pushpita Das and Namrata Goswami, ed. *India's Northeast,*pp-241-257, (New Delhi: Manas Publications, 2008) *and* Wasbir Hussain, *Insurgency sans Borders : An Analysis of Separatist insurrections in India's Northeast*in Wasbir Hussain ed. *Order in Chaos*, (Guwahati: Spectrum Publication, 2006), pp-109-125. Their writings can also be seen in various articles in *Faultlines* –a security centric journal published by Institute of Conflict Management, New Delhi.

[12] Leo E. Rose, *The Politics of Bhutan*, (New York: Cornell University press, 1977), pp. 7-72.

[13] Stefan preisner, "Bhutan in 1997: Striving for Stability.", *Asian Survey* 37 : 2 (February, 1998), p158.

KLO were located in Sandrup Jongkhar, Kalikhola Dungkhag and Samtse.

However three factors had forced Bhutanese governments to put pressure on ULFA, NDFB and KLO to leave and shift their camps in 1998[14]:

1. Continuous pressure from India.

2. Increasing disturbances in Southern Bhutan.

3. The Lhotshampa issue.

Bhutan resisted India's pressure till 2000. From 2001 to 2003 a number of dignitaries from India visited Bhutan. Both the India's National Security Advisor and the Chief of Army of Staff visited Bhutan in 2003 to raise India's deep concern. India in very categorical terms told Bhutan that such huge presence of Insurgents is not acceptable to India and was on the verge of an adverse relationship if Bhutan does decide to crack down ULFA and other insurgents. [15]

Meanwhile ULFA and the other militant groups took the Bhutanese government too lightly and started their own dominance in Southern Bhutan, including extortion and threatening to the traders in the area. In his speech the Bhutanese Prime Minister Lyonpo Jigme in the 12th Summit of South Asian Association of Regional Cooperation (SAARC) in Islamabad, in January 2004, complained that the rebels had impeded trade, forced the closure of several large industries an educational institutions, prohibited general development and conducted unprovoked attacks within the Bhutanese territory. [16]

The Lhotshampa (ethnic Nepalis) issue in southern Bhutan also prompted the Bhutanese Government to take action against the ULFA. The Bhutanese nation wide survey in 1991 had shown large increase of the ethnic Nepalese who increasingly settled in the fertile southern areas. The

---

[14] Arijit Majumder, "Bhutan's Military Action against Indian Insurgents,", *Asian survey*, Vol. 45, Issue-4, 2005, pp-566-580

[15] Rajesh Kharat, "Bhutan' s Security Scenario", *Contemporary South Asia* , 13; 2, June , 2004, p-181.

[16] Referred in Arijit Majumder, "Bhutan's Military Action against Indian Insurgents", *Asian survey*, Vol. 45, Issue-4, pp-570.

Bhutanese thought the increasing rise of the Lhotshampas might precipitate a disturbed situation in the Himalayan Kingdom. Interestingly Bhutan was reminded of the role played by the Sikkimiese Nepalis in their revolt against the Sikkimese monarchy which ultimately resulted in the merger of Sikkim with India in 1975.[17] The royal Government in order to prevent such a scenario to happen attempted to impose Bhutanese Dzongkha language, style of dress and the dominant Drukpa Buddhist religion. Many of the Nepalis were taken away their citizenship and nearly 100,000 fled the kingdom. The Lhotshampas resented such action and had drawn lot of international reaction.[18] The Bhutanese Government did not want the Lhotshampas to align with ULFA and NDFB and pose a larger security threat to Bhutan. The Bhunatese did not want the ULFA to supply arms and lessons of dissent to the Lhotshampas. From 1998 till 2001 the Royal Governments have been in five rounds of talks with ULFA and three rounds with the NDFB. In spite of repetitive requests and agreements ULFA closed down only one out of nine of their camps in Bhutan. [19] The top level leadership of both the organizations never bothered to talk rather middle level office bearers were sent to negotiate when their counterparts was the Prime Minister of Bhutan himself and in some occasions the King himself. [20] In 1999, the National Assembly of Bhutan adopted four pronged approaches to put pressure on ULFA and NDFB. These included talks with the armed groups, curtailing supplies to the miltant camps and the prosecuting those Bhutanese who assisted the insurgents. [21] Only as the last option military action is contemplated. The Bhutanese government did not want to go to a military confrontation with only 6000 odd soldiers of the Royal Bhutan Army who did not have any practical exposure to jungle warfare.

---

[17] Kharat, Bhutan's Security Scenario, *Contemporary South Asia,* 13; 2, June 2004, pp-177-178.

[18] Amnesty International, Nationality, Expulsion, Statelessness and the Right to Return, New York, Amnesty International, 2000, p-4.

[19] By December, 2001, ULFA was supposed to close four out of their nine camps. Later on it increased its numbers to 15.

[20] Thierry Mathou, "Bhutan in 2001: At the Crossroads,", *Asian Survey,* 42:2 (January/ February), 2002, p-193.

[21] Arijit Majumder, "Bhutan's Military Action against Indian Insurgents,", *Asian survey*, Vol. 45, Issue-4, pp-572, 2005

Meanwhile the presence of the militants hampered the business interest of Bhutan dearly. The Dungsum Cement project had to close down and the trade routes with India were seriously hit. The 900 megawatt Mangdechy Hydopower project to be built with Indian assistance was also stalled. [22] Both the India's National Security Advisor and the Chief of Army of Staff visited Bhutan in 2003 to raise India's deep concern. India in very categorical terms told Bhutan that such huge presence of Insurgents is not acceptable to India and was on the verge of an adverse relationship if Bhutan does decide to crack down ULFA and other insurgents.[23] India also offered its military help but was skeptical to intervene as it might draw reverse international public opinion to conduct operations in a sovereign country. The Bhutanese Government made one last ditch effort in the 81st session of the Bhutan National Assembly on June 28 that continued till August 18 by taking two resolutions. The first was to request the armed groups of the Northeast region to leave the country voluntarily or expel them by using military force if they don't pay heed to the first one. As expected this time too the brothers in arms failed to recognize the gravity of the situation.

On 15th December the RBA launched attacks on ULFA, NDFB and KLO in the southern parts of Bhutan. The last war the Buddhist Bhutan fought was 138 years ago when they fought British in the Anglo-Bhutanese war of 1865 in which Bhutan was defeated by the crown's Army. [24] However the kingdom did not have to try hard to oust the Indian insurgents. The ULFA's Central headquarters at Phukaptong and the group's General Headquarter at Merengphu both in Sandrup jongkhar was destroyed in three days and it also captured the NDFB camp at Tikri and also KLO camps in Samtse district. According to Timeline Bhutan Year 2003, by December 19 all 30 camps had been captured and more than 90 insurgents were killed and 100 captured. However another account says at least 650 rebels were

---

[22] Ibid-p-573.

[23] Rajesh Kharat, Bhutan's Security Scenario, *Contemporary South Asia*, 13; 2, June, 2004, p-181.

[24] Bhabani Sen Gupta, *Bhutan; Towards a grass root participatory polity*, (New Delhi, Konarak, 1999), pp-25-26. Referred in Wasbir Hussain, *Insurgency sans Borders: An Analysis of Separatist insurrections in India's Northeast* in Wasbir Hussain ed. *Order in Chaos*, (Guwahati: Spectrum Publication, 2006) pp-113.

neutralized –killed or captured. [25]

The Indian Army 4 corps based at Tezpur sealed the 266 kilometer international border and 20th Mountain division, Siliguri helped in the medical evacuation. India's role was more in terms of providing logistics, medical evacuation, surveillance, hot chase around the border and communication. Major General SS Dhillon, Commandant of the Indian Military Training Team coordinated the whole operation with the Chief of Operation officer, RBA, Lieutenant General GG Lam Dorji in the Bhutanese capital Thimphu and reported directly to the King Wangchuk. The top most leaders of ULAF who were captured and handed over to India were Bhimkanta Buragohain,— the senior most cadres and one of the members since the foundation of the organization in 1979, Mithinga Daimary-the publicity secretary Robin Neog. Around 64 family members, women cadres and children of these organizations who were residing in the camps were handed over to Indian authorities. However the fate of many top most ULFA leaders is not yet known whether they were killed or in the custody.

ULFA in Bangladesh

According to Subir Bhowmick, Bangladesh had started providing shelter to the rebels of Northeast from 1978 three years after India started arming the *Shanti Bahini* to fight in Chittagong Hill tracts.[26] The ULFA after being flushed out of Bhutan has set up minimum 8 bases in the Mymensingh region bordering the Indian state of Meghalaya.[27] Initially the ULFA's presence in Sherpur was very temporary but after the Bhutan episode it's presence in the area increased substantially. ULFA's leadership was however based in Bangladesh.

Why Bangladesh has started providing such huge support to the insurgent groups of Northeast. Is it just because of porous border –or Dhaka's inability to control its periphery? Is this to revenge India's support to the

---

[25] Provin kumar , cited in Subir Bhowmick, *Troubled Periphery-Crisis of India's North-east*, (New Delhi: Sage Publications, 2009), p-179. *The Assam tribune* on January, 3, 2004 quoted General Vij who also gave the figure of 650.

[26] Subir Bhowmick, *Troubled Periphery-Crisis of India's North-east,* (New Delhi: Sage Publications, 2009),p-169.

[27] Ibid-p-173.

Shanti Bahini to fight in Chittagong Hill tracts? Whether India's hegemonic role in the South Asia is responsible for keeping Northeastern India disturbed? How far is it to do with the growing Islamic fundamentalism in Bangladesh? To what extent China and Pakistan is responsible. These issues require deeper analysis for which we shall have to look into the politics of Bangladesh.

After playing a decisive role in ensuring Bangladesh's independence in 1971 India immediately pulled out its forces from Bangladesh and was the first country to recognize her as an independent Sovereign country. In 1972 both the States signed an agreement "Treaty of Friendship and Peace" for a term of 25 years. By the agreement both the Sates would respect each others independence, sovereignty and territorial integrity while refraining from interfering in each other's internal affairs. However after the death of Mujibur Rehman in 1975 there was a gradual transformation of Bangladesh from linguistic nationalism to Islamic nationalism. From the stated objectives of nationalism, secularism, democracy and socialism Bangladesh embraced Islamic ideology as the means to legitimize the subsequent regimes. The Bhratiya Janata Party's coming to power in 1998 with a proclaimed Hindutva ideology triggered Bangladesh's apprehension about India. [28]

India's gigantic size, economy and military power is a great source of concern for Bangladesh. Bangladesh shares a 4095-km international border with India. Of this the state of West Bengal has a border length of 221 kms, Tripura 856 kms, Mizoram 318 kms and Assam 262 Kms. India is also deeply concerned about Bangladesh's strategic alliance with Pakistan and China. There is suspicion that Pakistan's President Pervez Musharraf's visit to the country in 2003 was to forge strong military ties and ensure smooth operation of the Inter Service Intelligence (ISI) from the territory of Bangladesh. To meet his objectives he surveyed the possibility of harnessing insurgent forces that could be utilized for anti-India activities in her Northeastern border. It is also widely reported in the regional and national News papers that Musharraf in his visit met with ULFA's General Secretary Anup Chetia who has been detained in Bangladesh jail since 1998 for illegal

---

[28] Harsh V. Pant, India and Bangladesh-Will the Twain Ever Meet ? in *Asian Survey*, Vol 47, p-233, 2007.

stay in Bangladesh.[29] The allegation was made by Local Government Minister and Awami League General Secretary Syed Ashraful Islam while accompanying the Prime Minister Sheikh Hasina who visited India on January, 9, 2010.[30]

India's suspicion of Bangladesh also increased as the latter tried to woo China to prevent India from asserting hegemonic position in the region. Manish Dabhade and Harsh V. pant have argued that the smaller states in the region have utilized China as leverage in their dealings with India. [31] China is too happy to increase its interventionist role as it would keep India engaged in the regional issues and would effectively prevent her aspirations to become a global power. China did not recognize Bangladesh till 1975 – however China's relations with Bangladesh were determined by Pakistan factor. Growing Islamic resurgence in Pakistan and Bangladesh bring them closer. Because of their common security perceptions both are happy to be a part of China's 'encirclement policy' towards India. Bangladesh's increasing defence cooperation with China might divert India's attention from the western sector to the eastern sector. Very soon China tried its best to wean over Bangladesh from India's influence. The Defence Cooperation Agreement signed between the two countries in 2002 in Beijing can be considered to be the most significant steps in bringing the two countries together. China is also helping Bangladesh in the construction of a deep water port at Chittagong.

Like Pakistan, Bangladesh's domestic politics is largely determined by India. Bangladesh Nationalist Party (BNP) and other political parties have defined themselves in opposition to India portraying the Awami League as India's stooge. Beside the Islamic religious parties have gained ground in the electoral politics of the State by adopting a harsh anti-Indian line. Bangladesh's help to the insurgent outfits of Northeastincreased substantially

---

[29] Musharaf's meeting with Anup Chetia was widely reported in the News papers of Assam on 10th January, 2010. See *Assam Tribune*, January, 10, 2010.

[30] http://www.thaindian.com/newsportal/world-news/clear-evidence-of-musharraf-meeting-militant-anup-chetia_100301721.html accessed on June 15, 2010.

[31] Manish Dabhade and Harsh V. pant, "Coping with challenges to Sovereignty : Sino Indian Rivalry and Nepal's Foreign policy" in *Contemporary South Asia*, 13:2, June, 2004, 157-169.

after the BNP led coalitions assumed power in 2001. Immediately after the election there was attack on the Hindus at the behest of the ruling party activists. The near silence of the Government had encouraged the non-state radical Islamic groups to make Bangladesh an Islamic state and fight against the infidels. The supporting alliances of the BNP governments were among the most radical groups in the country. The Jamat-e-Islami (Islamic Assembly) and the Islamic Oikya Joot (IOJ-Islamic Unity Front) were linked to various Islamic organizations of Bangladesh. Incidentally the Jamat-e-Islami opposed Bangladesh's liberation and took a pro-Pakistani stand.[32] The growth of radical Islam in Bangladesh owes a lot to the failure of parliamentary politics and weakening of civil society.[33] Frequent fighting between the political parties and their inability to resolve nagging problems of the people have prevented the democratic institutions to function effectively. The vacuum has been filled up by the radical religious institutions. According to Kanchan Lakhsman, 50, 000 Islamic militants belonging to more than 40 groups now control large areas of Bangladesh with the assistance of the radical elements of the BNP government who were the stakeholders of the government. [34] After the US intervention in Afghanistan in 2001, the member of the IOJ one of the constituents of the ruling BNP took the street chanting-"We will be the Taliban and Bangladesh will be Afghanistan". Bangladesh has the third largest Muslim population in the world, however 70 million populations live on less than $10 a day.[35] Besides, Bangladesh is the most densely populated State in the world with 1250 persons living per sq km. Population doubled in Bangladesh from 1961-1991 from 55 million to 111.4 million, which is now nearly 130 million. Because of such tremendous pressure on land and acute poverty Assam and other Northeastern states become the preferred destination of immigrations from Bangladesh.

The growing radicalization has great consequences for Northeast in

---

[32] Shahedul Anam Khan, "Bangladesh : Challenges to Peace" , in Wasbir Hussain, ed. *Order in Chaos*, (Guwahati: Spectrum Publications, 2006) p-39.

[33] Harsh V. Pant, "India and Bangladesh-Will the Twain Ever Meet?" *Asian Survey*, Vol 47, p-238, 2007

[34] Kanchan Lakshman, "Islamist Extremists mobilization in Bangladesh*"*, *Terrorism Monitor* 13:12, June 2005, p-6

[35] Harsh V. Pant,, referred above, p-242.

general and Assam in particular. Since the pre colonial period the issue of illegal immigration from then East Bengal (now Bangladesh) remains the core issue of Assamese identity[36]. In fact as we have argued in the first chapter Assam's growing demand as an independent country emanates from the inability of the Indian State to give this much needed security to the Assamese elites. Although the Bangladeshi scholars and security experts deny the existence of Bangladeshi immigrants in Assam,[37] but the fact is an objective analysis would clearly reveal that such movements of population is bound to happen as the border between the two was virtually non-existent and there are many pushing factors that pull the Bangladeshi immigrants to Assam.

In recent years several studies have analyzed immigration and its impact on Assam and the other states of north east India. Much of the available literature points to immigration being problematic for Assam and the North East[38] though certain studies hold that the illegal immigration issue has been exaggerated [39] and that post −1971 migration from Bangladesh is more a myth than anything else and that 'there is no need to generate hysteria about a culture-in-crisis in order to expel a few thousand "illegal" migrants.'[40]

What is the magnitude of illegal immigration from Bangladesh? On the basis of Indian & Bangladesh documents one estimate holds that not less

---

[36] The first chapter of the book and the conclusion deal with the issues of Immigration and Identity.

[37] Shahedul Anam Khan, Bangladesh : Challenges to Peace , in Wasbir Hussain, ed. *Order in Chaos*, Spectrum Publication, Guwahati, 2006, P-43 and also Prof Imtiaz Ahmed, "Image of the Other" Paper presented at the contemporary South Asia Lecture series, Queen Elizabeth House, University of Oxford, June 20, 2005.

[38] BG Verghese, G Desai, etc. ed. *Situation in Assam*, Gandhi Peace Foundation, 1980. Mimeo. New Delhi; Sanjay Hazarika, Bangladeshisation of India, *The Telegrpah*, 6th February, 1992.; Mahmmad Taher, Ethnic Situation in North East, *North eastern Geographer, 28,*1997 and Myron Weiner, Rejected Peoples and unwanted migrants *in Economic and Political weekly*, August 21, 1993; Anup Saikia, Global Process and Local concerns : Bangladeshi migrants in Assam, in *Dialogue*, January-March, 2002, Vol. 3 No. 3.

[39] SK Das, Immigration and demographic Transformation of 1891-1981.in *Economic and Political weekly*, May 10, 1983., Monirul Hussain, *Assam Movement-Class, Idelogy and Identity*, Manak Publication.; Anindita Dasgupta, Poltical myth making in post-colonial Assam, in *Himal South Asia*, 13 (8), 2000.

[40] Anindita Dasgupta, referred above, pp-14-23

than one third of Assam's 22.38 million populations are immigrants and their descendants and those 10-14 million Bangladeshi migrants were settled in India.[41] Another estimate by a former Governor of Arunachal Pradesh and West Bengal holds that about 5 million illegal migrants from Bangladesh are settled in Assam.[42] Central Home Ministry/Intelligence Bureau sources place Assam's alien population from Bangladesh at about 4 million. Another study estimates that "based on the 1951 growth rate, the state of Assam should have a population of about 15 million. It has more than 7 million extra, according to the latest (1991) census. The extra numbers can be accounted for by either immigrants and / or their descendants". This would seem very plausible considering the estimates of 4 to 5 million made by intelligence sources being of reference only to the Bangladeshi immigrants and not to the descendants of such migrants.

A scholar from the Institute of Development Studies, Dhaka, points out that about 4.65 to 5 million migrated from Bangladesh between 1961-1974 and that there was no reason to believe that the phenomena of migration ceased after 1974.[43] Though this estimate is very conservative compared to Indian estimates, this is a rare acceptance of emigration from Bangladesh. Myron Weiner pointed out that had Assam's population increased at the same rate as the rest of India from 1901 to 1971, at a rate of 130%, the net population would be 7.6 million rather than 15 million in 1971 and consequently the share of migrants and their descendants amounted to 7.4 million.[44]

Going by such analysis, had Assam's population increased at the same rate as India from 1901 to 1991 at 254.99 % her population would be 8.33 million rather than 22.4 million in 1991, the share of migrants and their descendants amounting to 14.03 million. [45]

---

[41] Sanjay Hazrika, Bangladeshisation of India, *The Telegrpah*, 6th February, 1992

[42] TV Rajeshwar, Migration or Invasion in *The Hindustan Times*, 7th February, 1996, New Delhi.

[43] Referred in Anup Saikia, "Global Process and Local concerns : Bangladeshi migrants in Assam" *Dialogue*, January-March, 2002, Vol. 3 No. 3.

[44] Myron Weiner, *Sons of the Soil: Migration and Ethnic Conflict in India*, (Princeton University Press, 1988,

[45] Anup Saikia referred above.

Population Variation in India and Assam (in %)

DECADE	ASSAM	INDIA
1901-1911	16.99	5.75
1911-1921	20.48	-0.31
1921-1931	19.91	11.00
1931-1941	20.41	14.22
1941-1951	19.93	13.31
1951-1961	34.98	21.51
1961-1971	34.95	24.80
1971-1981	23.36	24.69
1981-1991	24.24	23.82
1991-2001	18.85	21.34

Source: Census India, various years.

Though such analysis is indicative of the migrant population in Assam, it is not useful in estimating the illegal immigration from Bangladesh. For this the rate of growth of Muslim population in Assam proves more useful, though this would ignore any non-Muslim immigrants from Bangladesh. It is apparent that growth rate of Muslim population in Assam has been far higher than the all-India aggregates. Such high growth rates can be attributed only to illegal immigration from Bangladesh. Fertility rates of the indigenous Assamese Muslims, who are educated, have high economic and income levels are in no way higher than Muslims across other parts of India. On the contrary it is likely, given their high literacy rates, that fertility rate of the indigenous Assamese Muslims are lower than those of Muslims residing in other states of India. Finally, since Muslims from other states of India are not unduly attracted to migrate to Assam, it establishes beyond reasonable doubt that behind the abnormal growth rate of Muslim population in Assam lies the Bangladeshi factor.

Proportion of Muslim Population in India and Assam (%)

DECADE	INDIA	ASSAM
1911	22.39	16.23
1931	23.49	22.78
1951	9.91	24.68
1961	10.71	25.30
1971	11.21	24.56
1991	12.12	28.43

Source: Census of India, various years.

While the 1991 and 2001 censuses show low population growth rates in Assam, the religion wise data of 1991 provides insights to the proportion of illegal migrants from 1981-91. Growth rates of Muslim population in Assam have been inordinately high vis-à-vis the non-Muslim population. Using the figure estimated by other sources, the quantum of illegal Bangladeshi immigrants in Assam of 4 to 5 million, would mean that between 18 to 22 percent of Assam's population comprises of illegal aliens.[46] Few regions in the world have such a high proportion of its populace as illegal aliens.

The problem of immigration from Bangladesh is over a century old. Only with India's independence did the migration become 'illegal'. While the fact remains that several states of India face a similar problem, such as West Bengal and Bihar, the larger base populations of these states in a way alleviates the intensity of the problem. In Tripura, another north eastern state of India, the local populations have been turned into a minority community over time by the sheer numbers of cross border migrants from Bangladesh. In 1947, 56 per cent of Tripura's population consisted of tribal (or indigenous) population. Today this stands at a quarter of the total.[47] Bengali Hindus had become 71 percent by 1971 and by then political and administrative power had passed from the indigenous tribal population to

[46] Anup hazrika , Referred above.
[47] H. Narayan, "Tribal tribulation in Tripura", *The Statesman,* 20 March, 1997.

migrant Bengalis; transfer of land to the Bengali migrants proved to be the critical factor in deteriorating social relations and in the June 1980 riots hundreds lost their lives. The tribals of Tripura have today been reduced to numerical non entities and are engaged in armed conflict against the migrants whom they see as the usurpers of their homelands. With political and administrative power in the hands of the latter, the tribals are engaged in a losing battle for survival. The perception in Assam is that just as the tribals of Tripura were economically, politically and numerically marginalized, the same fate may befall them. A veritable 'Tripurisation of Assam' in the coming decades cannot be ruled out.[48] Unfortunately, such fears have been treated lackadaisically, perhaps due to political compulsions, both by Delhi and Dispur.[49] We shall have occasion to discuss about the issue of immigration in our last chapter where I shall argue for a more pragmatic approach as a state of denial or an exaggerated figure of immigrants are landing us nowhere.

Whatever the numbers of the immigrants in Assam, the fact is Bangladesh occupies a significant position in the contemporary political history of Assam. However from 1995 onwards the issue is more directed towards Bangladesh's role in providing sanctuary to the militants of the Northeast and their design in doing so. Is it linked to the process of Immigration or the creation of Brihot Bangla[50] as some writers have argued? Jaidip Saikia has termed one of his chapters in his book "Terror Sans Frontiers" as "Swadhin Asom or Brihot Bangladesh".[51] Saikia has argued—

"Bangladesh is the main abettor for the new interest group, with a section of its intelligentsia, backed by the "barrack politics" of the country, which seeks annexation of Assam to be a greater Bangladesh....the new interest group's technique is to exploit Islam in order to consolidate the annexation from illegal migration from Bangladesh into Assam that is happening for reasons of economics."[52]

---

[48] Anup Sakia, "Tripurisation of Assam" Assam Tribune, 15 May 1996.

[49] Mahmmad Taher, Ethnic Situation in North East, North eastern Geographer, 28,1997

[50] Greater Bangladesh.

[51] Jaideep Saikia, Terror Sans Frontiers, Vision Books, New Delhi, 2004 ,p-66, Chapter -3.

[52] Jaidip Saikia 'Asom : Quest For Peace' in Pushpita Das and Namrata Goswami, ed. India's Northeast,pp-248, Manas Publications, New Delhi,, 2008

The greater Bangladesh and Islamic alarm may be too early and seem to have grossly neglected the moderate section of the middle class and intelligentsia in Bangladesh. Security experts give us an impression as if the entire Bangladesh is engulfed with Islamic radicalism and Taliban's taking over the country is just matter of time. As a perceptive Bangladeshi scholar has opined—

> "Bangladesh can also take solace in the fact that the deeply religious but moderate Bengali Muslim would not allow this to happen (radicalization of Bangladeshi society). It is their attitude to religion that makes them conform to the liberal values that Islam preaches that will militate against obscurantism and the distorted ideology of the extremists prevailing in the country......"[53]

Shiekh Hasina's coming to power in 1999 and the massive loss of BNP and other radical Islamic forces is a testimony to the fact that Islamisation or radicalization of Bangladesh society is taking place with a section of groups only. Too much reading of Islamisation of Bangladeshi society might hamper a durable conflict resolution process through people to people contact and Track II initiative.

However the elitist and the radical elements in the military establishment and intelligence establishments had definitely played a pro-active role in providing logistical and strategic support to the ULFA and other militant groups of the region. A scholar has argued in the journal Asian Survey—

> "Bangladesh, in fact, has long been a willing host to militant outfits operating in Northeast India. Even before the emergence of Bangladesh as an independent state, the Chittagong Hill Tracts were used by the Pakistani Army to train and shelter Mizo and Naga insurgents fighting against India. It has been suspected that Bangladesh, and Pakistan's ISI, has been coordinating anti-India activities along with outfits like the United Liberation Front of Assam, the National Socialist Council of Nagaland, the National Liberation Front of Tripura, and the All Tripura Tiger Force."[54]

---

[53] Shahedul Anam Khan, "Bangladesh: Challenges to Peace", in Wasbir Hussain, ed. *Order in Chaos*, Spectrum Publication, Guwahati, 2006, p-39.

[54] Harsh V. Pant,, referred above, P-243.

Recent evidence suggests that the ISI is now executing a much wider strategy of encirclement, exploiting every potential area of conflict, and the extensive, sensitive and poorly managed land borders all along the East and Northeast of India. It is under this larger programme that the ISI now operates training camps near the border in Bangladesh where separatist groups of the Northeast, collectively known as the 'United Liberation Front of Seven Sisters', are trained in terrorist activities. These groups include the National Socialist Council of Nagaland (NSCN), People's Liberation Army (PLA), the United Liberation Front of Asom (ULFA) and the Northeast Student's Organisation (NESO).[55]

B G Verghese in his seminal work 'India's Northeast Resurgent' gives an account how ULFA received support from Myanmar, ISI and DGFI support in Bangladesh and less successfully with LTTE. Indian Government was successful in putting pressure at Myanmar government for withdrawing their training camp by the Kachin Independent Army (KIA).[56] Verghese further remarks –

"Pressures in Myanmar led ULFA a couple of years later to establish contacts with the ISI and the Afghan Mujahideen in Pakistan and still later with the Bangladesh Field Intelligence in Dhaka and, less successfully, with the LTTE."[57]

The first comprehensive report on the subject was placed before the Assam State Assembly on April 6, 2000 by Chief Minister Prafulla Kumar Mahanta, after almost a year-long engagement with the ISI's activities throughout the State.[58] The Report followed the penetration and eventual dismantling of one of the Pakistani intelligence Agency's network in the State. On August 7, 1999, the Assam Police achieved a major breakthrough

---

[55] www.fas.org/irp/world/pakistan/isi/

[56] Operation Golden Bird by both Indian and Burmese armies in April-May 1995 killed 50 insurgents and a substantial number was arrested. The major engagement took place in the champai and Chhimtuipui sectors of Mizoram . ULFA's foreign secretary Sasadhar Chaudhury was among those caught later on to be released on bail. The value of shipment captured with delivery costs was placed at $250,000. obtained through Intelligence sources.

[57] BG Verghese, India's Northeast Resurgent, p-58.

[58] ISI activities in Assam, statement laid on the table of the house of Assam Legislative Assembly under item no 12, dated 6.4.2000. The full text is available at WWW.satp.org.

and arrested two officers of the ISI as well as two other agents of the same Agency from a hotel in Guwahati. The police also arrested twenty seven other persons belonging to different Islamic militant groups. The four ISI operatives arrested were identified as Mohammad Fasih Ullah Hussaini alias Mamid Mehmood alias Khalid Mehmood of Hyderabad (Sind), Pakistan' Mohammad Javed Waqar alias Mohammad Mustaffa alias Mohammad Mehraj alias Abdul Rahman of Karachi, Pakistan; Maulana Hafiz Mohammad Akram Mallik alias Muzaffar Hussain alias Atabullah alias Bhaijan alias Abdul Awal of Mukam Shahwali village of Jammu and Kashmir; and Kari Salim Ahmad alias Abdul Aziz alias Sadat of Mehilki village of Muzaffarnagar, Uttar Pradesh.

The Chief Minister's Report to the State Assembly - while seeking to establish the scale, nature and degree of the ISI threat - was mainly a glossary of the events which had occurred in the period following the August arrests of 31 persons. In the interregnum, according to the Report, the State police had exposed the *modus operandi* of the foreign Agency. The 16-page Report identified the activities of the ISI mainly in the following areas:

1. Promoting indiscriminate violence in the State by providing active support to local militant outfits.

2. Creating new militant outfits along ethnic and communal lines by instigating ethnic and religious groups.

3. Supply of explosives and sophisticated arms to various terrorist groups.

4. Causing sabotage of oil pipelines and other installations, communication lines, railways and roads.

5. Promoting fundamentalism and militancy among local Muslim youths by misleading them in the name of *Jehad*.

6. Promoting communal tension between Hindu and Muslim citizens by way of false and highly inflammatory propaganda.[59]

---

[59] Ibid-the report.

The Report goes on to state that the Assam Police has adequate evidence in its possession to show that the top ULFA leadership is in close touch with certain officials of the Pakistani High Commission in Dhaka. ULFA leaders have also been travelling to Pakistan regularly and Pakistani agencies have already imparted arms training to hundreds of ULFA cadres. According to the Report, the confessional statements of many ULFA leaders, including its Vice Chairman, Pradip Gogoi, have revealed that the Pakistani officials in their High Commission at Dhaka make arrangements for their passports under various fake identities.

The Chief Minister's Report further speaks of the ISI being involved in the provision of different passports for the ULFA Commander-in-Chief, Paresh Barua. Providing a facsimile of Paresh Barua's passport, the report also reveals that the ULFA leader has been travelling to Karachi under the name of Kamaruddin Zaman Khan.

The Special Brach of Government of Assam have chalked out the following details of ULFA's contact with Bangladesh and ISI.[60]

- In the month of November 1990, ULFA decides to send Munin Nabis and Partha Pratim Bora alias Jabed to Bangladesh to contact the ISI at Dhaka, to arrange the supply of arms and ammunition. They were instructed to set up a base camp in Bangladesh.

- Munin Nabis sets up a base camp in Dhaka in 1990 with the help of a certain Colonel (Retired) Faruque of the Bangladesh Freedom Party and Gani Shapan of the Jatiya Party. Nabis rents a house at Mogbazar in Dhaka.

- Munin Nabis assumes the name 'Iqbal' and contacts Samsul Siddique, the Second Secretary in the Pakistan High Commission at Dhaka. Contacts with the ISI are established through Siddique.

- Munin Nabis visits Pakistan to negotiate with a terrorist group headed

---

[60] For detailed account of ULFA's contact with Bangladesh and Islamic terrorism see Jaidip Saikia, *Terror sans Frontiers-Islamic militancy in NE India,* Vision Books, New Delhi, 2004, pp-74-85.

by Mustafa Ali Jubardo to negotiate training for ULFA cadres on payment.

- The Vice Chairman of ULFA, Pradip Gogoi visits Dhaka in January 1991 and contacts an ISI officer called Haque and signs an agreement for the training to ULFA cadres. He also meets another ISI officer, Jalal, there.

- After the agreement with the ISI, Munin Nabis calls a group of ULFA members for training in Pakistan in April 1991. Pradip Gogoi accompanies a six-member group to Islamabad for training with the ISI.

- Hari Mohan Roy alias Rustar Choudhury of ULFA, along with ten other ULFA cadres, undergoes training in camps organised by the ISI in Pakistan in 1993. Hari Mohan Roy obtains a passport under the name of Jamul Akhtar son of Akhtar Hussain of Bangladesh. [61]

The ISI had also organised training for ULFA cadres in association with the Directorate General of Field Intelligence of Bangladesh, at a camp located 35 kilometres west of the Karnaphulli Hydro-electric project in the Chittagong Hill Tracts in 1993. The training was supervised by Brigadier Joimullah Khan Choudhury. The ISI had reportedly also imparted specialised training to 48 ULFA cadres in Pakistan Occupied Kashmir (PoK) along with Muslim United Liberation Front of Assam (MULFA) cadres.

Bangladesh's role in providing shelter and other infrastructural facilities to the terrorist groups of the Northeast is a great source of concern in the South Asian region. In this regard I had the opportunity to interview Prof. Imtiaz Ahmed of Dhaka University. His main argument is in developing countries, particularly in South Asia the countries like Bangladesh has very little control in the peripheries. In the peripheries of Bangladesh a strong illegal arms racket exist which does not require the patronage of any country. Therefore in areas like Chitagong or Rongpur or Sylhet might have the bases of some terrorist groups. In addition Prof. Ahmed argued that the

---

[61] See Jaidip Saikia, 'The ISI reaches east Anatomy of a conspiracy' *Faultlines,* pp-61-75. ICM, Vol.6, 2000.

people of Bangladesh might have a soft corner for the 'oppressed groups' of Northeast as Bangladesh's struggle for liberation against the West Pakistan is too recent to be forgotten. In this regard he cited one Bangla Group that became very active for providing support to the Ireland cause.

However this kind of analysis completely overlooks the role of the State in such patronage. It is extremely difficult to accept that Bangladesh does not have any role to play. Our interaction with ULFA cadres as well as the surrendered militants of ULFA clearly demonstrates that not only the ULFA cadres but also members of other outfits of the Northeast region have been receiving the official patronage of Bangladesh particularly its intelligence wing DGFI.

Bangladesh's such anti-Indian posture has to do with its growing Islamic fundamentalism in that country. It looks like what Pakistan used to do to India five ten years back is now being repeated by Bangladesh. The politicians in Bangladesh try to gain legitimacy by maintaining an anti-Hindu and anti India stand. Bertil Linter of the Far Eastern Economic Review remarks:-

> "A revolution is taking place in Bangladesh that threatens trouble for the region and beyond if left unchallenged. Islamic fundamentalism, religious intolerance, militant Muslim groups with links to international terrorist groups, a powerful military with ties to the militants, the mushrooming of Islamic schools churning out radical students, middle class apathy, poverty and lawlessness – all are combining to transform the nation."[62]

ULFA: Getting entangled in the politics of Bangladesh and International Arms Network

ULFA while taking shelter in Bangladesh made certain monumental mistakes:-

1. It came to be identified with the Islamic radical groups of Bangladesh.

---

[62] Bertil Linter, "Bangladesh: A cocoon of terror" *Far Eastern Economic Review*, April 4, 2002.

2. It started funding and patronizing political parties for its survival.

3. It came to be identified more as International Arms dealer particularly for the insurgent outfits of Northeast region.

4. ULFA's involvement in the 2004 Arms Haul case –which is the biggest arms seizure not only in the history of the country, but also in entire South Asia, hastened the Bangladeshi establishments to tighten the screws against ULFA.

5. The final nail in the coffin was the attack on Sheikh Hasina's political rally in which 23 people were killed and she narrowly escaped on 21ᵗʰ August, 2004.

The *Assam Tribune*, the oldest and the most premiere English daily of Assam has published a sensational news item on 26ᵗʰ February, 2007 regarding ULFA's investment of $6 million among the major political parties of Bangladesh. The paper presented a report from Strategic Foresight Inc, better known as Stratfor which was released on January 31, 2007. The report indicated that ULFA leaders might find itself on a sticky wicket because the state Department officials in Washington have been keeping a close watch on ULFA's activities in Bangladesh. The Stratfor report said, besides the Islamist parties, the Awami League and Bangladesh Nationalist Party also are receiving substantial support from one of India's most prominent indigenous militant groups, ULFA. ULFA has developed into a powerful, moneymaking machine that relies on Bangladesh for its protection, making it all the more important for ULFA to ensure that its interests are satisfied in the upcoming elections.

By supporting both parties, ULFA is hedging its bets in order to protect its militant and business operations in Bangladesh should either party win. On ULFA's money making business in Bangladesh the report further said-

> "ULFA's core leadership is believed to have been living in luxury in Bangladesh for 15 years under the protection of political allies in Dhaka. As long as ULFA can continue funding the appropriate candidates, it can ensure that the Bangladesh government will

resist caving into Indian demands to crack down on the militant group." [63]

The paper said ULFA's commander in chief is said to have amassed an amount of worth approximately $110 million. Paresh Barua is said to have business operations throughout India, Bangladesh and the Persian Gulf, including hotels, consulting firms, driving schools, tanneries, department stores, textile factories, travel agencies, investment companies, shrimp trawlers and soft drink factories.

Interestingly ULFA has not offered any contradiction of the report in the News papers of Assam which it generally does immediately as the ploy of the Indian State or the intelligence officials.

ULFA is the only insurgent groups in Dhaka that has ventured into such an exercise. Almost all the insurgent groups of Northeast have their base in Bangladesh. But none had embarked into such activities. Dr. Anand Kumar, a prominent security analyst of India in one of his papers said that ULFA was involved in the assassination attempt of Sheikh Hasina on August 21, 2004. Dr Kumar said—

"It (ULFA) acted as a tool in the hands of certain political forces of Bangladesh who despise a major political alliance in that country led by Sheikh Hasina. Interestingly, ULFA also despises this alliance, though it rarely says so openly. In these circumstances, it is hardly surprising that the outfit made a common cause with the opponents of Hasina led alliance and tried to eliminate her in a public rally."[64]

On August 21, 2004, a lethal attack took place on Sheikh Hasina while she was addressing a public rally in Dhaka. In this incident 23 people were killed. One of the victims was Ivy Rahman, a close associate of Sheikh Hasina. Sheikh Hasina herself narrowly escaped with some injuries. Many people believed that this attack had the sanction of former four party alliances led by BNP. Without their support, it was almost impossible for the attackers to escape from such a huge gathering.

---

[63] Assam Tribune, 26th February, 2007.

[64] http://www.southasiaanalysis.org/papers22/paper2129.html accessed on June 16, 2010.

The one-member government judicial inquiry commission of Justice Joynul Abedin linked a foreign enemy with the attack but his report was not made public. The judicial inquiry commission claimed to have identified the perpetrators but its head declined to disclose their identity. Dr Kumar argues that the foreign enemy is ULFA. To quote him-

"A private news agency of Bangladesh BDNews24.com quoted Assam police intelligence chief Khagen Sharma as saying that a ULFA commander, Pallav Saikia, has confessed about the involvement of his group in attacking the Awami League rally. Saikia, arrested in Shillong on December 14, 2006, said that he led 11 men from his group. He reportedly said, "Some Bangladesh intelligence officials helped us plan the assault and even gave us the vehicles for the assault but I don't know these Bangladeshis".[65]

In fact, on the 8th and 9th February, 2007 various news agencies in Dhaka have reported that former National Security Intelligence (NSI) chief Maj Gen Rezakul Haider Chowdhury assisted the ULFA in carrying out the attack on August 21 and Jama'atul Mujahideen Bangladesh (JMB) later in raising bomb attacks. The official was transferred and then dismissed from service earlier this month. If all those allegations are true, question arises why ULFA went berserk? Such meddling is unheard of from any other insurgent outfits. I tried to cross verify it with some of the ULFA leaders who were there in Dhaka during that period of time. Their argument looks convincing. One of the leaders have said ULFA's cadres may not have been directly involved in such attacks. But surely Arms and ammunitions have been provided by ULFA.

ULFA's frequent meetings with the political leaders, particularly with *Mukti Judha Sanmilon* a wing of BNP began in 1995 and it is Anup Chetia—the charismatic General Secretary of the organization who took the lead in generating support, brought the organization closer to BNP. The tussle between the two parties (between AL and BNP) had become more intense and some sleeper cells of BNP in collaboration with Islamic radical parties even contemplated extreme actions to discredit the AL.

---

[65] Ibid. Paper no-2129. Published on 9/2/2007.

ULFA's gradual intervention into the politics of Bangladesh has, later on, been taken over by Paresh barua after the arrest of Anup Chetia in 1996. After 2000, especially after the NSCN-IM's peace process with Government of India in 1997, Paresh Barua by dint of his excellent connection in South East Asia became the undisputed leader of Arms dealing and Arms selling. Apart from the insurgent groups of the Northeast, even the Maoist leaders were dependent on Paresh Barua for arms and ammunitions. Since then politics and grievances of Assam took a back seat and a violence driven industry gained preponderance. Henceforth violence has become an independent variable, it found its own clientele and logic. Paresh barua became an island unto himself. In order to understand this character one must look at the 2004 Chittagong Arms case.

April 2004 Chittagong Arms case: ULFA's nexus with intelligence and other fundamentalist forces in Bangladesh

A huge cache of arms were seized in Chittagong in April 2004 by security teams of Bangladesh –the huge transaction was supposedly done and supervised at the behest of ULFA's Army chief Paresh Barua. The Chittagong arms haul case refers to police seizing ten trucks of arms and ammunitions with 4,930 different types of firearms, 27,020 grenades, 840 rocket launchers, 300 accessories of rocket launchers, 2,000 grenade launching tubes, 6,392 magazines and 11,40,520 bullets, weapons and ammunition. They were being loaded on 10 trucks from two engine boats at the jetty of Chittagong Urea Fertilizer Limited on April 2, 2004.The seizure has been described by the Bangladesh News paper as the "most sensational and biggest-ever arms and ammunition haul" in the history of Bangladesh.[66] The case, filed with the Karnaphuli police station in Chittagong got a new start following the confessional statements of the two prime accused, Hafizuddin Rahman and Deen Mohammed, recorded on March 2. [67]

Two prime accused in a big arms haul in Chittagong in 2004 have confessed in court that the weapons were being smuggled for the United

---

[66] "2 NSI Ex-DGs placed on fresh remand" *The New Age*, May 21, 2009 available online at http://www.newagebd.com/2009/may/21/index.html

[67] I have got the Photostat copy of affidavits of the accused Md Hafijur Rahman where he gave a detailed account how he met with Zaman alias Paresh barua and how he made the deal on behalf of Paresh barua.

Liberation Front of Asom and under the direct supervision of its leader
Paresh Barua. In the statement to the Metropolitan Magistrate, Chittagong,
Mohammad Hafizur Rahman and Din Mohammad said the then Ministers
for Home and Industries under the four-party government led by Khaleda
Zia and some high officials of the intelligence agencies and the coast guard
were well aware of the smuggling which also involved a former MP of the
Jatiya Party of Gen. H.M. Ershad and a film director. The Ministry of
Home was then led by a high-profile state Minister, Lutfozzaman Babar of
the BNP, and the Ministry of Industry was led by Jamaat-e-Islami chief
Maulana Matiur Rahman Nizami. Mr. Babar is in jail after he was convicted
in another case. [68]

The entire lot was confiscated on 1-2 April, 2004 by the Bangladesh
police. Bertil Lintner argues that ULFA arranged these weapons with the
help of a Pakistani businessman in Dubai. Lintener referred to Jane's
Intelligence report that (In July, 2004) the shipment originated from Hongkong
and reached Sittwe in Myanmar, where the weaponry was transferred to
smaller vessels and shipped to Chittagong. The shipment was worth US $
4.5m-$ 7m.[69]

The Internal Schism in ULFA: Clash between the Chairman and Commander in Chief

ULFA's internal contradictions became more intense after 2004-2005 when
Paresh Barua started taking many decisions unilaterally and organizational
meetings and decisions have mere become a formality. In fact it would not
be an exaggeration to say that ULFA is practically run by Paresh Barua
since 1995-96. After the arrest of Anup Chetia, no body had the charisma to
question Paresh and the Chairman always played a second fiddle in front of
the Chief of army Staff. Unquestionably Paresh is the most powerful person
in the organization because of three factors:-

1. He is in charge of Arms—practically all the military cadres are
    personally loyal to C-in-C. The chairman's influence was restricted
    to the executive meetings of the organization only.

---

[68] For details see,Haroon Habib, "Chittagong Arms were for ULFA", The Hindu, March 8,
2009

[69] Bertil Lintner, "ULFA: Radar-less Rebellions" in Look east , May, 2010, p-18

2. Practically he in charge of all expenditures, including providing logistical support to the Chairman and other members of the central Executive committee. From 2004 onwards as the financial collection from Assam and the recruitment process to ULFA came down, Paresh had to look for other sources to run the organization. He did not have many options in front of him. He selected the one which he can do most efficiently, i.e. Arms dealing and providing them to the national and international clientele.

3. In the process he developed a rapport with all the Arms net work in China, Myanmar and other parts of South East Asia. In order to do so he had to overcome all the pressures and limitations he had on him from the organization. To maintain his relations with the network he had to be the absolute controller of the organization. Practically he took over the powers of everyone, including the Chairman and other powerful members like Sasha chaudhury, Chitrabon hazarika and Raju Barua. From 2006 onwards all the office bearers of the organization at Dhaka had become useless. Even for petty errands the Chairman had to request the C-in-C. The only person with whom Paresh had conversation was the Chairman and his few handful loyal cadres. Paresh's dynamism, maneuverings, diplomatic shrewdness and impeccable anticipation helped him to become the unquestionable authority of the organization as the others were counting days for a better future—recollecting their golden days in Assam.

The Chittagong Arms case has given tremendous fillip to the international connection of Paresh barua –he is now one of the most well known names in the annals South Asian Arms history. However –both Paresh and the organization had to pay a heavy price as the former got practically alienated from the organization and in order to be in the international net work he facilitated the arrest of many of his compatriots.[70] According to the sources from the organization, Paresh had left Dhaka a few days before the arrests of Sashadhar Chaudhury and Chitrabon hazarika. Paresh's safe departure

---

[70] The writer could access to some E mail letters among the top ULFA leaders particularly after the Hasina Government came to power in 2008. Obtained through series of interviews with ULFA leaders.

from Dhaka was at the cost of a price. ULFA's anti-Hasina's activities resulted in a tough stand by the AL government that came to power in 2008. Paresh's close aides in DGFI and Military wings in Dhaka made it abundantly clear that the pressure from GOI is too much to withstand and the establishments in Dhaka have no way out but to capture a few leaders. There are unconfirmed evidences to believe that both Sasha Chaudhury and Chitrabon Hazarika were made to arrest from within the organization.

A major confrontation started between Paresh Barua and Aurobindo Rajkhowa from 12th November, 2009. This is the only occasion when the Chairman of ULFA dared to confront the C-in-C in all conceivable ways. After the arrest of Sasha and Chitraban , the Chairman along with the left over members took a resolution. It says "today, i.e. 10/11/2009 at the Central Headquarter an emergency meeting of the central executive (*kendriya Samiti*) was held. The following resolutions were taken at the meeting— the three fourth Central Executive Council members of ULFA are either arrested or are at large. At the central shelter zone (i.e. Dhaka) we witness a situation similar to Bhutan in 2003. At the Bhutan attack entire Central Command Headquarter (CCHQ) was destroyed which resulted in a big vacuum at the administrative level. Whatever Battalions have been left; they are incapable of executing any decisions. The organization and the armed struggle are gradually becoming alienated from the masses. In such a situation the meeting considers that it is essential to strengthen the collective leadership and in the interest of the struggle it is imperative to take a few emergent decisions. In order to ensure the release of the arrested leaders and to ensure the safety of the left over leaders, the meeting has decided to start the peace process for the effective political solution of the Indo-Assam conflict which got halted in 2007". [71]

For that purpose following decisions were taken—

1. To resolve the Indo-Assam conflict and to hasten the halted peace process it was decided to constitute two groups, one is to appoint a 'group to act as the interlocutor' with the Government of India and

---

[71] The write has obtained resolutions and other transcripts through series meetings, interviews and visits to some locations of ULFA—that includes Dhaka.

the other is a 'unit from within the organization' to prepare the primary modalities for talks. For that purpose Reboti Phukon and Dr Brojen Gogoi have been appointed as group to act as the interlocutor. In order to prepare the primary ground for resolving Indo-Assam conflict the following members from within the organization have been given the responsibility—The Vice-Chairman Pradip Gogoi, the general secretary Anup Chetia, the Finance secretary, Lt Col. Chitrabon hazarika and the foreign secretary, major Sashadhar Chaudhury . Other members were barred from articulating their opinion.

2. The above mentioned resolutions have been sent to various Battalions, central leaders of the organization for immediate compliance.

3. It has been decided to stop all kinds of armed activity till the peaceful talk process continues and till further instructions from the Headquarter.

4. The women and Children members of Rupohi (code name for the camps in Bangladesh) camp have a greater responsibility. In the event of male members being arrested or shifted to different place, they have the responsibility to face the situation by contacting various national and international Human Rights organizations.

Rajkhowa made frantic attempts to give effect to these resolutions. The plight of the Chairman and other leaders in Dhaka was quite palpable as the security agencies in Dhaka were dreadfully after them. Rajkhowa had a tough job—on the one hand he has to face the most intractable C-in-C who is unlikely to follow the resolutions, on the other hand starting the peace process was the only option in front of him. Apart from trying to contact his counterparts in Assam he did two things, first he wrote a letter to the Prime Minister of Bangladesh so that his stay in Dhaka remains secure at least for a few days, secondly he wrote another letter to the Prime Minister of India. In the letter to the PM of Bangladesh he tried to invoke emotional cords so that Sheikh Hasina develops some soft corner for ULFA. The letter can be divided into three parts. In the first part he tries to depict the contribution of Assamese forefathers to the cause of the liberation of Bangladesh. He wrote:-

"Historically conscious every Bengali is aware of the help and support of the people of Asom in the freedom struggle of Bangladesh. Birajananda Choudhury was one of those who trained your Mukti Bahini is an Assamese. He is the uncle of the Foreign Secretary of the ULFA Shasha Choudhury. Dulal Hazarika ended being a disabled soldier fighting the Pakistan army in creation of Bangladesh is none other than one of the brothers of our Finance Secretary Citrabon Hazarika. Both of them were arrested in Dhaka on 1 November 2009 and handed over to India on 5 November 2009."

Then Aurobindo Rajkhowa tries to depict how the entire state of Assam was overwhelmed by the liberation of Bangladesh. He wrote—"People of Asom has indelible memories of distributing food and medicine to the refugees from your land sheltering in Asom singing Bhupen Hazarika's song,

"Zoi Zoi Nabajata Bangladesh

Zoi, Zoi Mukti Bahini" …"

In the third part—he tries to minimize or deny ULFA's role in the fundamentalist activities of Bangladesh. "Therefore ULFA is not harmful to Bangladesh. We are always against terrorism and religious fundamentalism. So ULFA never trained or supply arms to any fundamentalist organization. Till today we are not doing any arms activities in Bangladesh. We shall maintain this principle in future too. That is our cordial commitment…..."

In the last part Rajkhowa expressed his commitment for peaceful resolution of the conflict and urged Hasin'a support for expediting the peace process—"Honourable Prime Minister, the raging conflict in Asom has damaged the social fabric and the local economy immensely. The majority in Asom are getting poorer day by day. My organisation the United Liberation Front of Asom(ULFA) has been making efforts to bring a peaceful political solution to the conflict and confrontational state of affairs. But our efforts have been thwarted repeatedly by some conspirators. Therefore, on behalf of my organisation I am appealing to your good office to support our efforts in seeking a peaceful political conflict resolution process with appropriate assistance in bringing peace to Asom, upholding the human rights in general and the birth rights of the our people in particular. Your positive contribution at this juncture for the cause of the oppressed people of Asom will be greatly appreciated."

In his second effort Rajkhowa wrote another short letter to the Prime Minister of India urging to initiate the peace process. Interestingly in that letter dated 21 November 2009, Rajkhowa reiterated Assam's non-negotiable rights of Sovereign Asom. In that letter he wrote—"In 2005 under your leadership and the perceived sincere efforts shown by your good self, a process for the peaceful political solution to the Indo-Asom conflict was embarked upon with high hopes. The process came to a halt unexpectedly in 2007. I am writing to you to apprise you of the decision of the ULFA to restart the stalled process. I would like you to know that my organisation has appointed Mr. Rebati Phukon and Dr. Brajen Gogoi as interlocutor between us and your government. Moreover, to take the peaceful political solution process to its decisive conclusion i.e. restoration of the sovereignty of Asom, my organisation has formed a seven member committee comprising of 1. Mr. Bhim Kanta Burhagohain, Political Adviser 2. Mr. Pradip Gogoi, Vice Chairman 3. Anup Chetia, General Secretary 4. Lieutenant Colonel Citraban Hazarika, Finance Secretary 5. Mr. Shashadhar Choudhury, Foreign Secretary 6. Mithinga Daimari, Publicity Secretary 7. Mrs. Pranati Hazarika, Cultural Secretary. I trust you will receive the two interlocutors entrusted by my organisation and the leaders of the same with due respect and genuine effort with total sincerity to reopen the peaceful political solution of the conflict meaningfully."

What was the reaction of the all powerful C-in-C Paresh Baruah to these peace initiatives? Paresh Baruah was never serious for any peace initiative. In fact ULFA's peace agenda was always guided by the crisis of the situation –peace effort was an alibi to come out of danger that the organization was facing from time to time. Naturally in this occasion also Paresh opposed the move on various grounds. It would be interesting to look at the exchange of letters between C-in-C and the Chairman.

Paresh Barua (PB) writes—"your meeting on 10/11/09 was not correct because before that it was essential to dissolve and reconstitute the emergency Executive Council. Even for that it is essential to know my opinion. Likewise I feel that it is your moral duty to inform me before convening the meeting of the Central Committee."

Aurobindo Rajkhowa (AR) says— "it is absolutely wrong –according to our constitution, if any members of the central committee is arrested or remain absent, the responsibility lies on the Chairman. So the question of dissolving the emergency Executive Council does not arise here. On the other hand, a day before you had left Dhaka, I told you that day after tomorrow, all three of us must seat together (i.e. the Standing Council). There is a need for it. You had never told me that you were leaving on the next day, only just before leaving you told me,."Sir, the preparation for my departure is complete". I was very pained to know how much significance you attach to my request. You never told me that you would discuss later on. In fact we wanted to discuss how to meet the emergent situation before us for which you had to leave. We were all facing similar situation. .....you tried all along to create such situations within the organization so that after being insulted thoroughly, Raju Barua and Sasha Chaudhury were forced to leave the organization. ...When I insisted you to talk to them, you shouted like mischievous boy—"I would never ever talk to them (Sasha and Raju)". As if your voice is the last voice in the organization. For having not agreed to your directions you have given me a treatment which I can never divulge to any one in my life. It's now beyond our apprehension that you are not the same Paban or Dukaba (the nick name of Paresh Barua). We have discovered a new Paban Barua who is now listening to no one—he listens to himself. The other day when you telephoned me with so filthy language I felt humiliated. I bear everything in the name of the organization –this is not the language used with the chairman of any organizations. As if I took the Chairmanship after oiling and messaging your legs. The day after my arrival from Malaysia, you rebuked me in front of your family members –I kept quite all in the interest of the organization. On that day in Sherpur when you telephoned me at night when I insisted on formal meeting, you said you would never sit for talks with Bana Hazarika (Chitra Ban Hazarika). Initially you said you would not talk with Sasha and Raju and now you have included Bana. ...We can't go out, talk to any one, telephone any one, can't check neither mail nor can we send it to any one. At any point of time we may face a crackdown—danger is engulfing us all the time. In such a situation holding of emergency Executive Council meeting with the available members in the central Head quarter can never be an anti constitutional.

PB writes: I have no doubt that decisions on 10/11/09 were a mistake. Had they been mere proposals I would have nothing to say.

AR : It shows that you consider yourself to be above the organization. Will the Chairman send the proposal to the CS? Yes you have the right to ask questions—but you can't interpret in other manners. More than that you don't have rights to instigate lower cadres against me. We sent the resolutions to you and GS. You could have sent your opinion to me—rather you started mobilizing cadres against me. I would have appreciated had you utilized your promptness in rescuing us rather than mobilizing cadres against me so quickly."

Till the last moment Paresh did not listen to voice of the Chairman. Finally Aurobindo Rajkhowa was arrested on the first or second day of December, 2009. ULFA chairman's arrest looks like a drama (the preparation of which must have begun much earlier) and lot of parleys took place before he was handed over to Indian authorities. After his arrest the Ministry of Home Affairs and the RAW officials insisted on a talk with ULFA where there will be no mention of sovereignty and the organization would agree to abjure violence. The MHA and RAW officials did not have the sensitivity to understand that it was too early for the Chairman to give up the demand of 'Sovereignty' for which he has been fighting for thirty years. Since he was adamant he was handed over to the Assam police.

So let us conclude this chapter by looking at the issues from where we had begun. The transition of United Liberation Front of Asom (ULFA) from 1979 till 2009 can't be analyzed from the exclusive prism of 'Greed or Grievances' model. The militant organization started its journey relying on the grievances of the Assamese people against the centre. However, in the later phase the organization made substantial compromises on its autonomy and reliance on unregulated financial collections which have alienated the organizations from the masses.

Transition of the group cannot be explained or limited to the choices of greed and grievances. Various political sociologists have advanced the salience of relative deprivation, resource mobilization and opportunity structures to account for the formation of or the use of violence. In addition, international Arms network, trans-national state and non-state actors play pivotal part in the sustenance of neo form of terrorism. Policy errors of the State, lack of control over resources, mis-use of laws; repression, recognition, misrecognition etc. are vital variables for the study of violence as our analysis on ULFA has shown.

It needs mentioning that those material incentives for leaders—"greed", in the form of pecuniary advantages or lootable resources was never critical in initiating the insurgency by ULFA. Control over resources and checking of illegal migration were the twin objectives for which the organization demanded secession of the state from the Indian Union. Unlike many other Armed Groups however, ULFA however, was quick in negotiating its autonomy and from 2004-05 its integration with International terror network had become complete. Today the organization is considered to be a major source of arms dealer in South Asia. Commenting on similar situations Briendan O'Leary and Andrew Silke commented-"The leaders of ETA, Hamas, Hezbollah, the IRA, JKLF, LTTE, PKK, FARC, or Nepal and Peru's Maoists have not led luxurious lifestyles, nor have their volunteers or cadres, including their forcibly conscripted cadres. The leaders of GAM...were hardliners in constitutional negotiation because of their secure status in Sweden, not because of their control over lootable resources or pecuniary stakes in conflict..."[72] That analysis is not applicable with ULFA who couldn't resist the trap of international terror network—the result is the organization today stands discredited in the eyes of the people of Assam. We believe that the causes matter more in initiating a group like ULFA — however—the "supply side explanations" [73]can't be set aside in explaining the transition of an armed Group like ULFA.

---

[72] For details see Conclusion-*Terror, Insurgency and the State—Ending Protracted Conflicts"*-ed by Marianne Heiberg, Brendan O'Leary and John Tirman, (Philadelphia: University of Pennsylvania Press, 2007), pp-401

[73] ibid—p-400.

5

India's Northeast: The Post 'Pacification' Era[1]

Samir Kumar Das

India's Northeast is now in a peace mode particularly since the late 1990s. The incidence of insurgency and violence has reached a new low and the societies of the region – in spite of their significant variations – have been passing through a process of pacification. The mood is clearly upbeat and celebrationist amongst the strategists, policy makers and perhaps a section of civil society activists. This work seeks to strike a somewhat discordant note and is intended to (a) examine how prolonged and chronic conflicts acquire newer forms in course of their evolution; (b) closely study the nature and quality of peace and pacification in the Northeast that has returned to the region and find out how older and traditional modes of managing conflicts and governing conflict resolution by the state have been rendered redundant and the newer technologies of governing the region are being introduced, explored and experimented with since the 1990s; (c) find out how peace processes in the region at the same time push continuously out of circulation many a concern for rights, justice and democracy and finally (d) focus on how all this has brought the agenda of rights, justice and democracy into the centre of today's public agenda. For reasons of convenience, this paper proposes to drive home the above arguments by way of making a study of two cases of conflicts in Mizoram and Assam with only occasional reference to a few others.

[1] An earlier draft of this paper was presented for discussion to the Discussion Meeting on 'Ethnic Issues and Political Management of Internal Conflict' organized by the Centre for Security Analysis (CSA) in Chennai in collaboration with Macarthur Foundation on 14-15 March 2012. I thank all the participants for their comments on the draft. Usual disclaimers apply.

Accordingly the paper is divided into four albeit unequally divided parts: The first two parts make an attempt at studying the insurgencies of Mizoram and Assam respectively. The third seeks to present the main arguments of these two case studies within a wider, comparative framework. The fourth seeks to draw attention to the newly emergent concern for rights, justice and democracy in the Northeast and how it has been playing a critical role in triggering off a series of new social movements in the region particularly in Assam. In so far as the public agenda is being redefined, a new citizen seems to be surfacing in the region – a citizen who harps less on her distinctiveness from the outsiders or the foreigners as seen in course of the Assam movement (1979-1985) but more on the three key issues of rights, justice and democracy. The process is likely to be a trendsetter for the future - although it is highly unlikely that it will not face any reverses – given that the region has until recently been a standing witness to ethnic schism occasionally erupting into acute xenophobia, violence and insurgency.

Mizoram: From Famine Relief to Insurgency

As India became independent in 1947 Mizo leaders were still undecided on the question of whether Mizoram should be part of India or Myanmar or the proposed 'Crown Colony' under the British rule or should simply become independent. Mizoram however remained as an administrative unit of then undivided state of Assam.

History of insurgency in Mizo Hills is believed to have its origins in the famine that struck large parts of the district towards the end of the 1950s. In October 1958, the Mizo District Council predicted the imminence of famine (*mautam*) following the flowering of bamboos. The much dreaded flowering of bamboos pushes up the rodent population - eating the flowers and procreating fast - that in its turn creates havoc to the standing crops in the field. The Council requested the Governor of Assam to sanction a sum of Rs.150, 000 as a precautionary measure for providing relief to the famine affected people. The Assam Government rejected the request, dismissing the prediction as 'a tradition of the primitive people'. One of the top leaders of Mizo National Front (MNF) who was also actively involved in the insurgency that followed it confessed to me in an interview that 'it was not the famine – but the way it was handled by the Assam administration with ridicule and contempt towards the Mizo people - that played a catalytic role in triggering off the movement for Mizo independence'.[2] When the famine really struck, the administration was simply caught unawares.

A welfare organization called the Mizo National Famine Front (MNFF) was formed in 1960 and it became highly popular by the dedicated work of its young cadres who collected donations from each house and helped the people in distress. The district administration also took the help of the Front in their work of relief and rehabilitation during the famine. On October 22, 1961 the MNFF dropped the word 'famine' from its name and became the Mizo National Front and emerged as a force with the demand for the creation of an independent and fully sovereign State of Mizoram.

Large scale insurgency broke out in the Mizo hills between 10.30 and 3.00 AM on 28 February - 1March in 1966 ('Operation Jericho'). All the major Mizo towns including its capital Aizawl, Lunglei, Vairengte, Cahwngte, Chimluang, Kolashib, Champai, Saireng and Demagri were captured by the armed cadres of MNF and it came to be known on March 1 that the MNF had declared independence. In the words of V. S. Jafa – himself a bureaucrat with the experience of having served the region during this time: "There was only a semblance of Indian authority in the Mizo Hills during 1966 ..."[3].

According to the Government sources, the MNF rebels were allowed to operate from the then East Pakistan. Although Pakistan denied giving arms and arms training to the Mizos, the Government of India continued to charge it of having incited rebellion in Mizo Hills and the northeast in general. As a result of the liberation of Bangladesh in 1971, MNF lost its base. According to the rebel accounts, Pakistan was hardly interested in Mizo independence; all that they were interested in was to keep Indian Army engaged in an internal warfare and thereby weaken India from within. As Pu Bualhrenga aptly points out: "They (Pakistanis) were so much afraid of us making peace with the Indian authorities! Their policy was – we should not be too weak so that Government of India (GOI) may neglect us. But we should not be too strong so that our demand for autonomy is granted to us

[2] Interview with Pu. Bualhrenga on 1 November 2010 in Aizawl, Mizoram.

[3] V. S. Jafa: 'Counterinsurgency warfare: The Use and Abuse of Military Force' in *Faultlines: Writings on Conflict and Resolution*, vol. 3. 2000, p 105

and our struggle thus comes to an end."[4]

The whole district was declared a 'disturbed area' under Assam Disturbed Areas Act, 1955. The Government of Assam clamped 'Armed Forces (Special Powers) Act, 1958. As a counterinsurgency measure, the Army also experimented with the patented Malayan experience of 'regrouping' villages under army surveillance in a bid to isolate the rebels from any social interaction with the villagers. As there were about 1000 villages most of which had a population of about 100 or so each, it was therefore 'considered reasonable to shift the population from the interior villages to some vantage points particularly by the side of the main roads' (Ray 1987:169). A 'regrouped village' was called "Protected and Progressive village' (PPV). In each of them a security post of armed forces was set up. Grouping, according to one estimate, affected about 80 percent of the rural population and 65 percent of the population in the district. The Scheme was cleared in December 1966 and between 4 January and 23 February 45,107 inhabitants of 109 villages were relocated in 18 group centers on the main road. The process continued till 1972. This further alienated the security forces from the common Mizo population. In Jafa's words: "One hopes that the Indian government would not allow the use of such outdated colonial military strategies while dealing with our own ethnic minorities who have not been able to finally settle their terms of political association with India"[5]. All the ex-insurgents - whom I had had the opportunity of interviewing between November, 2010 and March, 2011 - admitted that the grouping of villages helped MNF in an unintended way in so far as it led to the massive alienation of the Indian state from the Mizo people.

Peace with the MNF was a long haul and had a roller coaster character. As Pu. Rualchhina – an ex-insurgent leader – pointed out to me: "Some people especially our leader Mr. Laldenga wanted talks with India right from day one. He did not believe in the agenda of achieving Independence through armed struggle right from the beginning. His policy was to fight for the formation of the State of Mizoram within the Indian Union and he was

---

[4] Interview with Pu. Bualhrenga on 1 November 2010 in Aizawl, Mizoram.

[5] V S Jafa, 'Counterinsurgency warfare: The Use and Abuse of Military Force' in *Faultlines: Writings on Conflict and Resolution*, vol. 3. 1998, p. 127

more interested in becoming its first Chief Minister."[6] The Government of India agreed on a political settlement in 1971 and came out with a proposal for constituting the then Mizo Hills district into a Union Territory. Accordingly the Government of India passed a legislation entitled North Eastern (Areas) Reorganization Act by amending the Constitution (Twenty Seventh Amendment Act) under which the district of Mizo Hills was upgraded into a Union Territory on January 22, 1972.

In November Laldenga sent two of his aides – Zoramthanga and Zal Sangliana to contact the Indian mission in Kabul. In 1974, MNF first proposed talks for a solution to the Mizo problem, which turned out to be ineffective. As Indian security forces tightened their grip on the Mizo rebels, Laldenga offered peace talks in 1976. New Delhi readily agreed to the proposal. An understanding was reached between MNF leaders and the Government of India on 18 February. The understanding was followed by the MNF convention held in Calcutta (now Kolkata) that ratified its terms and authorized its president to negotiate with the Government of India. This agreement was not found to be acceptable to a section of rebels and Laldenga gradually backed out of it saying that it was merely an 'understanding' and not an 'agreement'.

Laldenga again came back in 1977 with a proposal for talks. He demanded statehood for Mizoram with himself as the chief minister of an interim government. The Government rejected the conditions and asked him to leave the country by 26 November 1977. Laldenga resurfaced with the proposal of laying down arms on 28 January 1978 although the MNF National Council refused to ratify the proposal. On 20 March 1978, the Government broke off the talks on the ground that 'Laldenga could not be trusted' (Nag 2002:264). Subsequently, he was arrested.

When Indira Gandhi came back to power in 1979 as Prime Minister of India, the charges against him were dropped and the prospects of continuing talks with him brightened. The talks meanwhile continued in New Delhi between G. Parthasarathy – her emissary and Laldenga. The revised list of 23 demands put forward by Laldenga included among others full statehood

---

[6] Interview with Pu. Rualchhina on 2 November 2010 in Aizawl, Mizoram.

for Mizoram, inclusion of all Mizo-inhabited areas of Burma (now Myanmar) and East Pakistan (now Bangladesh) in the Indian Union, a separate flag for Mizoram, membership for Mizoram in the UN, and a separate University for the state etc. The government agreed to grant statehood and a separate university for Mizoram but rejected all other demands. The Government of India was intrigued by the frequent changes in Laldenga's attitudes. On 12 January, 1982, it terminated the talks, and declared MNF an unlawful organization. Laldenga was ordered to leave the country and military operations mounted the pressure on him and his Front. It was at this point that the Mizo Church made an appeal for peace and called upon both sides to desist from armed campaigns.

Laldenga offered peace talks again from his exile in London in 1985 when a new Congress ministry took over in New Delhi under the leadership of Rajiv Gandhi. The Government invited him to talks and on 25 June 1986 a political agreement was signed between New Delhi and Laldenga on behalf of MNF. According to the agreement, the then Congress (I) Ministry in the state was to be dissolved and an interim coalition ministry consisting of Congress and MNF headed by Laldenga would take over. The then chief minister Lalthanhawla was to be made the deputy chief minister of the interim ministry and Mizoram, a separate state within the Indian Union.

The Mizo case is interesting. It shows at one level how a crisis like famine – if badly handled and responded to with ridicule and contempt eventually triggers off violence and insurgency. Once violence and insurgency set in and the demand for independence defines the political charter of the organization, these outlive the root cause and the 'original sin' of not having responded to the crisis with sensitivity. Sensitivity – more than success – in making the response plays a key role in governance and preempting violence and insurgency. The same lack of sensitivity was revealed when villages were regrouped as part of counterinsurgency operations. This is the single most important state initiative that turned out to be fatally counter-productive. It at another level shows how violence and insurgency survive the root cause of famine in this instance. It also plays a mnemonic role in reminding the people once the same crisis returns. A section of Mizo Farmers' Organization wanted to go back to the jungles and take to arms once the same famine returned sometime in 2008. In simple terms, one instance of 'bad governance' cannot be undone by many other instances of 'good governance'.

Deconstructing Peace in Mizoram

Mizo Accord has been hailed as one that was successful in bringing about peace with the stroke of a pen. According to Ghosh, this is the 'only accord that has not fallen apart or spawned violent breakaway groups' (Ghosh 2001:234). Nunthara attributes the success to the unity and homogeneity within the MNF ranks and the deftness with which it could handle – if not completely eliminate - internal schisms. He calls it 'entrenchment' and defines it as a process whereby constitutive ambiguities and schisms associated with the formation of an ethnic subject considered eligible for signing an accord with the state are reduced and avoided. As he puts it: "The MNF thus remained representative authority of both the underground organization and the overground politics in the peace process". [7]

What Nunthara calls 'entrenchment' is believed to have slowly produced an 'illiberal' society in which individual dissent is more or less throttled and the dissenters are forced to acquiesce to the commands of MNF and its satellite organizations. Laldenga has partly been blamed for this. As Jafa notes: "Laldenga tended to be authoritarian in his attitudes towards the office-bearers of the MNF, and often took important decisions without consultations with other members of the Front" (Jafa 2000:70). This was the reason why by 1970 there was serious 'internal rift' within the Front.[8]

The so called success story of the Accord will have to be read together with many other stories that compel us to read it against its grain. The Hmars – the erstwhile allies of the Mizo movement – fell apart from the Mizos the moment the separate state of Mizoram had come into existence in 1986 on the ground that the accord contained hardly any provision for the Hmars. The disillusioned Hmars met in Aizawl on July 2, 1986 and formed the Hmar Association under the leadership of J Laldinliana – significantly

[7] Interview with Pu. Bualhrenga on 2 November 2010 in Aizawl, Mizoram.

[8] It was divided between two groups. The hardliners were led by Laldenga and S. Lianzula while the moderates included C. Lalnunmawia, the MNF vice president, C. Lalkhawliana, Thankima and R. Zamawia.

an ex-MNF leader. On December 8, 1986 the Hmar Association was changed into 'Hmar Peoples' Convention'. The demand for 'Hmar Ram' to be carved out from the newly formed state of Mizoram made by the Hmar Peoples' Convention (HPC) raised first in October 1987 symbolizes a deep ethnic divide between the two hitherto friendly communities of the Mizos and the Hmars. It was in 1990 - when Mizoram's new Governor Swaraj Kaushal took over – talks began with the HPC. On July 27, 1994 after 15 rounds of talks, a five-point agreement was signed by the Mizoram Chief Secretary Lalfakzuala and Himgchunhnun – the HPC president that led to the formation of Hmar Autonomous District Council. A radical section of the Hmars however did not agree with the terms of the accord and stuck to their original demand for statehood and continued their struggle under the HPC (Democrats).

The Reangs or the Brus of Mizoram have been targeted by the Mizos reportedly on the ground that they are outsiders. They on the other hand claim that they are neither foreigners nor recent immigrants to the state. In a Memorandum submitted by Bru Students' Association (BSA) to the Chief Electoral Commissioner in 1997 in New Delhi, it pointed out: "historical records proved that the ever-peace loving Bru people have been peacefully living in the state (Mizoram) since the time immemorial past (sic)" (BSA 1996:1). The first Bru conference held in 1997 passed a resolution for the creation of an Autonomous District Council for the Brus in Mizoram. This move was opposed by Mizo Zirlai Pawl. Faced with the persecution and ethnic cleansing, a section of Brus of Mizoram formed Bru Liberation Front of Mizoram (BLFM) – an armed outfit – in 1998 that was expected to provide security to the Bru people. The clashes that broke out in Mizoram as a result of all this forced an estimated 33000 Bru people to leave Mizoram and take shelter in the forests of adjoining state of Tripura. The National Human Rights Commission after a visit to the Bru camps in Kanchanpur in Tripura in 1998 came to the conclusion that the camp dwellers were 'the lawful residents of Mizoram and the Government of Mizoram was obliged to take them back in accordance with the agreement with the Union Home Minister in November 1997'.

The Reangs in Mizoram are encouraged by the Mizos to embrace Christianity (Saha 2004:167). Being non-Christians, their difference from the Mizos is only too visible and after the formation of Mizoram as a separate state, the Reangs are supposed to be part of the Mizo mainstream. Many of their names have allegedly been struck off from electoral rolls and in the Mizo assembly polls held in November 2003, only 637 voters – a dismal 14.93 percent of them cast their votes 'because of the failure of the Mizoram government to provide adequate security' (Chakma 2004).

The Government of Mizoram concluded a Peace Agreement with the Bru armed outfit for laying down arms in July 2005. The agreement came about after four years of struggle and 12 rounds of discussion with the State Government. The Accord contained a commitment from the Government of Mizoram that it would take back 33000 Brus who had left the state as a result of the clashes in 1997. It took more than twelve years for the Mizoram Government to actually repatriate only one batch of refugees.

The Chakmas form the second largest tribe in Mizoram – second only to the Mizos. Following the movement by the All-Arunachal Pradesh Students' Union for the expulsion of the Chakmas from that state in the 1990s, the Mizo Students' Union too raised the demand for their expulsion on the ground that the Chakmas, according to them, were the infiltrators. The Asia Centre for Human Rights in its report entitled 'India: Human Rights Report 2009' released in New Delhi accused Mizoram of practising "systematic discrimination" against the minorities. The report further stated that minorities were denied employment, basic healthcare, education and rights to development. It alleged that Chakma minorities outside the jurisdiction of Chakma Autonomous District Council had to face "more discrimination and neglect".

The migration of the Mizos from Myanmar serves as a case in point. A post-Accord Mizoram which experienced heavy inflow of money from the Centre for the reconstruction and development of the state seemed very attractive to this otherwise poverty-stricken, poor Mizos from Myanmar crossing the porous border and by the beginning of the twenty-first century, according to Sajal Nag, there were about 1 lakh (=100,000) such Mizos (Nag 2011 mimeo). The matter came to a head when in July 2003 a six-year old Mizo girl was raped and found murdered reportedly by a Mizo immigrant from Myanmar. In 2010 again, Henry Vanneichung – allegedly a

Myanmarese national – was accused of having raped and murdered a six-year old Mizo girl. In both cases and as an instant reaction, the migrants from Myanmar were served 'quit notice' by the village councils.

Mizo society's intolerance to dissent is exemplified when Vanramchhaunvy – a leading Mizo woman activist, was threatened in May 2005 by Young Mizo Association (YMA), while protesting against the deaths of four persons and cruelty towards many others for their alleged involvement in peddling drugs and liquor. The YMA had launched a programme of curbing drugs and liquor and the victims who had died or had to suffer other forms of cruelty were 'punished' by the organization as part of its campaign for meting out instant justice to the deviants and offenders in the society. When she saw two women on the roadside apparently accused of some offence and made to wear large placards around their neck, she pleaded for turning them to the appropriate authorities and trying them according to the Constitution and the law of the land. She was summoned the next day by the YMA and nine local YMA leaders descended on her place as per the orders of the Central Committee and threatened her. In an open letter she pointed out that she was under pressure and made a reflection on the Mizo society:

> "These faith-based and community-based organizations dictate our lives since they are so powerful and there is no scope for the development and flowering of individuality and individual freedom. We have seen so much of unique talents and personalities being suppressed because of fear of these organizations."

While commenting on the role of YMA in Mizoram, Nag points out:

> Its advantage was that it did not have any opposition or counter-organization … YMA became the refuge of MNF youth who by virtue of their party affiliation could obtain favours and posts from the government. A position in the executive body of YMA, either central or local, became a route to power and prestige. What is worse the YMA soon started to moral police (sic) the Mizo society. When liquor sale and drinking were banned in Mizoram, the YMA took upon itself the responsibility of watching (sic) its violation.

Their area of monitoring also included prostitution, indecent behaviour and violation of social codes. They would often barge into houses, hotels and government lodges to detect violation and take the law in their hand to punish the offenders by beating them, public lynching, seizing the funds and humiliation ... Women were the special targets. Mizo society is strongly patriarchal. The extra-judicial power to the YMA only worsened their vulnerability (Nag 2011, mimeo).

Today when the Peace Accord MNF Returnees' Association (PAMNFRA) accuses the Government for not implementing the provisions of the accord, it blames itself for having signed it in good faith and more than any of its rival factions or members of other communities. As one of its documents lashes out:

The Strong Christian faith was perhaps one of the most important factors that decided our mind to give peace a chance. ... if it was not for the fact that the Mizo people have chosen peace and that their hearts are saturated with the horrors of insurgency, perhaps we might have taken up our guns if that is the only way to make powers-that-be listen to our woes. If we had known that the Memorandums would end only on paper, we would have never signed it, certainly not just to see Mizoram rejoin life in the mainstream as one of its poorest sections (PAMNFRA 2005, mimeo).

Peace process in Mizoram at one level underlines the importance of recognizing the variation in the theme of peace. While peace has returned to Mizoram, it per se poses an obstacle to such crucial questions as those of rights, justice and democracy. Peace per se may have its importance but one has to understand that it has a lot to do with the quality of peace. One has to make a distinction between peace that is established by way of gagging dissent and marginalizing the smaller communities and turning the multicultural nature of the society around and peace that respects dissent, recognizes the rights of the smaller communities and does not establish itself through marginalization.

Assam: From Anti-Foreigners' Upsurge to Insurgency

By all accounts, the Ganga-Meghna-Brahmaputra basin of the once-undivided subcontinent had had a long history of peasant migration since the pre-colonial times. Assam was considered as one of the most favourite points of destination of the migrants by the end of the 19th century. On the one hand, the population explosion in the eastern part led vast masses of land-hungry peasants to migrate to Assam and settle there. On the other hand, Assam had had much to offer to them whether in terms of surplus land and abundance of resources or in terms of land fertility and its alluvial nature. Although, according to Amalendu Guha, the middle class Assamese intellectuals woke up to the problem only at the beginning of the twentieth century, large-scale immigration continued unabated even after their protest albeit with varying degree. Immigration becomes a problem only after the international borders were reorganized in the wake of Partition and the large-scale migration has started being perceived by the natives as a threat to the fragile ecological and demographic balance of the region, their language and culture, their land and livelihood resources. Immigration in Assam is believed to have (a) created pressures on land, (b) caused unemployment to the 'Assamese' people claiming 'native' to the region and (c) their percentage decline vis-à-vis the immigrants and as a result (d) fomented social tensions and often sparked off ethnic and communal riots (Das 1993:165-175). This also poses a threat to the democratic setup of the state. As a result of the population movement from Bangladesh, out of 126 Assam Assembly constituencies, minorities are said to be a deciding factor in as many as 40.[9]

There is hardly any authentic estimate yet available to us, on the actual number of 'foreigners' settled in Assam. The Census practice of enumerating population according to their place of birth serves only as an unreliable pointer. In his report to the President of India in 1998, the Governor of Assam assessed the growth rate of Hindu population at 41.89 percent and that of Muslim population at 77.42 percent in Assam during 1971-91. The Muslim growth rate is more than the national average and was found to be disproportionately larger in the districts bordering Bangladesh. Dhubri – as

---

[9] Reported in *The Hindustan Times* (New Delhi), 27 September 2000.

the report notes - has already become a Muslim-majority district. This could not have been possible without immigration of largely Muslim population from across the borders.

The six-year long Assam movement (1979-1985) – one of the longest in the history of post-Independence India – was keyed to the threefold objective of detecting, disenfranchising and deporting the foreigners settled in Assam. The organizations involved in the movement were not in complete agreement on the question of the exact number of foreigners settled in Assam. All the estimates made during the movement ranged between 4.5 to 5 millions. The Asom Gana Parishad (AGP) that emerged from out of the movement and formed the government in 1985 did little in deporting the 'foreigners'. Its performance, as I put it elsewhere, was 'dismal'. The AGP Government during its tenure of office (1985-1990), according to official figures, could only deport 157 persons (Das 1998:122-26). Immigration continues to haunt the minds of the Assamese. They make claims to preferential policies in jobs. As recently as in early 2005, the Chirang Chapori Yuva Mancha (based mainly in Dibrugarh, upper Assam) launched a campaign asking the Assamese not to employ the 'illegal migrants', not to sell land to them and also not to use the vehicles owned or driven by them. The campaign was so successful that an estimated 10,000 Bengali-speaking persons were believed to have fled upper Assam as a result of this.

It is for instance argued that the intense police and army atrocities during the Assam movement - particularly during its closing years from 1983 to 1985 - led a section of its leadership and ideologues to embrace a more militant course. In fact, there were many precursors to the United Liberation Front of Assam (ULFA) in the form of such organizations as Brachin National Liberation Army (BNLA) and Assam Peoples' Liberation Army (APLA). The violence and repression seem to have persuaded them to believe that in the face of massive repression and atrocities committed by the security forces some sort of a resort to violence would be necessary to realize the objectives of an otherwise non-violent movement. This at one level led BNLA to emphasize the importance of building solidarity across the region while putting up a unified struggle against 'New Delhi'. The term 'Brachin' highlights the conjunction between the two rivers of the Bra(hmaputra) in the Northeast and the Chin(dwin) in Burma. But at another level, the growing resort to violence also prompted them to question the monopoly of the state over the legitimate instruments of violence – in short the State's sovereign power. There is reason to believe that ULFA did not view sovereignty as an end-in-itself; for it, sovereignty was a means to the end of establishing a state free from repression and exploitation. An ULFA document reproduced verbatim in *Budhbar* in 1990 unambiguously points out:

> "… [O]ur objective … is to create a society which is devoid of any exploitation; we are not for Sovereign Assam for the sake of it. We shall have no compunction to give up the demand for separation if we can establish exploitation-less society within India" (*Budhbar* 4 March 1992)."

In simple terms, the twin issue of pan-Mongoloid solidarity cutting across the Northeast and Burma (now Myanmar) and Assam's sovereignty (contingent however on India's failure in meeting the demand for an 'exploitation-less society') provides the template of insurgency in Assam after the Assam movement. Eventually a more militant fringe of the movement broke away, drawing from alleged police repression of the movement enough justification for setting up a separatist group called ULFA on 7 April, 1979.

Although ULFA was born in 1979, it was not until 1983 that ULFA surfaced in the public arena and people became aware of its political presence in Assam.[10] It seemed to have slowly distanced itself from the legacy of the Assam movement in the early 1990s, when it brought out a longish pamphlet entitled 'Asombasi Purbabangeeya Janagoshthiloi ULFAr Ahvan' (ULFA's call to the groups from East Bengal living in Assam). In that pamphlet ULFA redefines the concept of 'the Assamese' (*Asomiya*) as 'a people of all communities, the mixture of people who are determined to work for all-round progress of Assam'. Thus the scope of the concept no longer remains restricted only to those who speak the Assamese language as their mother tongue. Obviously, the immigrants from Bangladesh being the largest group of immigrants are 'an indispensable part' of them (*Budhbar* 1992).

---

[10] For a brief biography of ULFA between 1979 and 1990, see, Das (1994: 68-89).

As Assam movement ended up in a fiasco and only few of the estimated migrants could be detected, Nagen Saikia – the former president of Asom Sahitya Sabha and one of the principal ideologues of Assam movement – criticized ULFA for its turn in these terms:

"One vital question that erupts in (the mind) of every conscious person of Assam today is how much ULFA itself is independent – the organization that wants to make Assam sovereign by armed struggle ... It is most unfortunate for the Assamese people that ULFA which emerged form the anti-foreigners' Assam movement (against the Bangladeshis) is now taking shelter in Bangladesh ... the whole world knows that Pakistan stands nowhere vis-à-vis India's military might – not to talk about Bangladesh. In such a situation, can any militant organization even dream of liberating Assam with the help of Pakistan's military might and the population of Bangladesh? If that unthinkable ever happens, whose Assam will be this? In that case, Assam will be an extension of Bangladesh! ... What an erosion of self-respect and dignity!" (Saikia 2005).

The Long and Short of Peace with ULFA

1990 mark a watershed for it was in this year that ULFA was invited by the Government of India to come and join the peace talks. The reference to talks has been made intermittently right after the first-ever army operation against the outfit. ULFA shot down the offer as 'a clever means employed by the capitalist groups and the State of disarming ULFA' and of creating 'rift within its ranks'.

Again in 1991 when the second military operation was in full swing, the Government and ULFA were reportedly engaged in dialogues with the help of mediators consisting mainly of the locals from the central services and the journalists. It seems that by the middle of 1991, ULFA was clearly divided on the question of whether to enter into dialogues with the Indian State or not. According to *Budhbar*, it was possible to identify the 'moderates' and 'extremists' on this crucial question (*Budhbar*, 30 October 1991). In an interview with *Budhbar*, Raju Baruah – then chief of ULFA's Nalbari unit, observed: "There has been no change in our position on (the issue of, the author) freedom (*swadhinata*). The struggle will continue. The question of compromise with the treacherous State or its representatives is absurd" (*Budhbar* 8 January 1992). On the other hand, there were reports that five ULFA leaders under the leadership of Arabinda Rajkhowa acquiesced to the Constitution and signed what Parag Kumar Das termed 'a treaty of compromise' with the Government of India (*Budhbar* 22 January 1992).

In 1992 immediately after 'Operation Bajrang', a section of ULFA leadership was involved in peace talks, which however broke off when one of its delegations led by Arabinda Rajkhowa decided to withdraw due to 'the pressure from his uncompromising "commander-in-chief" Paresh Barua (Misra 2000:139). Baruah is said to have expressed his 'dissatisfaction' with the 'unconditional surrender of arms' and 'one-sided acquiescence to the Constitution of India'. Rajkhowa subsequently walked away from the talks describing his compromise-seeking colleagues as 'Government revolutionaries'. Finally on 22 July 1992, a full-house General Body meeting of ULFA was held at an undisclosed place in Bhutan. The meeting was attended by Arabinda Rajkhowa, Paresh Baruah and Anup Chetiya etc. All the 18 District units including that of Karimganj took part in it. The meeting arrived at a 'unanimous decision' that the question of 'falling into the trap laid by the Indian State through deceit and treachery in the name of discussions does not arise' (*Budhbar* 29 April 1992). The meeting also decided to prepare a list of compromise-seeking leaders, described them as 'counter-revolutionaries' but did not assign to itself the responsibility of punishing them. It resolved that the people would 'judge and punish' them. It seems that the hardliners prevailed over the moderates.

In a signed statement issued by Mithinga Daimary – its publicity secretary in July 1996, it again extended an offer of peace to the Government and set immediate stoppage of 'the forceful Indianisation of the people of Assam' as one of the preconditions. The organization reiterated that the talks would centre on the issue of 'Assam's sovereignty' and be held in 'a third country' under the UN supervision.[11]

Again in 1999, a section of S(urrendered)ULFA cadres reportedly sent

---

[11] ULFA has more or less consistently stuck to these three conditions since 1992 until recently.

'feelers' to the Government circles expressing its willingness to enter into some form of peace negotiations with the central Government. Immediately after the operations in Bhutan that led to the busting of its headquarters and killing of a number of its top-ranking cadres in December 2003, an offer of peace was made by the organization although the same issues of 'sovereignty of Assam' and 'venue of third country' were set as preconditions by Paresh Baruah. The Government of India's response was very cautious in the sense that it accused ULFA of trying to initiating peace talks with a view to regroup itself usually after any army operation.

Indira Goswami – one of the highly respected Asomiya litterateurs based in Delhi - in her letter to the Prime Minister written in November 2004 urged New Delhi to take steps for holding talks with the insurgents. Arabinda Rajkhowa – the outfit's Chairman - also expressed his willingness to begin dialogues provided it receives a formal invitation on "the Government of India's letterhead with a signature and office seal". In an email message to the media Rajkhowa made a case for holding plebiscite on the contentious issue of 'sovereignty' of Assam as 'sovereignty', according to ULFA, rested with the people of Assam. The need for initiating an ULFA-Centre peace process was highlighted in a Jatiya Mahasabha (national conclave) held in Guwahati. Organized under the aegis of the people's Committee for Peace Initiatives (PCPI), the two-day conclave urged the Centre to start talks with ULFA on the issue of Assam's 'sovereignty' or hold a plebiscite. The Assam Government however rejected the demand for plebiscite. Chief Minister Tarun Gogoi rubbished it as "a futile exercise" on the ground that the question of plebiscite did not arise since elections were held democratically and the people had been exercising their franchise despite calls for boycott of elections by various outfits including the ULFA. ULFA seems to have moved a step ahead by dropping the first two conditions and Paresh Baruah had reportedly agreed to come over to New Delhi or Dispur to attend such talks. As he pointed out in a statement issued in August 2004: "Sovereignty is the core issue for us and we are willing to sit for dialogue anywhere if this is discussed."

On 16 November, 2004 Goswami met Prime Minister Manmohan Singh and handed over a memorandum drafted in consultation with the academics from Delhi University. The Government of India was reportedly consulting legal experts for an interpretation of 'sovereignty' and its place in the Indian Constitution. She also consulted Soli Sorabjee – the then Solicitor General of India. *The Telegraph* commented on the draft in the following terms: "Legal opinion seems to be that there could be various kinds of sovereignty, some of which are not against the Constitution. Economic sovereignty is a possibility, for instance."[12]

The Prime Minister however put to rest any speculation of talks and said in Guwahati on 22 November 2004 that "if they shun violence, then I will invite them for talks but violence and talks cannot go on simultaneously." Responding to Singh's categorical rejection of ULFA's 'sovereignty' demand on 22 November, the ULFA commander-in-chief Paresh Baruah said, "The commitment made by the PM was not unexpected and not different from that made by his predecessors. It is evident that the Centre's colonial policy will continue."

Sometime in early 2005, Indira Goswami again met Prime Minister - Dr. Manmohan Singh (who happens to be one of her ex-colleagues from Delhi University) - requesting the start of a dialogue between ULFA leaders and the Government. An 11-member People's Consultative Group consisting mainly of well-known civil society activists was set up by ULFA to conduct negotiations with the Government. This is the first time that ULFA inducts the civil society persons into the peace process. The Prime Minister met them in late November 2005 and the members of PCG expressed satisfaction over their first meeting with the Prime Minister.

The talks broke down abruptly when both sides got involved in armed engagement. The military operations against ULFA in the Dibru-Saikhowa forests of upper Assam were enough to jeopardize the peace process. While according to one estimate at least 13 rounds of talks were held between the Government of India and PCG, no less than 36 ULFA cadres were killed by bullets of the security forces ('ULFA-kendra katha ...' 2006). ULFA too went on a rampage and claimed responsibility to the carnage that killed over 70 'Hindi speakers' – most of them Bihari brick kiln workers whose families, as subsequent findings bear out, had migrated to and settled in Assam more

---

[12] http://www.telegraphindia.com/1050222/asp/frontpage/story_4408414.asp

than 100 years ago. ULFA'a attacks were meant mainly for avenging the alleged death of five ULFA cadres in Kakopathar in early January that year by the Bihar Regiment deployed there.

Although 'deadlocked' from September 2006 with the resumption of army operations on 24 September 2006 and PCG backing out from talks, the Government never ruled out the possibility of holding peace dialogues even at the height of army operations. Even in early January 2007, Prime Minister Dr. Manmohan Singh offered 'safe passage' to ULFA leaders, should they come for direct negotiations. After the recent army operations began, V. K. Duggal - the then Home Secretary to the Government of India, for example observed: "Let them (ULFA) come for talks". He also dismissed a question whether there was lack of will on the part of the Centre to open talks with ULFA. The war game is clear from the army brief - the objective of which this time is to exert pressure on the insurgent outfit to give up violence and come to the table. J.J. Singh – the Army Chief for example pointed out: "The Army has been given as assignment to perform. If we can compel them to come to the negotiating table and abjure violence, the peace and prosperity will come back to Assam" (quoted in Pandit 2007:7). Peace, according to this understanding, can only be achieved by completely defeating ULFA.

ULFA's 28th Battalion – the pro-talk group – made the offer of peace talks in 2007. The A and C Companies of the Battalion under the leadership of Mrinal Hazarika, Mrinal Dutta and Prabal Neog declared cessation of war on the security forces. The Battalion went on record saying that it did not subscribe to ULFA's demand for 'Swadhin Asom' in the following terms:

"… [W]e the pro-talk ULFA group looking at the (a) global political and economic situation, (b) continuous threat from the neighbouring countries surrounding Assam. (c) possible terrorist attacks in Assam by anti-Indian religious and fundamentalist groups, (d) age-old religious and cultural ties with India have adopted a resolution in favour of Full Regional Autonomy instead of Independent Assam as a pragmatic approach". (Manifesto 2009:1).

The cadres of the Battalion after their surrender have been living in the designated camps of upper Assam and the Pro-Talk group started popularizing its agenda in order to create appropriate conditions for peace by way of holding workshops, seminars and contributing newspaper articles etc. It seemed to have brought back the issue of immigration. As put in its letter to the Prime Minister of India:

> "… it is the prime duty of central and state government to protect and safeguard the interests of the citizens from foreign invasions and check infiltration. By performing this duty a state can maintain its territorial integrity and safeguard the interests of citizens. We believe, Sir, you will agree with our painful observation that in the last 61 years, the government of Assam has failed miserably to discharge responsibilities sincerely. Sir, nowhere in the world, it has been witnessed that, for preserving and protecting the regional language, building up refineries, Tea Auction Centres, roads and bridges, sealing of borders, protesting against the illegal migrants; has the youth started movements and thousands of youth have laid their lives fighting for the above causes … Sir, we sincerely believe that, full autonomy to the State of Assam will not only remove the fear and insecurity from the minds of the indigenous people and will provide safeguards to land, language, economy and right to self-determination. This will reduce the resentment towards the Indian government and will help to refrain from hostile activities." (Charter 2009)

The major initiative was undertaken by Assam Jatiya Mahasabha which organized is first national convention on 24 April 2010. More than 109 organizations, activists and intellectuals across the state gathered in Guwahati on this day to meet and chalk out the modalities of possible talks between Government of India and ULFA. The draft resolution of the convention made a plea to the top leaders of both the Government and ULFA for sitting together to resolve all issues: "All core issues of the ULFA, including the issue of sovereignty, can be discussed. However, both the government and the ULFA should shun violence."

It is interesting to note that many organizations representing communities other than the Assamese like the Bodos, the Dimasas, the Mataks and the Morans did not participate in the Convention. The All-Bodo

Students' Union (ABSU) did not participate on the ground that they considered it as 'too ULFA-centric a forum' to allow the ventilation of their concerns. The Matak-Moran leaders considered it as an attempt at isolating Paresh Barua – who is a Moran. They urged Prof. Hiren Gohain – the President of the Convention – to play a proactive role in bringing Paresh Barua to the negotiating table.

Indeed, there is a difference between the PCG, which was appointed by ULFA in 2005 and Prof. Gohain-led National Convention (*Sanmilit Jatiya Abhiwartan* or SJA). Whereas PCG looked upon itself as a facilitator bringing only the rivaling parties to the negotiating table, SJA actively evolved the framework for developing certain ground rules for talks. PCG did not give up the idea of 'Sovereignty of Assam'. But SJA categorically set 'sovereignty' aside as the main demand.

In a paper written about a year back (Das 2010 mimeo), I pointed out that the Government's twin strategy of getting Bangladesh to detain and hand over the ULFA leaders to the Indian authorities subsequently to arrest them and release them on bail on condition that they promise to sit for peace talks might not help at least on two counts: First, there still remains a not-too-insignificant section of leaders under Paresh Barua, its Commander-in-Chief, who are yet to join peace talks if not completely opposed to it. Secondly, the pro-talk leadership that - according to its own admission – has 'not surrendered' - might run out of steam if it does not develop some synergy and come to terms with the larger social body that comprises many other stakeholders. The society in Assam has changed beyond the recognition of its cadres since ULFA was banned and they went into hiding.

An eight-member ULFA delegation led by its chairman Arabinda Rajkhowa met the Home Minister and Home Secretary in February 2011. Although this was regarded as the first round of talks held for the first time directly with the ULFA leaders there is no denying that it was more of an attempt at breaking the ice. The first round is expected to be followed by many more such rounds in the near future. However, by all indications, 'informal talks' with ULFA, according to Chief Minister Tarun Gogoi, are being held on a 'positive note' almost on a regular basis ('Ulfa talks likely …' 2011:8). Talks are reportedly being held without Paresh Baruah, ULFA's

'Commander-in-Chief' who is still at large and the Chief Minister makes it clear that they "would not wait for him for an indefinite period."

It is interesting to note how ULFA's original demand for 'sovereignty of Assam' got translated into 'sovereignty of the People of Assam' within the framework of the Constitution of India. As Sasadhar Choudhury, ULFA's Foreign Secretary points out in an interview given immediately after the first round of talks:

> We want to explore the viability of protection and enforcement of the sovereignty of the people of Assam in all its dimensions within the flexibility of the Indian Constitution as proposed by the Prime Minister Dr, Manmohan Singh (Deb 2011: 20).

ULFA emphasizes the need for exploring the option of 'full autonomy' within the purview of the Constitution of India. While elaborating on the idea, Pradip Gogoi, ULFA's Vice Chairman informs Swati Deb in an interview:

> We want (to put) utmost stress on the true federal structure of the Constitution. This has to be worked out. Ethnic reconciliation is needed in Assam and that can be ensured only through genuine Constitutional mechanism (Deb 2011: 19).

On the occasion of ULFA's thirty-second anniversary in April 2011, Arabinda Rajkhowa – its President – in his address to the people of Assam welcomes the 'promise' of a 'respectable and acceptable solution' that he claims to have received from the Government of India and argues:

> Although the United Liberation Front of Assam harbours an armed resistance programme in Assam, it wants a peaceful political, solution to the Indo-Assam conflict. Any military solution to the conflict is a position opposed to ULFA's principles and Constitution (Sanjukta Mukti Bahinir ..., 2011:24).

While strongly disputing that they have ever relinquished their demand for 'Swadhin Assam', he highlights the importance of discussion and negotiation in order to find out a 'durable solution to the question of Assam's existence' (Sanjukta Mukti Bahinir ..., 2011:18).

On 7 May 2011, a National Convention was organized in Guwahati and a voluminous document containing the charter of demands was produced. The Convention describes it as 'a letter of advice' (*paramarsha patra*) to ULFA. An abridged version of 37 pages of this otherwise voluminous document was circulated through the local press. The document revolves around the demand for 'full autonomy' (*purna swayattasasan*). The Constitution of India does not have any provision of 'full autonomy' – although it has it provisions for Sixth Schedule and local self-government institutions. If the demand for 'full autonomy' is to be addressed, it is important that the Constitution is appropriately amended. The demand for 'full autonomy' is modeled on Article 370 that applies to the State of Jammu and Kashmir – although a concern is expressed that the provision might not work if what is granted by the Constitution is taken away through frequent Presidential interventions.

The document significantly does not regard 'political independence' (*rajnaitik swadhinata*) as the key to the solution of all of Assam's problems. It, for instance, makes the point that 'political independence might not make development possible'. It also states that 'Assam and the people of Assam may achieve its right to control its destiny even without political independence'. The document makes a distinction between 'political independence' and 'political power' and argues that 'political power is necessary for the enjoyment of economic independence.'

According to Sabhapandit, ULFA took up the arms - without seeking any guidance and advice from any National Convention. But if it were to be in the 'national interest' (meaning in the interest of Assam and the Assamese), then the guidance and advice from the National Convention presently set up are more than necessary (Sabhapandit 2011:13).

What if the talks fail and the pro-talk leaders fail in achieving what they intend to do? One may get a hint when Jiten Dutta – one of ULFA's top ranking leaders – back in 2009 argued:

> We will not say now what we will do but we will take some decisive steps. The government has turned a deaf ear towards the issue. Despite repeated requests to clear its stand, there is simply no response from the government. This will be our final meeting with the government as we want to clear the air once

and for all (Barman 2009:110).

On 5 August 2011, ULFA leader Arabinda Rajkhowa submitted the charter of demands, which ULFA hardliners have completely rejected. Their patience seems to be running out. Paresh Baruah has reportedly refused to join the peace process saying no talks could be held unless the issue of sovereignty of Assam is discussed. On 6 August 2011 Arunoday Dohutia who is in charge of hardliners' publicity wing pointed out: "ULFA does not recognize the charter of demands that has nothing to protect the rights of the indigenous people of the state" (quoted in *Times of India* 'Paresh Faction' ... 2011:14). Their stand may dash the hopes of pro-talks faction led by Arabinda Rajkhowa and his associates.

Dis/Re-appearing Conflicts

While insurgency and violence are only more congealed and hardened forms of conflict along a scale of intensity, these acquire certain momentum in the sense that the cause/s that are said to have inspired them are gradually being pushed into the background without consequently resolving them. The irony of peace in today's Northeast is that peace has returned without the issues and problems being addressed and solved. Earlier I made a distinction between peace that is fragile and constantly haunted by the spectre of war and peace that is durable in the sense that it seeks to address the concerns of rights, justice and democracy (Das in Samaddar ed. 2004: 19-31). I have shown how conflict everywhere in the Northeast exists as a 'complex cacophony' of voices and how all these voices become gradually articulated into a mega-conflict rendering many other voices hitherto involved in the cacophony redundant. Prolonged violence and insurgency are seen to requisition newer 'causes' in order to sustain themselves or these are simply 'forgotten' and dry up. Sanjib Baruah designates the process as the 'disappearance of conflicts'. Few conflicts in world history, as he puts it, get resolved – most of them get 'marginalized' over time (Baruah 2008:46-48).

The Mizo case illustrates how the objective of the insurgency got redefined – from an innocent-looking issue of famine relief to complete independence and subsequently to incorporation into the Indian Union as a separate state, while the Assam case points out how the way the Government sought to resolve the conflict by way of signing the Assam Accord (1985) as it were opens up the Pandora's Box and catalyzes a new set of conflicts represented by the politics of ULFA. One has to take note of the protean nature of conflicts in the region so as to appreciate the need for dynamic solutions.

Peace Impasse

Peace, as we emphasize, is not the end of conflict. Indeed, as we argue in this paper the way peace is brought about produces newer conflicts. Peace and conflict form a continuum and their distinction gets blurred as is evident in almost all the peace processes now underway. For instance, the very way peace talks are conducted plays – perhaps more than any other factor - a key role in influencing and shaping the outcome of such talks. In simple terms, peace defined as an end of war acquires a dynamic of its own and often posits itself as an obstacle to rights, justice and democracy that are expected to inform the accords, such peace talks are likely to culminate in. Peace is understood here as a strategy of disarming the militant non-state actors and pacification of the society.[13] Peace in the sense of pacification becomes an obstacle to the question of rights, justice and democracy. The ceasefire that was agreed between the Government of India and the National Socialist Council of Nagalim (IM) back in 1997 has now met with the fate of perpetual deferral.

On the other hand a respondent cited in a recently conducted survey (Nag 2011) aptly sums up the Mizo accord (1986) in the following terms: "We are happy with the accord. But we are unhappy with the provisions of the accord." Similarly to quote an ex-insurgent from Mizoram, who later became the state's chief minister and now the leader of the opposition: "In principle people wanted independence; in practice they wanted to have

---

[13] Many of the participants present in the Discussion Meeting underlined the importance of moderate pacification as the gateway to the establishment of the triadic principle of rights, justice and democracy. Some even described pacification and paece as establishment of the triadic principle as two distinct yet simultaneous processes. I however argue that the very acts of defeating and disarming the 'enemy' seem to posit the claimants to rights, justice and democracy first of all as *enemy*, paint them in adversarial terms and therefre are a stumbling bloc to what I call the triadic principle. As Sahadevan puts it in course of the Discussion Meeting 'pacification is necessitated by resistance from the armed militant groups'.

peace talks." He continues: "The people instructed us to try to come to a peace settlement – whatever the nature of that settlement becomes. The present settlement is not up to the wishes of the people but still we found it as per middle road (sic), acceptable solution. Otherwise we will be crushed"[14] In both cases, the cadres seem unwilling to go back to the jungles and undergo the pain; the people in general have developed an enhanced stake in the peace that emerges after the war comes to an end. But this enhanced stake does not mean complete eradication of the roots of disaffection. This disaffection persists because peace howsoever acceptable it is eventually turns out to be an obstacle to rights, justice and democracy. The dilemma is that the insurgents are not all too comfortable with the peace that exists post the conclusion of the accord but are too unwilling to return to jungles and resume the warfare. Unlike peace that presumably is of more durable nature, I propose to describe it as 'pacification', that is to say, peace that is constantly visited by the spectre of conflict and war.

A survey conducted in 2001 on a sample representing such background variables as religion, geographical distance, demographic composition, literacy rate, caste etc of as many as 29 of Assam's 126 Assembly constituencies as part of a pre-election survey indicated the declining support base of ULFA. 91.23 percent of the respondents were of the opinion that ULFA's support base did not exist any more and 76.40 percent refuse to give credence to the view that Assam is not part of India as claimed by ULFA (*The Sentinel* 1-5 May 2001). A survey conducted on a fairly representative sample drawn from across the people of Assam points to the flagging support base of ULFA. A whopping 87 percent do not lend support to ULFA's concept of 'Swadhin Asom' while a significant part of the sample sympathizes with the issues of 'neglect' and 'colonial extraction of Assam's economy' highlighted by ULFA (Barman 2009: 103). One problem with these surveys is that they do not shed light on the question of whether declining support base of ULFA necessarily implies swelling support for the state. Unlike the survey on Mizoram, these surveys designed in the way they have been are singularly incapable of capturing the dilemma that lies at the centre of the pacification campaign now under way in the region.

---

[14] Interview with Pu. Zoramthanga on 2 December 2010 in Aizawl, Mizoram.

We introduce the concept of 'peace impasse' in order to capture this dilemma that marks much of the pacification campaign whether in Mizoram, or in Assam, Nagaland or in Tripura. The concept is helpful in understanding how peace might turn out to be stumbling bloc to the trinity of rights, justice and democracy.

Peace and the New Technologies of Governance

Much of the theoretical literature on International Relations in general and Conflict Resolution in particular is based on the commonplace assumption that peace emerges from out of mutually hurting stalemate. In the Northeast however, peace talks begin to be held when the asymmetry between the Government of India and insurgent organizations is at its highest. The former rebel leaders of MNF - whom I had had the opportunity of interviewing only recently - uniformly pointed out to me that their objective was never to win war against India – but to make her negotiate and listen to them.[15] In other words, peace talks are not held unless the enemy is softened – if not completely defeated. Peace talks start when the war ends and by the time insurgents join the peace talks they are as it were militarily defeated. The same story was repeated – as we have already noted - when the army was briefed to bring the ULFA leaders to the negotiating table or as in more recent times the captured ULFA leaders were bailed out of prison only on condition that they would join peace talks. A commentator puts it: this is peace 'at the point of a gun'. Pacification unlike peace is only a continuation of war.

In the first phase of insurgency, state measures consisted predominantly of (a) counter-insurgency campaigns including full-scale military operations, village grouping and driving a wedge between different sections of people etc; (b) responding to the independentist demands of the insurgents by way of granting some degree of autonomy (ranging from statehood within the Indian Union to the formation of an Autonomous District Council (ADC)

---

[15] Pu. Rualchhina in an interview on 3 December, 2010 in Aizawl, for example told me: "Ours was a national army – its task was to defend our people rather than anything else." In an interview held in Aizawl on 4 December 2010, Pu. Tawnluia, formerly the chief of Mizo National Army (MNA) pointed out: "We were sure that we could not win but what we definitely could was inflict some casualties".

and conferment of recognition on the traditional institutions, so on and so forth); (c) initiating development by creating dependency of the insurgency-affected states through grant of doles and subsistence, recognition of their special category status and doles and subsistence eventually feeding into the insurgent coffers and their economy.[16]

Tripura, to my mind, is the latest example following the same trend. Although there is hardly any scope for any detailed study of the Tripura case, the key to pacification lay in (a) the consolidation of the Communist Party of India and in the proliferation of Gana Mukti Parishad particularly in tribal-inhabited areas; (b) relocation of minorities in areas closer to the Tripura State Rifles (TSR) camps and vice versa, that is to say, relocation of camps in areas closer to minority settlements – a kind of modern grouping of settlements so to say and (c) driving a wedge within the tribal society and playing a section of them (like the Halams) against others.

Such pacification campaigns have developed certain anomalies in both Mizoram and Assam. First, in both cases – particularly in Assam, military campaigns are accused of having routinely violated human rights. While in Mizoram the issue of human rights was yet to emerge as a public discourse – although by all accounts it turned the Mizo masses against the state, in Assam examples of people and human rights groups protesting against such violations became more vociferous particularly during the 1990s. Indeed, as we have seen, the rise of a more militant form of politics in Assam since the beginning of the 1980s may at least in part be explained with reference to such routine violations of human rights especially during the closing years of the Assam movement (1983-1985). Such protests definitely cut into the legitimacy of military operations. Secondly, in each case autonomy granted or promised to a particular group in preference to others led others to voice their resentment against the majority community and press for some form of autonomy for them. The Bodos were the first to fall out in Assam -

---

[16] G. Das has shown how development and insurgency form a nexus and how the nexus has actually tied the economies of this region down to a 'low-equilibrium trap' (G. Das 2009 mimeo). Chakraborty shows how increasing dependency of the hill states on the Centre cuts into the states' ability to spend – particularly on social sector and foments the 'movements for autonomy, exclusive ethnic homelands and right to self-determination in order to attract more share of the state expenditure' ((2010:14-15).

followed closely by the Ahoms of upper Assam, Dimasas, Karbis and others in Karbi Anglong and North Cachar Hills. In Mizoram, almost all the other communities living there remained an integral part of the Mizo movement but subsequently walked out and formed their respective militant organizations. The autonomy logic is carried to an extreme where it looks not only impossible but incredibly ludicrous.

No region of India has been subjected so much to such dense and unprecedented policy interventions as the Northeast has been in recent times. Since I had had the occasion of writing rather elaborately on Look East policy, in this paper I propose to confine myself to an analysis of primarily two major policy documents viz. *North East Region: Vision 2020*, volumes I & II prepared by the Ministry of the Development of the North east Region (MDONER), Government of India and *Natural resources, Water and the Environmental Nexus for development and Growth of Northeast India: Strategy Report* prepared by the World Bank.

Although the first document traces Northeast's present status as 'one of the most backward regions of the country' to its 'history and geographies', it holds such factors as 'frustration and disaffection from seclusion, backwardness, remoteness and problems of governance' responsible for breeding 'armed insurgencies' (MDONER 2005:2). While it identifies 'weak administrative capacity' as the single most important factor, this is what makes armed insurgencies highly profitable and yield 'high rates of return' (MDONER 2005:9). The problem is not so much that violence and insurgencies mark the region's politics but very much that violence and insurgencies yield 'high rates of return' so much so that it becomes difficult to break the vicious cycle and end them.

"By 2020", as the document declares, "they (the people) aspire to see the region emerge peaceful, strong, confident, and ready to engage with the global economy" (MDONER 2005:9). Its objective is to steer the economy and help the region develop in a way that invests it with the ability to compete in the global economy. While most of the Northeast is as much peaceful as the rest of India, the region has been a victim of bad publicity and newspaper reports reproduce the image of the region as one afflicted by chronic insurgency and extortion. Insurgency and extortion have been a 'major deterrent' in holding back 'private sector initiatives in economic activities'. Insurgency is viewed in this document as an aberration for having 'taken a heavy toll on economic progress and people's happiness in the region'. As it puts it: "The people of the North East would like peace to return to their lives, leakages to cease and development to take precedence" (MDONER 2005:18). The document in other words creates the impression that insurgency has no real basis in the society and economy of the region and will come to a stop once development and economic progress are undertaken. Although it feels the necessity of 'dealing with the issue of insurgency where it exists in a spirit of accommodation, pluralism and subnationalism' (MDONER 2005: 16) – most significantly without elaborating on it, the underlying economism that runs through the vision should not escape our notice.

The Vision Statement highlights that attracting private investment in the region needs a shift from the current protective policies of assistance and subsidies to more market-friendly policies of incentives, easy credit facilities, tax holidays, export promotion parks and capital investment subsidies. The inflow of private capital is directly related to responsive administration and governance, availability of critical inputs like power, connectivity and other infrastructure, access to markets and well-defined procedures to ensure accountability, transparency and good governance. The natural and human resources of the region, in other words, need to be mobilized in a way so that it can be 'an asset for economic returns' (Bhattacharya 2011:164).

'Enabling conditions' must be created so that the region's economy becomes competitive and can engage with the global economy. This first of all requires 'protection of people's property rights'. While development and economic progress are left to private sector initiatives, such initiatives can thrive only when the inalienability of property rights is guaranteed. Insurgency and violence are considered by it as a direct threat to such rights. The headway that tourism in Sikkim could make in recent years is 'due to the lack of any insurgency in the State' (MDONER 2005:164). The whole idea is to trump insurgency and violence by rapid economic development that can make good the lost time and help resolve the crisis. The document calls for massive public investment in order to attract and encourage private enterprise in this context:

> Public investment alone will help in the creation of a critical mass
> which will facilitate private investment from outside the region.
> Thus the role of the State would be to ensure certain basic minimum
> prerequisites: free and unhindered mobility of goods and services
> (infrastructure) across the region as well as within the region,
> well-defined property rights; and law and order and security of
> life such markets can function and reflect the true scarcity costs
> for goods and factors (MDONER 2005:327).

In simple terms, it envisages a critical turnaround only by putting the region's economy on the fast track. The idea is to tap the resources of the region in a way that these can be marketed by way of improving connectivity and ensuring institutional reforms particularly with the twin objective of opening the region to the 'powerhouse' economies of Southeast Asia and securing private property. While marketization of resources is expected to make the economies of the region competitive, so long as prices are determined in the global market, poor and backward hill states of the region have 'no role to play in determining them' (Chakraborty 2010:15).

By contrast, the World Bank report views reestablishment of community ownership and control over such resources as forest and water as the means for solving the problem of insurgency. As it points out:

> The demands of local communities to retain control over their
> natural resources are typically supported by more than 20 armed
> insurgent groups that reject national efforts to exert control over
> indigenous areas. Effective efforts to develop a conservation area
> network in that region will necessarily be required to involve these
> cultural communities as "owners" of the land, rather than following
> a North America model of State-sponsored and managed national
> parks and wildlife areas (World Bank 2006: 94).

By all indications, the introduction of newer technologies of governance in the second phase of peace does not address these larger questions of rights, justice and democracy. Strangely enough, the newer attempts at setting the region free from its present landlocked status by way of linking it with the 'powerhouse' economies of Southeast Asia are likely to make many groups and communities of the region vulnerable to further isolation and primitive accumulation. This, as I argued, is likely to set off a fresh series of conflicts in the region (Das 2005:65-69).

Peace in the negative sense of managing conflicts and pacifying the society has indeed run the full circle in the Northeast. But unless the larger questions underlined here are addressed, the gains of pacification will not take time to get dissipated and a new series of insurgency might ensue. This peace that has 'arrived' is likely to be fragile and is constantly haunted by the threat of conflict and war.

Dialogical Democracy and the Emergence of a New Citizen

It is now being increasingly realized that each of these measures has its snowballing effects on violence and insurgency in the region. The Assam/ Bodo problem is a case in point. Pacification and the democratic idea of justice therefore seem to move in opposite directions. While peace accords set off ethnic consolidation and homogenization, the democratic agenda of justice highlights the necessity of reconciliation by way of recognizing difference amongst individuals and communities. On the other hand, the agenda of justice has to do with, as Plato puts it, 'giving one one's due'. The task involves incorporating these claims and counterclaims into an integral whole – an order that is considered as just by those who are its constituent parts. While division-based ethnic accords seek to do the impossible of ethnicizing and homogenizing the space in a region that is irreducibly plural, justice seeks to 'give them their due' by making them an integral part of a just social order that includes many others. Justice therefore is not what one considers as just – it precisely involves transcendence of many a singularity. The binary between the self and the other that has hitherto defined many a social movement in the Northeast is slowly giving way to the movements of a different kind – movements that supersede the self-other opposition. In the movements against injustice, the other plays a crucial role. As Balibar argues:

"The experience of injustice (which of necessity is a lived experience, which is not to say a purely *individual* experience:

on the contrary, it must involve an essential dimension of "mutuality", sharing, identifying with others, and witnessing the unbearable in the person and the figure of the other), is a necessary condition for the *recognition* of the reality and existence of the institutional injustice." (Balibar 2008:33).

All of us know how the Naga Reconciliation Process ended up in a fiasco (see for details, Das 2007:22-35). These fail not because of any innate social division in the society – but because claims to self-determination are seen to outweigh the imperative of reconciliation. The civil society institutions that get involved in reconciliation are unwilling and/or unable to prevail over the claimants to exclusivism and extreme self-determination. Naga-Kuki clashes in Manipur Hills in 1993 are a case in point. The post-accord society in Mizoram is often identified as 'Mizo society' and self-determination claims of other non-Mizo communities refuse to subscribe to such a simple identification. Similarly, the Assam Accord (1985) was signed without the Assamese and the Bodos – otherwise comrades-in-arms in the Assam movement – coming to terms between themselves.

While insurgencies in the Northeast are based on the claim to some form of exclusivism and self-determination, this claim is officially responded to – by conceding to these claims *only if* these become unmanageable and cross a certain threshold. In our understanding of peace this concept of threshold is very important. Nagaland (1947, 1960, 1975), Mizoram (1986) and Bodoland (1993, 2003) are illustrative of the point. In other words, claims and responses reinforce each other and hit what I preferred to describe as 'homeland bind'. The post-accord scenario in Mizoram, Assam (1985) and Bodoland is a case in point.

The struggle for justice as evident in a spate of new social movements for transparency and accountability in governance, movements against displacement induced by development projects etc seems to bring about a unifying impact on the otherwise conflicting communities. Now that internal pacification is nearly complete and the state has been able to establish its hegemony over the body politic - thanks to the subsidence of insurgency all over the Northeast, the agenda of rights in the region seems to have shifted from citizenship being defined in contradistinction with the outsiders to a new citizenship being defined as people's right to equality and equal opportunities and right over natural resources (like oil, coal, forests etc.). According to this new notion as evident in the series of movements led by Akhil Gogoi and his Krishak Mukti Sangram Samiti established in 2005, the presently established 'centralized control over resources' must go. Besides, the people also raise their voice of protest against the government's inability to protect them against such natural calamities as floods and droughts, against man-made disasters like massive population displacement induced by so-called development projects and dams. Fight against corruption has developed into a popular movement. People's right to tenure over land and control over forest resources is high on the rights agenda. All this highlights the failure of the government in providing 'civic governance' and the success of the popular movement in 'shaking off self-absorption and melancholia associated with radical dissent in Assam' so far (Barbora 2011:22). In the context of Assam, the rights are increasingly being perceived as ones pertaining to not just *an* ethnic community or as being exclusive to any group of them to the point of depriving others of it. Today rights are being claimed for the entire 'public living in Assam' (*Asombasi Raij*). The KMSS stands for the *ganadebata* (the public as the God) – as Akhil Gogoi calls it.

Assam's 'new voice of dissent' brings a new citizen into existence – a citizen who makes a departure from the earlier citizenship movements in the region on two counts: One, unlike in 'the anti-foreigners' upsurge' today's citizen harbours a concern for the moral basis of her self. Citizenship has become more inwardly directed than it had hitherto been. The citizen today is unhinged from the obligation of being pitted against an *other*. It is less about how and what others should be deprived of and more about what we succeed in achieving for ourselves while becoming what we want to become. Never before in the recent past history has the imaginary of citizenship been invested with so much of self-reflexivity and inspired by the project of making of the self. Two, citizenship is not simply a matter of Constitution, body of laws and judicial pronouncements – as Roy and Sigh make us believe when they point to Assam's reversion to a more narrow and ethnicized version of citizenship, but it over and above is about people and their struggle for a new agenda of rights.

By all indications, the Northeast is quietly undergoing a regime shift towards a new citizenship that is yet to arrive but is continuously announcing its imminent arrival.[17] To say that it is a shift towards global citizenship is premature; yet the region's uneasiness with the older version of citizenship is only too discernible.

The new citizen is caught somewhere between two extremes: On the one hand, she refuses to accept that the parliamentary democracy with all its representative institutions is the be all and end all democratic politics. The majoritarian argument has lost much of its edge. Justice is not necessarily expressed through the rule by the majority. The contemporary popular movements in the Northeast are only a pointer in this direction. On the other hand, there are many more to violence and insurgency than the parties involved in them. The resolution of conflicts depends neither on pacification nor on rapid economic development through heavy dose of public investment – but by bringing into existence a social and political order that is considered as just not only by one community or by two rivaling communities but by the society as a whole. Northeast is showing albeit very early signs of the emergence of a new citizen who instead of belonging to any particular ethnic community in exclusion from another loves to situate her within a social order of many groups and communities.

Peace talks in other words are never held in a roundtable mode. A roundtable would have offered to various stakeholders – particularly those who have a stake in rights, justice and democracy - more than peace being defined in the minimal sense of merely signifying the end of war.

---

[17] As a participant points out that Assam has not moved 'an inch from its anti-foreigner sentiment'.

6

Changing Patterns of
Nepali Ethnic Movement

Uddhab Pyakurel

Janajatis in Nepal: An Overview

Though considered as a small country in South Asia, Nepal is a homeland of 100 ethnic/caste groups. The term "tribe" or "ethnic community" often used by western scholars and popular in the writings of Indian anthropology and administration, these groups are popularly known as Adibasi/Janajati (indigenous/nationalities) in Nepal (Dahal 1979; also see Dahal forthcoming). The ethnic groups, who have been popularly known as 'Janajati' in Nepal, alone comprise 59 groups in total. As per the official definition, "Janajati" or "indigenous nationalities" means "a tribe or community as mentioned in the schedule having its own mother language and traditional rites and customs, distinct cultural identity, distinct social structure and written or unwritten history"[1]. It is said that the categorization was based on the recommendation of a task force formed by the government of Nepal in 1996 for the identification and uplift of these social categories. However, the National Foundation for Development of Indigenous Nationalities NFDIN Act 2002 was brought into existence only after revision on the recommendation of the task force[2]. There is also a provision that the Nepal Government, on the recommendation of the Governing Council of the National Foundation for

---

[1] National Foundation for Development of Indigenous Nationalities (NFDIN), An Introduction, (Kathmandu: NFDIN, 2003), p 32

[2] So far the major revisions are concerned; the part of the definition proposed by the task force which stated that Janajatis were not part of the four-tier Hindu varna system has been omitted in the Act. Also the schedule published as part of the Act only lists 59 groups as indigenous nationalities even though the task force proposed 61 groups in the schedule (for details, see Onta 2006: 308-313).

Development of Indigenous Nationalities (NFDIN), can make change in the schedule of Janajatis by publishing a notice in the Nepal Gazette (NFDIN 2003:52-53).[3] As per the clause, the number is likely to increase in the near future as the list has been further updated to 81 groups by a recently formed Technical Committee of the Government of Nepal in 2010. (Dahal forthcoming).

The population size of identified Janajati groups in the 2001 census was 8,473,429. Also 5,259 people were placed under unidentified Janajati groups. If both the numbers are added, the total population of Janajati groups comes to 36.6 percent of the total population of Nepal. Of this, 24 per cent belongs to Tarai, and the rest to the Hills. Tharu alone comprise 58.8 percent of the Tarai Janajati population, and six Janajati groups, i.e., Magar, Tamang, Newar, Rai, Gurung and Limbu together comprise 65.5 percent of total hill Janajati population. In addition, there are 23 small Janajati groups, such as Kusunda (164), Yehlmo (579), Raute (658), Munda (660), etc., whose combined population size is less than 0.1 percent of the total population of Nepal (Dahal forthcoming). It is also stated that the identified 59 groups are not in similar status in terms of their socio-economic conditions . Having realized this, the 59 groups have been classified and put into five categories.

They are: (1) endangered groups; (2) highly marginalized groups; (3) marginalized groups; (4) disadvantaged groups; and (5) advanced groups. As per the classifications, 10 janajatis are listed in the first category whereas 12 are in the second, 20 are in the third, 15 are in the forth, and only two are in the fifth category. As far as regional (geographical) strength of the 59 identified Janajatis is concerned, some 18 are from mountain, 24 are from hill, 7 are from inner Tarai and 10 are from Tarai. (refer Table 1 on the next page).

---

[3] NFDIN, An Introduction, pp. 52-53

Table 1: Indigenous groups /nationalities with their process of marginalization

Classification of Janajatis

Region	Endangered	Highly marginalized	Marginalized	Disadvantaged	Advantaged
Mountain		Siya, Shingsawa (Lhomi), Thudam	Bhote, Dolpo,Lar-ke, Lhopa , Mugali, Topkegola, Walung	Bara Gaunle, Byanshi,Chhairotan,Marpaha-li-Thakali, Sherpa,Tangbe,, Tingaule Thakali	Thakali
Hill	Bankariya, Hayu, Kushbadiya, Lepcha, Surel	Baramu, Thami, Chepang	Bhujel, Dura, Pahari Phree,, Sunuwar, Tamang	Chantyal, Gurung,Jhirel, Limbu, Magar, Rai, Yakha , Hyolmo	Newar
Inner Tarai	Raji, Raute	Bote, Danuwar, Majhi	Darai, Kumhal		
Tarai	Kisan, Meche	Dhanuk, Jhangad, Satar	Dhimal, Gangai, Rajbanshi, Tajpuriya Tharu		
Total	10	12	20	15	2

Source: Tamang 2004; see also NEFIN 2005 cited in Dahal (forthcoming)

If we go through the history of Nepal, the Shah rulers used to pamper the ethnic groups to grab their support for the unification project, by saying that it is the 'homeland' of this and that ethnic groups. But once the 'unified' Nepal came into existence in 1769, the process of Hinduisation[4] (making Hinduism as a "state religion") and Nepalisation[5] (Nepali as the 'official language', and thereby marginalizing other linguistic and religious groups) have become the major aim of the same rulers.

Let me first discuss the overall political scenario related to conflict of interest between the state and ethnic groups of Nepal before and after unification. In other words, I will focus on the ethnic groups and their access to power and other social domains in different political era. In doing so, this paper discusses the paradigm shift of state policy under five different periods - pre-unification, Shah Regime 1769-1846, Rana Regime 1846-1951, Pseudo-Democratic Period 1951-60, Panchayat regime 1960-1990, and Democratic System after 1990.

Pre-Unification: Background to the Process of Hinduisation and Nepalisation

Nepal's present international boundaries are of recent origin. In its present form, the boundaries were fixed after the Sugauli Treaty of 1816, which the government of Nepal and British East India Company had signed. Prior to that, Nepal's territory was unstable and unclear. In fact, it covered the whole of the sub-Himalayan hill area; its boundary extended from the border of Bhutan in the east, to Kangra in the west.[6] Before 1769, only the Kathmandu valley with three Malla rulers was known as Nepal. At least 56 small princely states, which were outside the valley, were not referred to as Nepal. In fact, even after the unification until 1909, 'Nepal was referred only to the Kathmandu valley. Today's Nepal were referred to as various 'countries' (desa) all subject to the house of Gorkha' (Burghart 1984 cited

---

[4] For details about the term, see Uddhab Pd. Pyakurel, Maoist Movement in Nepal: A Sociological Perspectives (New Delhi: Adroit Publishers, 2007).

[5] For details about the term, see Ibid.

[6] Leo E Rose and John T. Scholz, Nepal: Profile of a Himalayan Kingdom, (Boulder: Westview Press, 1980), p.3

in Gellner et el. 1997:5).[7] Ranas were credited to have given a single name
'Nepal' to avoid varied and ambiguity complex names. It is said that the
Ranas, for the first time, began to define the country (Nepal) 'as a nation-
state' (Ibid). Kathmandu valley was a great lake prior to human settlement.
It was known as Naghdaha (lake of snakes) and Naga tribes inhabited its
surroundings. They survived on fish, animals, and birds which were available
in the lake and its surrounding areas. When the lake dried up, it became a
valley with fertile land. Later, the Nagas along with Gopalas (cow-herders)
and Mahispalas (buffalo-herders) moved into this valley and made it their
dwelling place. At that time, king or ruler of the valley was appointed through
election.[8] 'A sage (muni) called Ne appeared on the scene as the protector
(pala) of the land and the founder of the first ruling dynasty. Thus, the
chronicles explain the origin of the name of the country Ne-pala, the land
protected by Ne'. Gopalavamsi Guptas replaced Ne Dynasty and ruled for
491 years (Shah 1992:7).[9] Gopalvamsis dynasty was replaced by
Mahispalvamsa regime (buffalo-herder dynasty) which lasted for a period
of eleven years and seven months. Later, the Kirats of the Mongolian stock
entered the valley and became the ruling dynasty by replacing the Gopalas
and Mahespalas. The Kiratas who ruled for a period of 1,581 year and one
month were replaced by Lichhavis who entered Nepal around the middle of
the 5th century B.C. from the republic of Vaishali in the present northern
Bihar of India. Lichhavi dynasty was based on some kind of divine right:
justice and morality were associated with the religion of the time. The judges
of civil and criminal courts were termed 'religious authority' (Dharmadhikari)
at that time. There was a provision for a state minister for religious affairs
or religious activities. Lichhavis are thus considered the first Hindu rulers of
Nepal. Before the Licchavis, the indigenous peoples, who were originally
Saiva and Vaishnava non-Hindu and casteless community,[10] were subjected
to influences. However, some ambitious Lichhavi kings like Amsuvarma

---

[7] David N.Gellner, Joanna Pfaff-Czarnecka, and John Whelpton (eds.) *Nationalism and
  Ethnicity in a Hindu Kingdom: The Politics of Culture in Contemporary Nepal,* (Amsterdam:
  Harwood Academic Publishers. 1997), p 5

[8] ISRSC, *District Development Profile of Nepal,* Kathmandu: Informal Sector Research and
  Study Center,2004

[9] Rishikesh Shah, *Ancient and Medieval Nepal,* (New Delhi: Manohar, 1992), p7

[10] Ibid, p28

tried their best to impose occupation-based caste system among the people.[11] Also, it is said that the Lichhavis made Sanskrit the official and literary language of Nepal, and extended it to the field of architecture and sculpture. These were hallmarks of the process of Hinduization and Nepalization by the Nepali rulers. On these counts, the Licchhavi period has been described as the golden age of the Nepali history by 'mainstream historians' and subaltern historians see it as 'a set-back to indigenous rights of people'. However, religious antagonism was not evident in the Lichhavi period. Rather, there was 'religious harmony' within the society as everyone was free to worship any of the deities they chose according to their personal preference. All the temples and monasteries of Saiva, Vaishnava and Buddhist sects made during the Lichhavi period were subsidized by the rulers without discrimination. [12]

The Malla Dynasty replaced the Lichhavi dynasty. When Jayasthiti Malla came into power, he restored order and stability, and managed a century-long anarchy of Kathmandu valley. He brought many Karnat priests from Mithila, and started social reforms by initiating many social rules and regulations.[13] Jayasthiti Malla started a long-term policy for consolidation of the Nepali society with the help of five Brahmans, who hailed from North and South India. He introduced a Civil Code, and classified people into 64 sub-castes, and introduced detailed rules with regard to their social activities and social behavior. Although Jayasthiti Malla's reformist activities aimed at consolidating the Nepali society within the orthodox Hindu religious framework, he is considered 'liberal' in the matter of religion because of his belief in polytheism and especially his devotion to Shiva and Vishnu.[14] In the Malla period, it is said that the two religions—Buddhism and Hinduism— were developed harmoniously and simultaneously. To summarize, prior to the unification, many principalities [states] had their existence in the present territory of Nepal. As many as 46 kingdoms were in the western part.

---

[11] Ibid

[12] Ibid, pp.29-31

[13] ISRSC, *District Development Profile of Nepal*, (Kathmandu: Informal Sector Research and Study Center,2004), p 4

[14] Rishikesh Shah, *Ancient and Medieval Nepal*,, p 57

Makawanpur, Vijaypur and Chaudani kingdoms existed as prominent states under the Sen Dynasty of Palpa in the southern and South-eastern part of modern Nepal. Kathmandu, Patan, Bhaktapur (also colloquially known as Bhadgaon) and even sometimes Nuwakot and Banepa kingdoms, were located in the middle and surrounding areas of the Kathmandu valley. There is still some debate about the Baise and Chaubise and other principalities and their territory being under medieval Nepal. Shaha (1992), referring to Francis Buchanan-Hamilton, considers Gorkha as one of the Chaubise states, but Joshi and Rose (1966) contest this argument and write that Gorkha was never under the Chaubise states.

In terms of linguistic/social features of Nepal, at least three major racial trends are visible. These are:

(a) Indo-Aryans, who migrated to Nepal from the plains or from the hill areas of India several hundred years ago in the wake of Muslim invasions of Northern India.

(b) The people of Mongolian origin inhabit the higher hill areas in the east and west including Kirat tribal communities like Rais and Limbus.

(c) A number of tribal communities may be remnants of indigenous communities whose habitation of Nepal predates the advent of Indo-Aryan and Mongolian elements. Among the three, the third one had gradually been driven back into the more isolated sections of Tarai jungles and the humid, malarial river valleys in the hill areas during the course of the Indo-Aryan and Mongolian incursions.[15]

Although there is not enough literature about religious affiliations of the above-mentioned groups, there are indications that they were practicing different religions like Buddhism and Shamanism. Buddhism came to Nepal in its Mahayan form from Tibet and had tremendous influence on the Nepalese society up to the 7th century A.D. The Hindu Lichhavi rulers imposed Hinduism on various tribal groups of Nepal. The Indian impact had also helped the growth of Hinduism in Nepal during the Lichhavi rule. Before the Hinduism got ascendancy in India, the old form of Hinduism and

---

[15] Leo E Rose and John T. Scholz, *Nepal: Profile of a Himalayan Kingdom*, p.10

Buddhism continued to survive, but later on, a majority of Nepalese reverted to the Hindu religion.[16] Rose and Schulz assume that during the Lichhebi period, a number of ethnic communities such as the Rais and Limbos in eastern Nepal, various Tibetan groups (Sherpa, Tamang, etc.) in the north, the Magars and Gurungs in the central-western hills, and the Khas in the far west, established themselves in areas of what is now Nepal. Those communities, except Chaubise states, had tribal culture, and culturally and economically, they were more dependent on the Buddhism in the north rather than on India or Kathmandu valley.[17] It is important to note that Buddhism was not only dominant among the Newars of Kathmandu valley but also in other Mongolian, and tribal and indigenous communities. Shaha has a different view. He writes that the Kirats, who are considered as ethnic groups with remarkable skill in archery and warfare, also used to celebrate the well-known Hindu epic, the Mahabharata, and the Puranas.[18] There is a saying that Buddhism co-existed with Vaishnavism and Saivism. Such a situation continued till the rule of Manadeva in Nepal. Manadeva seemed dedicated to both Buddhism and Hinduism, although he was a Hindu ruler. The Buddhist monastery, which is situated at Swayambhu, Kathmandu, is thought to have been built on Mandeva's order. It is said that the Vihar is named as Mana Vihar because it was constructed on Manadeva's initiation.[19]

Jayasthiti Malla of Kathmandu (1382-95), and Ram Shah of Gorkha (1606-33) were the orthodox Hindus who, before unification, attempted to codify the structure of Nepali society—both Hindus and non-Hindus—within an orthodox Hindu framework. The former imposed the social code on the Newars of Kathmandu valley. For this task, he received guidance or advice from the Indian Brahmans. The latter did the same thing to the non-Hindu tribal community of Gorkha. Jayasthiti Malla divided the Newars of Kathmandu valley into 64 sub-groups and imposed on them the essential characteristics of Jatis (caste) applicable in the context of the Hindu caste

---

[16] R S Chauhan, *Society and State Building in Nepal: From Ancient Times to Mid-*Twentieth *Century*, (New Delhi: Sterling, 1989) p1.

[17] Leo E Rose and John T. Scholz, *Nepal: Profile of a Himalayan Kingdom,*, p.12

[18] Rishikesh Shah, *Ancient and Medieval Nepal,*, p 8

[19] Ibid, p 14

system. These two incidents were considered as a setback to religious freedom so far enjoyed in Nepal. These incidents played a critical role in the ongoing 'Nepalization' and 'Hinduization' process among the Newars and other low-caste groups. The impact of the process was that the low-caste or non-Hindu communities gradually adopted the rituals and ideologies of high-caste Hindus. Another notable thing of Jayasthiti Malla's reform was that it had given similar status to the Buddhist Newars and Hindus. Such a social code was retained throughout the Malla period, which helped Newars to become closer to the Hindu religion. [20]

Post Unification: Hinduisation and Nepalisation

Dravya Shah, younger brother of the king of Lamjung (Lamjung is about 30 miles north-west of Gorkha), conquered Gorkha, in the middle of 1559. After assuming the position of the king of Gorkha, Dravya Shah began conquering the neighboring states. Invocation of the Rajput heritage was the driving force behind it. However, he succeeded in conquering only two small states—Siranchock and Ajirgarh—during his rule.[21] Evidence shows that the newly established Shah dynasty, with the exception of Ram Shah, had made continuous plans to expand the state territory. Nara Bhupal Shah, descendant of Ram Shah and father of Prithvi Narayan Shah, unsuccessfully tried to defeat the neighboring state of Nuwakot in 1737. His son Prithvi Narayan Shah ultimately conquered Nuwakot in the fall of 1744.[22]

The credit of unification goes to Prithvi Narayan Shah, who brought about the 'Central Himalayas' into a single state. Apart from his personal contribution, he used many strategies to make the unification process easy. He strategically maintained marital relations with the powerful Sen Dynasty of Palpa, and had *Miteri* relation (ritual friendship within the same gender) with other principalities. Because of such affection based on relation, religion, culture and traditions with the Gorkha principality, several other neighboring principalities accepted Prithvi Narayan Shah's request to help him in his dream to make a unified and great Nepal. Some weak neighbors helped

---

[20] Leo E Rose and John T. Scholz, *Nepal: Profile of a Himalayan Kingdom*, pp11-12

[21] S B Gyawali, *Prithvinarayan Shah*, (Darjeeling: Gyawali (in Nepali), 1935), p 3, 31

[22] Ibid, p 3, 83

Shah by submitting their states to Gorkha . There was an open declaration by the Gorkha regime that if a state accepted the offer to submit its sovereignty into the Gorkha regime, the rulers of the state could enjoy a broad degree of autonomous control over their 'subjects' on internal matters. Those local rulers and elites who surrendered to Gorkha continued to enjoy 'a fully autonomous status with a tenuous political authority'.[23]

In terms of strategies enforced by the Gorkha ruler to unify Nepal, there are many stories. The ruler used religion, relation, etc., as weapons to unify other states. Before unification, most of the rulers were Hindus in those small states. In the central parts of Nepal, there were some autonomous indigenous tribal areas under the Rajput-ruled principalities; however, they were under the domination of the high-caste Hindu elites. They started establishing socio-cultural relations among the neighboring kingdoms through marriage and Miteri relation as they belonged to the same religion and culture. This helped to promote the concept of 'we feeling', and led to a psychological bond of togetherness. Ultimately, this nearness helped in the 'integration into a unified nation-state system.' Ram Shah's 'first written legal code in the hill area' also brought the hill principalities closer to each other as the 'legal code evoked positive responses from other hill principalities.' The legal code was based upon the orthodox Hindu religion but 'suitably modified to accommodate the social and political traditions of the non-Hindu subject of the principality in the 17th century'.[24] There is a popular saying, 'if you are deprived of justice, then go to Gorkha.' It is presumed that the saying might become a reality after Ram Shah's legal code was applied to Gorkha.

Prithvi Narayan Shah could not capture Kathmandu valley easily. He was successful only after his third attempt because of the powerful presence of Malla rulers and Newars who defied the 'unification' process. However, when he captured the valley, he ordered that the ears and nose of the people of Kirtipur (the gateway to Kathmandu valley), should be slashed, which weighed 18 *dharnies* (equivalent to 42 kg) when collected. There is a debate as to whether Prithvi Narayan Shah's policy of a united Nepal was

---

[23] Leo E Rose and John T. Scholz, *Nepal: Profile of a Himalayan Kingdom*, pp 4-5

[24] Ibid, p 15

'unification' or a 'conquest'. After all, he used not only diplomacy and consensus but also military force in the name of unification of the state. Not only the rulers but also the people of the other states, which declined the offer of the Gorkha states, faced lots of violence and brutality by Gorkha soldiers. That is why the process was termed 'based on the right of sword'.[25]

In fact, it was the Gorkha regime which killed all the adult males and young boys of Khumbu-Kirat community of eastern Nepal, who had not accepted or surrendered to the proposal of the regime. Data collected by Hudson indicated that pregnant women, due to fear of giving birth to a male offspring, were compelled to go for abortion, and the fetuses were also snatched away and destroyed by putting them into an *Okhal* (mortar in which rice is husked). Such brutal behavior of the Gorkha ruler compelled all other people either to surrender to the ruler of Gorkha, or to leave their birthplace and enter the Indian territory (Dhungel 2006). Another example of such brutality was seen in Jumla. Jumla was one of the powerful principalities before unification, which is situated in mid-western Nepal. When it defied surrendering to the Gorkha ruler in 1794, the Gorkhalis ordered its local authority to 'kill all rebels above the age of 12 years.' They warned Jumla people by using very arrogant terms. The Gorkhalis threatened that if anyone engaged in rebellion or intrigue, the Jumla regime would degrade the 'culprit' into a lower caste, even if he were a Brahman. However, if the 'guilty party' belonged to other lower castes, enslave or behead him according to his caste. Chauhan termed it as 'obedieance elicited through reign of terror'. [26] People of different regions were not considered as citizens but as 'subjects' of unified Nepal. With the unification of the country, it was hoped that the people could do business at the place of their choice, but the government imposed religion, caste, and social code and wanted the people to adhere to the regime and their traditional professions of their respective places. The royal order of 1846 banning Jumla from visiting other places for trade [27] was an example of such an imposition, which made people frustrated in the so-called unified Nepal and became the major cause of the

---

[25] Krishna Hachhethu, "Democracy and Nationalism Interface between State and Ethnicity in Nepal". *Contributions to Nepalese Studies* 30(2) July, 2003, p 281.

[26] R Chauhan, *Society and State Building in Nepal: From Ancient Times to Mid-Twentieth Century*, p 111

[27] Ibid, pp112-113

marginalization of the region.

However, there are several sayings about Gorkha states and its rulers' flexibility or liberality towards the policy related to the ethnic and tribal community. Bista presents Prithvi Narayan Shah as an egalitarian who regarded Brahmans, Khas and Magars simply as different ethnic groups with none of them superior or inferior to the others. Sharma agrees with Bista's argument and writes that Prithvi Narayan Shah 'was able to rally a broad cross-section of Gorkhali society, including the Brahmans, the Khas, the Gurungs, the Magars and others to his cause.' According to Sharma[28] there was social harmony among the different caste groups. Whelpton[29] writes that the two ethnic groups, Magar and Gurung were found among the ruling elite of Gorkha house when there was the practice of *Chha Thar Ghar* (six family linage) system to support the king for policymaking. Even, one can assume such a feeling when one reads the famous quotation by Prithvi Narayan Shah. The quotation reads as, 'Nepal is a garden of four Varnas and thirty-six Jatis or castes'. There are many evidences that prove this quotation. Prithvi Narayan Shah himself says, 'I (Prithvi Narayan Shah) am king of Magars'.[30] Being the then king of Gorkha, Shah's expression should be considered as a radical expression in the society. It is because the Magars were considered as lower caste people by the society and high-caste-dominated society still treats the Magars not as citizens but as subjects.

To substantiate the above argument, Yogi and Acharya state that the king of Gorkha, prior to unification, used to listen to the voice of people before taking action. The Kings' hearing would be based on 'the local populace with its composition and function'. 'When the king had to choose

---

[28] Prayag Raj Sharma, "Nation-Building, Multi-Ethnicity, and the Hindu State" in David N. Gellner, Joanna Pfaff-Czarnecka, and John Whelpton (eds.), *Nationalism and Ethnicity in a Hindu Kingdom: The Politics of Culture in Contemporary Nepal*, (Amsterdam: Harwood Academic Publishers, 1997), p 477.

[29] John Whelpton, "Political Identity in Nepal: State, Nation and Community" in David N. Gellner, Joanna Pfaff-Czarnecka and John Whelpton (eds.), Nationalism and Ethnicity in a Hindu Kingdom: The Politics of Culture in Contemporary (Nepal, Amsterdam: Harwood Academic Publishers, 1997), p 43

[30] Harka Gurung, "State and Society in Nepal". in David N. Gellner, Joanna Pfaff-Czarnecka, and John Whelpton (eds.), *Nationalism and Ethnicity in a Hindu Kingdom: The Politics of Culture in Contemporary Nepal*. (Amsterdam: Harwood Academic Publishers. 1997), p 501

the minister, he obtained a consensus of his court and subject' (Yogi and Acharya 1953:5-9). Shah rulers, in the name of hearing the 'local populace' before taking action, used to take the consensus of six elite families (*Chha Thar Ghar*). These families, belonging to different castes and ethnic groups, were prominent in the social and political life of Gorkha.[31] However, after having a look at Prithvi Narayan Shah's long-term policy of Hinduization and Gorkhaization, one is inclined to conclude that his quotation was more of a slogan to draw the different groups for the 'unification process.' There is another quotation by Prithvi Narayan Shah, which was contradictory to the above mentioned quotations. The quotation says, '*Yo Asali Hindustan ho* (this is the pure land of Hindus)'.[32] This statement enlightened us about his actual position on the religion. After this quotation, one can easily argue that his earlier mentioned statements were only a strategy for getting support from the non-Hindu and lower caste people. In addition, his real position is reflected in his later statement. To Gellner, his role was neither as a wisher 'of becoming a garden of every sort of people' nor 'really a nationalist,' but he was 'very far from being a multiculturalist celebrating cultural diversity for his own sake.[33]

After he had successfully conquered the Kathmandu valley, he reduced the *Chha Thar Ghar*, his consultative body, into *Char Thar Ghar* (four family lineage) by excluding the two ethnic groups, the Magars and Gurungs. This exclusion also indicates his actual position on non-Hindus and lower caste people. The position was later converted into a state policy. The policy was the process of Hinduization (concept of Asali Hindustan) and Gorkhaization. The state tried to establish the Gorkhali peoples' hegemony over all the Gorkha defeated states. Prithvi Narayan Shah launched such a policy when he declared that Nepal was an ideal garden for flourishing of Hinduism along with its four Varna and 36 caste systems. For fulfilment of these objectives, the state began the process of granting new Guthis (the land donated to priests for performing daily Pooja to deities and for managing food, shelter etc., for the pilgrims during religious festivals) to the Brahmans.

---

[31] Leo E Rose and John T. Scholz, *Nepal: Profile of a Himalayan Kingdom,* p 26

[32] Harka Gurung, "State and Society in Nepal". p 501

[33] David N.Gellner, Joanna Pfaff-Czarnecka, and John Whelpton (eds.) *Nationalism and Ethnicity in a Hindu Kingdom:* The *Politics of Culture in Contemporary Nepal,* p 25

Most of the fertile lands were granted as Guthi. Such a practice was accelerated 'particularly in those areas where the Hinduism was nominal, i.e., towards the eastern region.' The settling of 28 Brahman families simultaneously in July 1811 in the Hattigisa of Morang, a part of eastern Nepal[34] (Chauhan 1989:89) was an example of such a policy initiated by the state.

Upon the emergence of Nepal as a nation-state in 1769 under the leadership of Prithvi Narayan Shah, the participation of two high-caste Hindu groups—Brahmans who were considered as the intellectual elite and spiritual preceptors, and Kshatriyas who were considered the warrior caste— started ruling the state where 'participation in the political process became virtually their exclusive prerogative' (Joshi and Rose 1966:23). The state enforced the ancient Hindu scriptural requirement where 'the ruler of the state should always be recruited from the Kshatriyas and that they should exercise their political function with the advice and consent of the Brahmans'. Brahmans were given the role of priests, lawgivers, astrologers, and diplomatic emissaries. Other governing and administrating posts were given to the Kshatriyas. Among the Kshatriyas, especially the members of four prominent families—the Shah, Pandeys, Thapas and Basnyats, enjoyed such privileges. This system continued until the emergence of the Rana Family in 1846.[35] For making Brahmans a respectable group, the then government implemented the royal order wherein the people were urged 'to respect Brahmans and not to take the flesh of dead cattle.' The government further ordered that 'only the Brahmans could perform religious ceremonies in the house of individuals and none else,' and 'Brahmans would not be put to death throughout the kingdom howsoever heinous his crime might be.' Although the death penalty systems was operative, Brahmans were exempt from such a penalty; 'he could be degraded from his caste and imprisoned, but he could never be executed'.[36] Caste discrimination was also extensively practiced. For example, the government employed 65 postmen during the year of 1825-26 and each one was allotted rice land on *adhiya* tenure as a

---

[34] R Chauhan,, *Society and State Building in Nepal: From Ancient Times to Mid-*Twentieth *Century*, p 89

[35] Leo E Rose and John T. Scholz, *Nepal: Profile of a Himalayan Kingdom,* pp 11-12

repayment for their service. However, the high-caste postmen were allotted lands measuring between 95 to 105 *Murris*, (one *Muri* is equivalent to 45 kg paddy and 50 kg corn), and the low-castes jobs were allotted only 35 to 45 *Muris* [37] as emoluments for doing the same work.

In the later Shah rule, the state policy became more rigid. The Shah rule started recruiting military and civil stalwarts only from one region of the country—the Gorkha, the name of 'the trusted' people. Gorkha was the dynasty's native land. Further, even from Gorkha, the dynasty was chosen exclusively from the high-caste Brahman and Kshatriya families. Regmi (1995) states that despite the phenomenal growth of the Gorkha kingdom, its leadership until the mid-19th century continued to come from a small set of families from the heartland of Gorkha. And, as the class was completely dependent upon the king for its economic security, modern Nepal, under the absolute control of the king, also functioned as a socially hierarchical Hindu polity with no legal or constitutional recognition of ideas related to the concept of equality until the mid-19th century.[38]

On account of such an established practice of the Shah dynasty, Chauhan defined the term 'Gorkha' 'as those progeny of Brahmans and Kshatriyas who had migrated from the southern plains and had come into contact with the Khas and Magars of this region, and who had accepted the Hindu religion, including diet and deity' (Chauhan, 1989:79).[39] Chauhan mentioned seven imbibed characters as the basic criteria to be considered as Gorkha people by the ruler. These were: (a) they had contempt against the elite of other religions; (b) they abhorred all religions except Hinduism; (c) they did not hold high opinion about the low castes; (d) they had no respect for the vanquished; (e) they did not regard trade, commerce and other business activities as respectable professions; (f) they had no esteem for art, literature

---

[36] R Chauhan,, *Society and State Building in Nepal: From Ancient Times to Mid-*Twentieth *Century*, p 93

[37] Ibid, p 97

[38] Pratyoush Onta, "The Growth of the Adivasi Janajati Movement in Nepal After 1990: The Non-Political Institutional Agents", *Studies in Nepali History and Society*, Vol. 11 (2), December. 2006, p 305

[39] R Chauhan,, *Society and State Building in Nepal: From Ancient Times to Mid-*Twentieth *Century*, p 79

and architecture; and (g) possession of land and military post was their prized holding. Examining the 'Gorkha' culture, Chauhan writes, 'in Gorkha there was no Gorkha in the sense that it was populated by the *Matwalis'*.[40] The Khas Magars, who had not accepted Hindu religion and its dietary restrictions, were not known as Gorkhas by that criterion. For general information, there is a trend in Nepal to classify people into *Tagadhari* and *Matwali* group on the basis of wearing the scared thread. Those who wear the sacred thread are called *Tagadharis* and the others *Matwalis*. Taking note of those seven characters, one can conclude that such a policy was introduced to ban other native and indigenous groups to be state elites to preserve the posts only for high-caste Hindus. There were Newars of Kathmandu valley, the Tamangs in the surrounding area of Kathmandu with good knowledge as entrepreneurs, skilful in arts, architecture and traders, but they got fewer chances to be in state mechanism.

Rana Regime, 1846-1951: Acceleration of the Hinduisation and Nepalisation along with new initiatives of Ranaisation

In the history of Nepal, the Rana hereditary system came to power in 1846 as a result of 'intrigues, counter-intrigues and conspiracies' within the members of four prominent Kshatriya families. Janga Bahadur Kunwar, backed by the then younger queen Lakshmi Devi, organized a massacre and 'established virtually dictatorial control over the government'.[41] The massacre was named *Kot Parva* (Kot Massacre) and Janga Bahadur is considered as an initiator of the Rana regime. In the *'Kot Parva* most of the prominent Kshatriya elites were either assassinated or compelled to leave the country. According to Acharya, 30 were killed, 60 fled the country, and 26 others were banished from prominent four Kshatriya families. Again, one-and-half-months later on October 13, 1846, at least 23 Basnyat prominent nobles of Kshatriya caste, were killed by Janga Bahadur. They were accused of being organizers of the *Bhandarkhal Parva* or 'Basnyat conspiracy'.[42]

---

[40] Ibid

[41] Leo E Rose and John T. Scholz, *Nepal: Profile of a Himalayan Kingdom,* p 40

[42] Baburam Acharya, *Aba Yesto Kahilyi Nahos* (Let such things never happen), (Kathmandu: Prof. Sri Krishna Acharya (in Nepali language), 2005), p107, 115

After establishing himself in power, Janga Bahadur combined in himself the roles of the chief of army, the prime minister and the *'Maharaja'* (His Majesty) of Kaski and Lamjung, two small principalities of Nepal. Then, the third title *'Maharaja'* was made as an inheritable title of the Rana family. Within 10 years in power, the Ranas ruled the country by their hereditary premiership system. The system was termed as the 'Rana oligarchy' in the history of Nepal.

With the coming of Janga Bahadur to power, a seven-decade long rule of four Kshatriya nobles disintegrated. However, the change did not move towards the inclusive and democratic system of government. Indeed, the Rana system had been more repressive towards the people. The regime sought to perpetuate backwardness and ignorance among the people by discouraging opening up of the education institutions. The system imposed orthodox and discretionary social rule. The regime not only tried to ban people from getting education but also banned travel abroad. Further, it controlled the people by intensifying communal disputes and rivalries through the social controls exercised by the royal priests. In the name of religion or *dharmashastra*, the priests were vested with the authority to punish any attempt on the part of the people to modify social, ethnic, and caste inequalities. As a political system, it was observed:

'The Rana political system was an undisguised military despotism of the ruling faction within the Rana family over the king and the people of the country. The government functioned as instrument to carry out the personal wishes and interests of the ruling Rana Prime Minister; its main domestic preoccupation was the exploitation of the country's resources in order to enhance the personal wealth of Rana ruler and his family. No distinction was made between the personal treasury of the Rana ruler and the treasury of the government; the Rana ruler, as private income, pocketed any government revenue in excess of administrative expenses. No budget of the government's expenditures and revenues were ever made public. As a system accountable neither to the king nor to the people, the Rana regime functioned as an autonomous system, divorced from the needs of the people and even from the historical traditions of the country, and served only the interests of a handful of Ranas and their ubiquitous non-Rana adherents.'[43]

The Rana regime, initially, promoted the process of 'Ranaization' or their hegemony over the society where, for assuming power and getting privilege, one required to be from the Rana family. For other people there was no opportunity; they were even banned from getting education. In the army, which was the key to the survival of the system, generals and colonels were appointed from Rana families soon after their birth, and sometimes even before their birth. Ordinary people were restricted from wearing clothes, ornaments, making houses, etc. For such a societal sanction, they used the orthodox Hinduism as a weapon. For middle and lower level job opportunities in the military and bureaucratic cadre, Brahmans and the earlier discussed noble family were selected. The selection itself was a strategy to win the support of those families.[44]

The Rana regime introduced the first Muluki Ain (Civil Code) in 1854. It was not new in the strict sense, because it was practiced earlier as a 'legal code' during the period of Jayasthiti Malla (1382-95) from late 14th century in Kathmandu valley, and during the period of Ram Shah (1603-36) in Gorkha from first the half of the 17th century. What was new was that the regime put it in a nationwide legal framework. Before being declared as a law, it was practiced as a tradition. By promulgating it as a civil code, the Rana regime compelled all the 'subjects' to obey it. It was part of their strategic policy to continue their regime for a long time. They were aware that they could control the people only by such religious code of conduct, which had already gained legitimacy as a tradition. The orthodox Hindus accepted it and even claimed it as a vital step for promoting the Hinduism as a national religion. The code had revised caste categories from the four Varna classical Vedic models into six categories. It had provisioned a different type of punishment system on the basis of caste; to the higher caste, there was one type of punishment, and to the lower caste people a different type was applied for the same crime. In other words, the system did not break the continuation of discrimination between the people of higher and lower

---

[43] Leo E Rose and John T. Scholz, *Nepal: Profile of a Himalayan Kingdom,* pp 38-39
[44] Ibid, p 40

castes. Another characteristic of the code was that it tried to accommodate the ethnic identities into Hindu Varna system, which 'translated diversity into inequality.'

Comparing the Shah rule and Rana oligarchy in Nepal, Chauhan termed Rana administration as 'less cruel and not that exploitative'.[45] However, no one is of the view that the system was not exploitative. The classification of Rana family into 'A', 'B' and 'C' classes on the basis of their purity of blood itself was a saleable example of the regime's exploitive nature. Later on, the classification was also made on the basis of caste of their mothers and kind of marriage (whether she was a concubine or formally married). Such a classification led the Ranas to divide themselves into three groups as noted above. The three groups started fighting amongst each other for power and position. In fact, the struggle within the Rana family became the most important cause for disintegration of their 104-year long rule.

Hinduism was practiced in a very orthodox manner in this period. Travelling abroad was termed as a 'violation of religious and social tradition' by conservative Ranas. Even Janga Bahadur, the initiator of the Rana regime, was accused of being a violator of the code. He was told that he had lost his caste by dining and socializing with Europeans when he visited Europe in 1850-51. After his return to Nepal, he visited important Hindu pilgrimage centers of India to be purified. Another intention of his visit to pilgrimage centers might have been to close the mouth of conservative people. Another example of the Rana's religious orthodoxy was that they were not even ready to reform Hinduism and when some Nepalese started reforming the movement of Hinduism in the name of Arya Samaj, they were socially disgraced, paraded through the street, beaten and sentenced to jail.

Ranas were more concerned about the impact of education and exposure. They knew that education and exposure would have helped in people's freedom and creating awareness. In this context, they seriously observed the returnees of 'Gorkha' army and western education holders. One of the threats to the Rana regime from those people was that they might bring modern ideas of freedom into their village and society. Therefore,

---

[45] R Chauhan,, *Society and State Building in Nepal: From Ancient Times to Mid*-Twentieth *Century*, p 119

the Ranas requested British authorities not to promote Gorkha recruits beyond the rank of sergeant and upon their return to the country rigidly enforced on them the rules of caste purification (Joshi and Rose 1966:52). Although the other religions were allowed 'except for doing acts prohibited in the code, including the slaughtering of cows', conversion of people from Hindu religion to others was prohibited. The permission to enjoy other religions was only for those who 'were already Muslims or Christians when they entered Nepal, and were born in Nepal from Muslim or Christian parents'. [46]

Linguistically speaking, the Rana regime not only continued the process of Nepalization of the Shah regime, but also accelerated the process. For the first time in history, Khas Kura or Gorkhali Bhasa was declared as the official Nepali language in 1930. Chandra Shamsher was the Prime Minister. The regime in the process gave rise to the idea of a 'nation'. Prior to that, Nepal was referred only to the Kathmandu valley, and the rest of the country was known by the individual names of the places. The job of Ranas during their period was on the pretext of the 'nationalist objectives'.[47] In aspect of other religions and languages, the Ranas again followed the path of Shah Regime. The late Dharmaditya Dharmacharya, a brilliant Buddhist scholar, was expelled from Kathmandu Valley in the 1920s for the 'crime' of publishing and circulating Buddhist and other books in the Nepal Bhasa (Newari language). Buddhist monks Mahaprajna and Amritananda were imprisoned, and Tsering Narbu Lama was expelled in 1937. In 1925, another four monks, and in 1944, eight more monks were expelled from Kathmandu.[48] The state sponsored rampant migration of people from the west hill area to east hill area during this period. The main objective of such migration was to spread Nepali speaking and Hindu people with a view to promote and expand their cultural hegemony all over the territory, especially in the eastern hill

---

[46] Marc Gaborieau, Muslims in the Hindu Kingdom of Nepal", *Contribution to Indian Sociology,* New Series, No. VI, December, pp. 84-105, 1972

[47] John Whelpton, "Political Identity in Nepal: State, Nation and Community" in David N. Gellner, Joanna Pfaff-Czarnecka and John Whelpton (eds.), Nationalism and Ethnicity in a Hindu Kingdom: The Politics of Culture in Contemporary (Nepal, Amsterdam: Harwood Academic Publishers, 1997), p 45

[48] Ranjana and Prem Kumar Khatry, 'Inter-Religious Dialogue: An Unbreakable Thread to Unite the Diverse Cultures of Nepal' in R.D. Bajracharya, K.B. Bhattachan, D.R. Dahal and P.K. Khatri (eds.) *Cultural and Religious Diversity: Dialogue and Development* (Monographs and Working Papers: No. 6) Kathmandu: UNESCO, 2005, pp 73-74

area where Rais and Limbus—the non Hindu indigenous group—inhabited.

In regard to the ethnic issue, both the Shah and Rana regime played the same role of suppressing the indigenous people. Earlier the regime wooed the indigenous people by distributing land as kipat (land given to indigenous community for enjoying as common land of the community) to encourage them to support the unification process, but later the regime abolished the *kipat* system. Many indigenous groups including Bhote, Chepang, Danuwar, Garung, Pahari, Majhi, Rai, Limbus Thakali had customary occupation of land. All except the Limbus got alienated by the land under the regime. In case of the Limbus, the land got alienated only after 1964. The regime faced several revolts like Gurung revolt against Ranas in 1857 because of such policy.[49]

Pseudo-Democratic Period (1951-60)

I have used the term 'pseudo' while examining the period of 1951-60 in the Nepali history. It is primarily because of the fact there it was the period, which had a character of both, democracy and autocracy. Another factor for using the term 'pseudo' has been that in democracy, government has been always elected by the people, but in this case, Nepalese could witness the elected government only for 18 months (May 27, 1959 to December 15, 1960) out of total of ten years.

During this period, Nepal became free from 'isolation' from the world, and it could witness a few constitutional and social changes along with people's movement in 1951. One of the significant changes was abolition of the 104-years-old Rana oligarchy. An interim government with the people's choice was constituted to change the existing system into a democratic system. The king, who was caged without rights in the palace by the Ranas, was also freed with the support of people. After the freedom, the king promised to let the democratic system run the country. The 1951 interim government made some important decisions in favor of democracy and the people.

It is well known that the NC was the only major political force which launched a nationwide protest against the Rana regime. Once the anti-

---

[49] Leo E Rose and John T. Scholz, *Nepal: Profile of a Himalayan Kingdom,* p 43

Rana movement was over the NC got an opportunity to be the part of the Interim Government in 1951. The interim cabinet abolished many feudal practices 'at the initiative of the NC', such as monetary exactions in the form of mandatory gifts and presents, and forced labor to maintain public work which had been an integral part of the Rana political system. Birta (rent-free land), the traditional base of the Rana economic power was abolished. The monopoly of Ranas in the high position of the army was brought to an end by the government. Further, those positions were made accessible to other castes/ethnic communities. All government schools were directed to open the gates of their school for children of untouchable castes. Prior to that, only the 'male children of elite families' were permitted to go to the school and 'mainly Brahman boys were taught in the classical Sanskrit Pathshalas or school'. [50]

Also, the ethnic activism was first noticed with the dawn of democracy in 1951. NGOs and other organizations like Pichadieka-Barga Sangathan (the backward class organization) including Gurung Kalyan Sangh, Tharu Kalyankari Sabha, Kirat League and Dalit Sangh were established during this period. The Tarai Congress, the first regional party in Nepal, was established in 1951. However, after few months rule of the Interim Government, the king tried to be active by making/sacking the government. And interestingly, the king-nominated government constituted a committee called Nepal National Education Planning Commission, 1955 which recommended the use of Nepali language in such a manner that other languages were gradually wiped out with an expectation 'to provide greater national strength and unity'. [51]

Though the primary objective of the NC of 1950s was to make a constitution through the election of the Constituent Assembly, it was never materialized. Rather King Mahendra, after mounting pressure from major political parties, decided to held first general election in 1959. Then, the first elected government was formed under the premiership of B.P. Koirala,

---

[50] Martin Hoftun, ,William Raeper and John Whelpton , *People Politics and Ideology: Democracy and Social Change in Nepal*, (Kathmandu: Mandala Book point, 1999), p 4

[51] John Whelpton, "Political Identity in Nepal: State, Nation and Community" in David N. Gellner, Joanna Pfaff-Czarnecka and John Whelpton (eds.), Nationalism and Ethnicity in a Hindu Kingdom: The Politics of Culture in Contemporary (Nepal, Amsterdam: Harwood Academic Publishers, 1997), p 49

who himself was reported to have 'antagonized orthodox Hindus and the conservatives'.[52] Once he formed his cabinet, he resumed the goal of strengthening democracy and Nepal prosperous.. He started implementing the programs promised in the election manifesto. The main slogan of the party was to 'end the very roots of the traditional social and economic inequalities.' The highlights of the Nepali Congress (NC) manifesto included: abolition of the proprietor system, abolition of Rajyas (small principalities which enjoyed the semi-autonomy), a ceiling on landholding and redistribution of the excess landholdings, forests' nationalization, promotion of co-operative farming, etc. Respect for religion and a guarantee of the right of any citizen to practice the religion of his/her choice and encouragement of the development of regional and local languages were other important highlights of the election manifesto of NC. In fact, the first elected government of B. P. Koirala tried to deconstruct the very notion of language policy recommended and implemented in 1955; the government, in doing so, had also given the status of national language to other languages like Newari, Hindi and Maithali. Again, for the first time in 1959, news was broadcast in languages other than Nepali. The motive behind such a decision was the promotion and appreciation of other languages.[53] Hindi was accepted for use in Parliament discussions in 1959.

Unfortunately, the first democratically elected government of NC, which was set up 'as the champion of the poor and indebted peasantry,' started facing disturbances shortly after its formation. It was assumed that the Gorkha Parishad, a political party that represented the 'feudal exploiters, cruel moneylenders, and profiteers,' backed such disturbances.[54] Also, the orthodox Hindu advocates and royalists like Yogi Narahari Nath backed those disturbances. Ultimately, the king dismissed the 19-month-old government and imprisoned all the political leaders on December 15, 1960 which led to a complete halt of the entire reformist program.

---

[52] Leo E Rose and John T. Scholz, *Nepal: Profile of a Himalayan Kingdom*, p 308

[53] David N.Gellner, Joanna Pfaff-Czarnecka, and John Whelpton (eds.) *Nationalism and Ethnicity in a Hindu Kingdom:* The *Politics of Culture in Contemporary Nepal*, p 29

[54] Leo E Rose and John T. Scholz, *Nepal: Profile of a Himalayan Kingdom*, p 357

Panchayat Regime (1960-1990): Extreme Face Of Hinduisation And Nepalisation

This period could be seen as a resumption of the early Shah dynasty. The Shah family ruled over the people absolutely. The only difference during the period was that the king started his rule by a system called 'Panchayat'. It was a party-less system made out to be 'suitable to the soil anc climate of Nepal. The system was innovated by the king after the dismissal of the elected prime minister and the democratic system.

The Panchayati ethos—*Euta Bhashsa Euta bhesh (one language , one dress)*— was a perfect example for examining policies and programs of the period in respect of the plural identity of the country. The process of Nepalization and Hinduization continued vigorously with the state declaring a Hindu state and making the King as the symbol of religion and politics. The Constitution of Nepal has more clearly enunciated this doctrine along with making Nepali as the only national language. It was declared by the King that "Nepalis were Panchas , all Panchas were Nepalis" thus making people and Panchayat system synonymous. It is said that the 1962 Constitution was written in accordance with the King's Interest. The king was considered as "symbol of national unity and source of political authority in accordance with the Hindu tradition and custom.[55] Once the constitution was promulgated along with the party-less Panchayat as system of governance, Nepali state tempo the Nepalization process also. For maintaining the hegemony of Nepali languages in society, the regime stopped the news broadcasting service in Newari and Hindi from Radio Nepal in 1964. The program was started by the first elected government in 1951.[56]

The state accelerated the process of Hinduization and Nepalization through internal migration. In the name of cultural assimilation, and to avoid the demand for autonomy raised by Tarai people since 1950, the regime supported the migration of hill Nepali speaking people to the Tarai. Indian penetration into the Tarai was singled out for encouraging people of the hills

---

[55] Lok Raj Baral "Participatory Democracy: Concept and Context", in Lok Raj Baral (ed.) *Nepal: Quest for Participatory Democracy*, (New Delhi: Adroit Publishers, 2006), p 3

[56] David N.Gellner, Joanna Pfaff-Czarnecka, and John Whelpton (eds.) *Nationalism and Ethnicity in a Hindu Kingdom: The Politics of Culture in Contemporary Nepal*, p 29

to migrate so that a balanced could be made vis a vis Indian domination. People of the Tarai were generally branded as Madhese or Indian origin. King Mahendra too followed the role of both his ancestors and of the Ranas for weaning away the support of the indigenous community to the regime. The differences between the roles played by the two kings were the strategies of Prithvi Narayan Shah that was based on community and King Mahendra's effort to enlist the support of various communities on individual basis. He took some elites individually from the indigenous community and vested some roles in them. The elites got privileges and power in the name of ethnic and regional representation. For such an opportunity, the elite had to support the Panchayat and surrender activism based on his/her community. As a strategy, Bedananda Jha, president of the Tarai Congress, was appointed as minister by the king in 1963. But it was made possible only after Jha dissolved his party. In the name of accommodation to diverse groups, some middle and higher class elites from indigenous communities were given state power and facility by the king, but the groups, as such, remained excluded. Panchayat policies towards other religions and ethnicity can be illustrated through some examples. To make Hinduism influential within other communities and to achieve its primary goal of Nepalization, the Panchayat officially declared Buddhism as a branch of Hinduism.[57] Gopal Gurung's book, the first blueprint for ethnic resentment, was banned by the regime for 'its allegedly communal overtones and for inciting mutual hatred between different cultural groups'.[58] Likewise, Limbu's traditional customary rights over the land, which was called *kipat* system, was abolished by the Panchayat regime. It is said that, because of the abolition of this customary right, the Limbus now face severe economy related deprivations and problems. In fact, 71 percent among them live below the poverty line.

National symbols and the national anthem are other examples which exposed the regime. In respect of set of national symbols—the crown, scepter, royal crest, royal standard, coat-of-arms, cow, national flag, pheasant,

---

[57] William Reaper and Martin Hoftun, *Spring Awakening: An Account of the 1990 Revolution in Nepal*, (New Delhi: Viking, 1992), p154 -163

[58] Prayag Raj Sharma, "Nation-Building, Multi-Ethnicity, and the Hindu State" in David N. Gellner, Joanna Pfaff-Czarnecka, and John Whelpton (eds.), *Nationalism and Ethnicity in a Hindu Kingdom: The Politics of Culture in Contemporary Nepal,* (Amsterdam: Harwood Academic Publishers, 1997), p 487.

rhododendron, and the red simrik (Tika) invented by the Panchayat system, seven out of ten were related to 'monarchy and Hinduism'.[59] The national anthem that was used for a long time copied the British pattern as if the British constitutional monarchy and Nepal's absolute monarchy shared the same values. lthough King Birendra was considered more democratic than other Kings, he also followed his father's path in the process of Nepalization and Hinduization. He tried to reform the Panchayat system after the referendum in 1980 but was not willing to change his father's policies. Indicating his belief in 'ethical code,' Birendra once said, 'the king cannot change the value system' of Hinduism. He further said, 'the monarch and his subjects have been governed by Dharma, a system drawn from Hindu religion'.[60] This statement pointed to the fact that he was also in favor of orthodox Hinduism to legitimize his rule. No fundamental change had occurred on ethnic, gender, regional and religious issues during his two-decades -long rule in Nepal.

Democratic System 1990-2002: An Era of New Ethnic Awakening

After 30 years of imposed autocratic Panchayat system, Nepal reinstated the democratic system as a consequence of the successful mass movement. In the wake of democratic upsurge , ethnic, lingual, and cultural issues once again surfaced in the public sphere.. This was obvious because the dominant issue in the pre-1990s was to restore the 'multi-party democracy' rather than the caste, ethnic, religious, linguistic and gender questions. Any autocratic regime does not allow such trends that purport to destroy the established ethos of the absolutist regime.

After the end of the Panchayat System, different groups started raising their own slogans and making demands on the state. When the new constitution making process began, the issues of language, religion and ethnic conflict came to public attention. During the six month transitional period, the above agenda was very influential compared to that of the power game.

---

[59] Harka Gurung, "State and Society in Nepal". in David N. Gellner, Joanna Pfaff-Czarnecka, and John Whelpton (eds.), *Nationalism and Ethnicity in a Hindu Kingdom: The Politics of Culture in Contemporary Nepal.* (Amsterdam: Harwood Academic Publishers, 1997), p 505

[60] *Newsweek*, 10 September, 1973

In the debate on secularism vs. Hinduism, not only the minority religious groups—Buddhists, Muslims and Christians—but also the Hindu fundamentalists became visible in public life and started to articulate their ideology. Although all the indigenous groups, including the civil society, were in favor of secular state, the constitution came out with the status quo provision of its earlier version of 1962 as the 'Hindu kingdom'. Several rallies and even demonstrations were organized for making a secular status of Nepali state. It is said that it was the largest one with 150,000 protestors was held in Kathmandu. Gellner mentioned this was the largest protest 'ever held in Kathmandu' (cited in Gellner 1997:178). Their demand to declare Nepal as a secular state was sidelined because of the neutral position of two main political parties— NC and CPN(UML), and 'the influential intervention' of the king backed by in-service and ex-service army officers, Hindu fundamentalist groups of Nepal and India[61]. It is said that King Birendra had a desire to retain Nepal as a Hindu state. This was proved when the king gave this to recommend the then cabinet minister Achut Raj Regmi, who went on hunger strike until death, because he was not in favour of Nepal as a Hindu state and wanted to change the religious status of Nepal.

Although the phrase 'Hindu Kingdom' remained unchanged, the Constitution of the Kingdom of Nepal 1990 accepted Nepal's 'multi-ethnic, multilingual' character. It recognized orphans, women, the aged, the disabled and incapacitated persons, as well as socially and economically backward groups and communities as marginalized groups, who deserved special treatment from the state in education, health, employment, and social security. The Directive Principles and Policies of the State of the Constitution of the Kingdom of Nepal, 1990 says, 'the social objective of the state shall be to establish and develop, on the foundation of justice and morality, a healthy social life, by eliminating all types of economic and social inequalities and by establishing harmony amongst the various castes, tribes, religions, languages, races and communities'. In the state policy, the constitution provisioned that 'the state shall, while maintaining the cultural diversity of the country, pursue

---

[61] Uddhab Pyakurel, *2046 Ko Paribartan ra Nyayapalika* (1990 Change and Judiciary), (Kathmandu: Nepal Center for Contemporary Studies. 2005), p 6 and also see Uddhab Pyakurel, "Identity Politics in Nepal", *Research Journal* Vol. 1 (1), January-July 2006, p110.

a policy of strengthening the national unity by promoting healthy and cordial social relations amongst the various religions, castes, tribes, communities and linguistic groups, and by helping in the promotion of their languages, literature, scripts, arts and cultures" Freedom of press, organization and expression, which the constitution guaranteed, were also better provisions provided to the people. It helped them to organize and to raise their common voices against the state. Many caste/ethnic and religious organizations sprang up during this period. The government identified 59 caste/ethnic groups and announced some affirmative programs for them. On the language issue, although Nepali was declared as the official language, all other languages spoken as the mother tongue in Nepal were also declared as 'national languages'. In addition, government committed itself to provide education in the language of the mother tongue till primary level, following the recommendation of the Rastriya Sanskritik Samiti, 1992.

In 1992, the government formed a committee called Rastriya Sanskritik Samiti to formulate programs for a national cultural policy. The committee recommended the formation of a national coordination committee. Recognizing the multilingual character of the state, Nepal for the first time started news broadcasting in eight minority languages. These were Rai, Gurung, Magar, Limbu, Bhojpuri, Awadhi, Tharu, and Tamang. Earlier, news was broadcast only in three languages—Hindi, Newari and Maithali. The government offered several scholarships for school going girls and boys of deprived and under privileged groups.

Although a lot was done by several democratically elected governments in Nepal from 1990-2002, the governments also showed some shortcomings, especially with regard to enforcing the spirit of the constitution, i.e., abolition of all kinds of gender, religion, region, caste and ethnicity related disparities and discriminations. Inclusion of Sanskrit as a compulsory part in lower-secondary and secondary level curriculum, as well as the decision of broadcasting news in Sanskrit from Radio Nepal are, according to the ethnic elites, other negative aspects of the democratic government. In fact, Sanskrit is termed as 'a dead language' by ethnic elites in Nepal. The NC and UML have been accused of giving space to Brahmanism by making Sanskrit compulsory in secondary schools and introducing newscast in Sanskrit in 1995. Both the decisions are criticized as a ploy 'to create government jobs for unemployed Brahman boys'.[62] More than that, the structure of Nepali elites and their continued domination in polity, society and economy do not allow Nepali state to be progressive and participatory both in form and substance.[63] In fact, all earlier marginalized groups, including ethnic groups did not show any change in the pattern of representation during the three parliamentary elections after 1990. On the one hand, the number of Brahmin in the House of Representative (HOR) increased from 39 per cent in the HOR in 1991-94 to 44.4 per cent in the second (1994-1999), and 43.6 per cent in the third (1999-2002). Chhetri, another dominant caste group of Nepal, had similar record as they were 17.1 per cent in 1991, 18.5 per cent in 1994 and 17.1 per cent in 1999. On the other, the representation of other hill ethnic groups declined from 16 per cent in 1991 to 11.7 percent in 1994, and 12.2 per cent in 1999. There had been a similar trends in Madhes as the representation decreased from 20 per cent to 18 percent to 17 per cent in 1994, 1996 and 1999 respectively.[64]

Also, the Supreme Court's verdict of 1 June 1999 against the use of local language as the official language along with Nepali has been criticized as a continuation of Nepalization process in the recent democratic period. The Court invalidated the announcement of Kathmandu Metropolitan city, Dhanusa District Development Committee and Rajbiraj Municipality to use their respective dominant languages as the official languages in addition to Nepali. Most of the people under these three local bodies speak their own language (*Nepal Bhasa* or Newari language in Kathmandu, and Maithili in Dhanusa district and Rajbiraj municipality) rather than the Nepali. The court's decision has been criticized as 'a clear case of linguistic discrimination' by the state. Apart from that, inability to get equal development of all the regions by allocating adequate budget and deploying sufficient manpower, lack of attention to prevent caste-based discrimination and untouchability in society, especially in public spheres, such as denial of access to the public drinking water trap, temples etc., are other grievances raised against the governments.

---

[62] Cited Malla in David N.Gellner, Joanna Pfaff-Czarnecka, and John Whelpton (eds.) *Nationalism and Ethnicity in a Hindu Kingdom:* The *Politics of Culture in Contemporary Nepal, 1997*

[63] Lok Raj Baral "Participatory Democracy: Concept and Context", in Lok Raj Baral (ed.) *Nepal: Quest for Participatory Democracy*, p 18

[64] Ibid p 19

In the meantime, it seems quite relevant to discuss on how the Maoist party became instrumental in popularizing the agenda of ethnic autonomy and federalism and what were the lacunae of political parties to address this very issue raised by the ethnic groups and other marginalized communities. Initially, the Maoist movement was confined to controlling anti-social activities such as anti-alcohol and anti-gambling campaign; it campaigned against polygamy, wife-beating culture, etc. The Maoist raised the issues related to caste/ethnicity, gender, region, religion, and language. They demanded ethnic autonomy, regional autonomy, inclusion of all marginalized groups, freedom for the promotion of own language and religion, declaration of Nepal as a secular state, etc.

In fact the communists in Nepal had attempted to take up arms twice before the Maoist started "people's war" in 1996. The first, in Jhapa district in 1971 was an attempt to replicate Indian Naxalite movement; the second was on the eve of 1990s Mass Movement. However, both these attempts failed, and its cause can be attributed to the exclusive focus on 'class' by Nepali Communists following the conventional script of Marxist ideology.[65] It seems that the Maoist party had a great realization from the past, and they had assumed   potential power of identity politics. That is why, the Maoist party took up an identity-related popular agenda in the 1990. To attract people from ethnic communities towards the 'people's war', the Maoist party formed All Nepal Nationalities Association in 1994 and adopted Ethnic Policy in 1995. In fact, ethnic groups mobilized themselves in 1991 around the twin agenda of secular state and linguistic/ethnic equality. However, the Maoists decided to take up the cause of ethnic right to self-determination in 1997, just to sell ethnic agenda to the people.

It is also witnessed that the 'people's war' seemed to be expanding relatively slowly during the first two years. It may be because of people's indifference towards the Maoist's political agenda, which the people had perceived as being not substantially different from those of other parties. However, when they started taking up the ethnic agenda in 1997, the support base of the Maoist expanded dramatically. Interestingly the influence of the Maoist got further expanded once it established Ethnic Department at the

[65] Uddhab Pyakurel, *Maoist Movement in Nepal: A Sociological Perspectives*. (New Delhi: Adroit Publishers, 2007)

central level and formed 11 ethnic/regional fronts. Out of 24 districts, where the Maoist formed District Janasarkars (people's governments) during December 2000 to June 2001, 18 districts had 33 to 68 per cent ethnic/Dalit population. Having a look at such a scenario, one can conclude that the Maoist have gained appreciative support from the ethnic/Dalit population. Once the Maoist leadership knew the fact, the Maoist formed about a dozen ethnic/regional front organizations between 1998 and 2000. These fronts were formed on the basis of nationalities and religions. Among 11 front organizations, only two (Madhesh and Karnali) were based on region, and the rest were formed on the basis of the different nationalities. The Maoist nominated all the heads of the front from the same identity. Needless to say that the Maoist applied the policy to lure support of 'marginalized' groups.

As we all know, Nepal's democratic system again went into 'coma' on October 4, 2002, when the king 'unconstitutionally' dismissed the elected government. During the period, the political parties were sidelined, people's rights provided in the constitution were made inoperative by the king. Such a situation ended on April 24, 2006 after the king was compelled to restore the parliament and give up all powers. For the change, millions of Nepali people came to the streets, protested against the four-year- long 'regressive and repressive action' of the king. During the democratic movement, approximately some 21 people lost their lives, hundreds were injured, and thousands of people were imprisoned and tortured.

Actually, the February 1, 2005 coup was the fourth invasion of monarchy against democracy. The first was by King Tribhuvan in 1952, the second by King Mahendra in 1960, and the third by King Gyanendra on October 4, 2002. Because of such interventions by the monarchy into democracy, people in general joined hands against it. According to them, only inclusive and substantive democracy could solve the identity issues arising out of disparities existing in the society. So all political parties were under pressure to include the agenda of inclusion. In April 2005, the Seven Party Alliance (SPA) of parliamentary parties reached an agreement on the issue. It focused on the democratic and progressive restructuring of the state to lay a solid foundation for social, political, and economic inclusion. Admitting their mistakes, they resolved that such a thing would not recur. On November 26, 2005, the SPA and the Maoist reached a 12-point understanding to end the king's absolute rule and to restructure the Nepali state. The SPA, with the backing of the underground Maoists, called for a four-day general strike as a protest against the king's autocratic regime in April. The strike continued for 19 days and the king finally agreed to reinstate the parliament, and to hand over power to the people. The reinstated parliament unanimously resolved to go to the Constituent Assembly (CA) to make the new constitution, and declared Nepal as a secular state. Also, while addressing the demands put forward by Madhes Andolan 2007, Nepal decided to amend the Interim Constitution 2007 to go for federal set-up. Today, all the ethnic communities, including Madhesis believe that the decision for the federal set-up will transform Nepal into an inclusive country. Keeping this in mind, the political forces, civil society, and other activists have been working together to restructure the state for transforming Nepal into a democratic state based on inclusion and empowerment of all sections of society.

In summing up, the ethnic movement has been one of the most influential social movements that Nepal has ever seen in the post 1990 era (Onta 2006).[66] The movement, which was initially launched by individual activists during the late years of the king-led Panchayat system, was strengthened after 1990 when some of those individuals and activists started to organise themselves under various ethnic institutions. Concerning the demands, the ethnic movement has been able to achieve a lot, especially after *Janaandolan* -II. For example, they are well represented in the CA. They are also being benefited by each and every government's steps in order to change its old structure from exclusive to inclusive one. Yet, their inclusion now needs to be qualitatively better along with the figures of increased representation.

Today, the following two issues are important from ethnic point of view:

(i) Nepali state should be restructured along federal, and it must also be based on the principle of caste/ethnicity. While doing so, they started claiming their ethnic territory within the federal set up with which they could safeguard their identity;

---

[66] Pratyoush Onta, The Growth of the Adivasi Janajati Movement in Nepal After 1990: The Non-Political Institutional Agents, *Studies in Nepali History and Society*, Vol. 11 (2), December 2006

(ii)   Social inclusion for the *Janajati* groups in every sector of Nepali society.

One can see a paradigm shift of Nepali ethnic movement along with these recently added demands. The shift seems to be more complicated and challenging, which may invite further conflict inside Nepal. In fact, it seems that the demand of having 'federalism based on ethnicity' is likely to bring much more complication not only in the Nepali political discourse but also inside the ethnic movement as a whole. Here it is appropriate to quote Thapa[67] , who rightly states:

> ...Nepali scholarship has evolved over the years; "ethnic groups" are now identified as those that are known by the generic term "Janajati". But ethnicity, and its Nepali equivalence *jati,* is surely more than that, and can also be defined by particularistic traits such as language (making Maithili-speakers within Nepal as well as Nepali-speakers in the UK ethnic groups), religion (Muslims), place of residence (Madhesis) and even caste (Chhetri). Any province that identifies with any of the above or similar characteristics is an "ethnic province".

It is because of the fact that all ethnic/caste groups are inter-mingled in any village or district throughout Nepal. It is therefore hard to find the concentration of the population of one Janajati group to be more than 20 per cent in the districts, except for a few districts. In this the obvious fact is that more than one ethnic group would claim to a particular territory as its traditional territory triggering off territorial clash resulting in disputes and violence over the ownership of the territory. As a result, the ethnic movement which has been, in a way, united movement of all ethnic communities till today, is likely to be fragmented into many movements. Also, the claims of more than one ethnic group over the ownership of the territory are likely to shift their violent activities to other areas.

The following table provides a basic feature of the recommendation by majority members of the High Level State Restructuring Commission (HLSRC).

---

[67] Deepak Thapa, "Generalized precision", *The Kathmandu Post*, March 1, 2012.

Table 2: Population Composition (in percentage) of Major Caste/Ethnic Groups in the Majority HLSRC Proposed 10 Territorial Provinces.

Name of Provinces	Brahmin	Chhetri	Gurung	Limbu	Magar	Newar	Rai	Tamang	Madeshi	Dalit
Karnali-Khaptad	11.47	48.04	0.65	0.01	6.42	0.33	0.05	0.12	1.14	19.50
Kirat	7.66	18.98	1.63	0.47	6.89	5.35	34.68	6.27	0.75	10.29
Limbuwan	12.18	15.06	2.79	27.38	4.55	3.07	13.30	6.64	0.49	7.27
Madesh-Awadh-Tharuwan	11.17	12.54	1.13	0.09	5.13	1.02	0.08	0.37	54.54	12.68
Madesh-Mithila-Bhojpura	7.51	5.44	0.44	1.25	1.53	2.19	1.67	2.09	69.31	14.83
Magrat	16.83	17.81	2.82	0.01	35.37	2.33	0.04	0.19	1.36	15.99
Narayani	30.60	14.45	7.20	0.02	10.67	6.92	0.34	2.86	3.52	14.23
Newa	17.54	19.36	2.09	0.45	2.94	35.63	1.74	8.46	3.94	2.98
Tamsaling	13.56	16.26	1.35	0.04	5.96	7.61	1.29	34.75	0.96	7.10
Tamuwan	19.70	13.12	32.22	0.06	4.97	4.49	0.65	4.25	1.27	13.56

Source: Census 2001, computed by the author as per HLSRC Report Submitted to the Prime Minister, 2012.

If one follows the modus operandi of state apparatus in order to handle ethnic aspiration in Nepal, he/she finds that the political parties including responsible state authorities perform in very immature manners which have been providing quite a lot ground for such violent future of Nepali ethnic movement. For example, the ruling Maoist party, which was initially advocating for 11 provinces, all of a sudden comes up with a proposal to have 14 providences. Similarly, the state restructuring committee of the CA puts forward a proposal to have 14 provinces with names and boundaries of those provinces. But, another constitutional body formed by the government in consultation with major political parties—the High Level State Restructuring Commission (HLSRC)-comes up with recommendation to delete some of the provinces from the list. Then, some of the ethnic groups took to the street to oppose the recommendation of the Commission saying that it had no right to delete names of the provinces decided by the CA committee.

Generally, being an elected body, the CA should be the final authority to decide what kind of state structure Nepal needs today. Before deciding those serious issues, the CA had to ask expert's opinions on those matters. And the HLSRC was provisioned in the constitution for providing expert's feedback to the CA. But, on the contrary, Nepal practiced differently. As the issue of state restructuring was first debated in the State Restructuring Committee (SRC) formed by CA, and once it came up with a proposal, then again the parties decided to form the HLSRC in order to seek experts' views on the matter. Unfortunately, the Commission also could not bring a unanimous recommendation. Rather, it submitted two separate recommendations to the Prime Minister. Coincidently, the commission members divided along ethnic lines— three members belonging to Brahmin and Chhetri group; took a position, and the rest six (five ethnic community members and a Dalit) took another position. The fact was that the stake holders were already divided when the SRC under the CA put forward its proposal. And, though the commission was termed as expert's commission, it was indeed a partisan Commission because all members were recommended by the four major parties and the Madhese Front. When the Commission itself was divided, there was no point of accepting its' recommendation by all stake holders. Thus, it was natural that, there was a widespread criticism after the report was made known to the public. Two members of the Maoist party including Lekh Raj Bhatta and Top Bahadur Rayamajhi have been opposing the delineation of boundary as recommended by the Commission. Bhatta is against the division of Far West into Khaptad-Karnali and Tharuwan, and Raymajhi has demanded a state called "Khasan" where Brahmins and Chhetris make majority of the population. He is in favour of calling Chhetris as *adibasi/janajati*. Also leaders of all three major parties, including Maoist supremo Pushpa Kamal Dahal opposed the division of Chitwan district as suggested by the Commission's majority report.

Finally, we could already see signals of a divided ethnic movement in which one Janajati group fights against another. In fact, the Tharu movement of 2009 has already set an example which by-and-large was the clash of two ethnic groups—the Tharus and Madhesi communities—in order to claim the Western and mid-and Far Western parts of Tarai as their traditional territory. Major party leaders of Far-Western region, in almost unanimous manner, are claiming Kailali and Kanchanpur districts for their "undivided Far West" province. Along with these assertions, we could see multiple ethnic groups which put their claim for a particular territory. Lately, the religious minority-the Muslim community has also demanded that they be recognised as a separate minority group — not under ethnic Madhesis. Till today, the Muslims of Nepal are demanding a separate status. But eventually they are likely to assert their self rule based on identity. It is because the Muslim organisations already say that the government's move to include Muslims in the Madhesi is a ploy to ignore the identity of Muslims[68].

These are major visible complications, for the Madhes. But, such opposing claims over the territory can also be made in many other areas as no single ethnic group commands a majority. Only a matured state apparatus can handle such a complexity. The State should bring all stake holders on board while deciding the division of provincial territory. And the solution should a comprehensive one through an intense discussion of all stake holders. But the modus operandi of Nepali state till today is just opposite. It acts on events or on an ad-hoc basis and on compulsion without seeing long-term impact of any of its decision. That makes the situation more complicated. That is why; Nepali state should change its working style while dealing with

---

[68] For details, see "Muslims Demand Separate Status", *The Himalayan Times*, February 1, 2012; also "Muslims demand separate identity", *The Republica*, March 22, 2012.

such new aspirations of various ethnic and regional groups. Once state starts dealing with them with the backing of major political parties, Nepali ethnic movement would be moderate. Any failure on the side of the state would only invite more violent, scattered and ethnic movements in the country which may eventually invite even a foreign intervention.

7

Nepal's Armed Conflict - A Narrative of Political Mismanagement

Chiran Jung Thapa

Conflicts are omnipresent in all societies. Most developed societies tend to have developed structural mechanisms to manage conflicts. Therefore, they are more capable of preventing an armed confrontation between the protagonists. In weaker societies, however, due to effete mechanisms, the likelihood of a conflict taking a vicious trajectory is immense. Nepal is a case in point. In Nepal, it was the failure to timely meliorate the dissention that lead to an armed confrontation between the State apparatus and the Maoist insurgents. As a result, Nepal was enmeshed in a bloody bout that hobbled the polity for almost a decade. The culpability rests greatly on the ruling political class' inertness and ineptitude to properly diagnose the severity of the circumstance and subsequently devise and implement a befitting response. This paper will illustrate the utter lack of a coherent and coordinated political will to earnestly seek a resolution that led to the intensification of the conflict. Today, although an armed confrontation between the former warring sides has come to halt following the peace accord, it has not resulted in durable peace. Instead, a rise in numerous unsavory trends continues to beset Nepal. The paper will also focus on the ineptness of the political leadership and their prominent role in stoking newer and more intractable conflicts in the post-conflict transitory period. Further, it will aim to highlight their unabashed power lust which is greatly responsible for the current stagnant political dispensation.

The narrative of Nepal's conflict, however, would be incomplete without the mention of the international intercession. India's role in particular is salient. Rather than just the willful intent of the Nepali protagonists, it was the Indian maneuverings to tilt the balance in favor of preferable protagonists that ultimately led a negotiated settlement between two protagonists of a tri-polar conflict. For better or worse, the shotgun wedding of the Maoist rebels with the Seven Party Alliance (SPA)[1] orchestrated by the Indian establishment radically altered the trajectory and dynamics of the Nepali conflict.[2]

This paper will further argue that a sustainable solution to the conflict would have rather entailed a timelier and synchronized national and international effort coupled with a more conciliatory approach at the initial stage of the conflict. Such an approach would have involved the participation of all major protagonists of conflict to ensure the sustainability of the resolution and would have averted huge losses incurred by the Nepali polity.

Conflict Chronology

A few years prior to the inception of the Maoist insurgency, two scholars had written foretelling articles citing that Nepal was a fertile ground for a Shining path like Maoist insurgency. Firstly, it was Andrew Nickson who in 1992 wrote:

> "the future prospects of Maoism in Nepal will depend largely on the extent to which the newly elected Nepali Congress government addresses the historic neglect and discrimination of the small rural communities which still make up the overwhelming bulk of the population of the country. As in the case of Peru, this would require a radical reallocation of government expenditure towards rural

---

[1] The Seven Party Alliance (SPA) was an alliance between the major parliamentary parties of Nepal. This political alliance was formed to counter the Monarchy that had usurped political power. This alliance comprised of a) Nepali Congress, b) Nepali Congress (democratic) c) United Marxist Lennists (UML), d) Rastriya Sadhvanan Party, e) Nepal Workers and Peasants party, f) United Left front and g) Nepal People's front. The SPA went on to sign 12 point agreement with the CPN (Maoists) in Delhi and then jointly launched a nationwide agitation against the Royal regime. After the collapse of the Royal regime, on November 2006, the SPA and the Maoists ultimately signed the Peace Accord.

[2] The 12 Point agreement was signed in New Delhi on 23 November 2005 between the Maoist insurgents and the SPA under the aegis of the Indian establishment. Through this agreement, the parties and the Maoists joined forces to put an end to the autocratic Monarchy.

areas in the form of agriculture extension services and primary health care provision. Successful implantation of such a program would mean a radical shake up of the public administration system in order to make it both more representative of the ethnic diversity of the country and more responsive to the needs of the peasant communities. However, such a scenario is extremely unlikely."[3]

A year after Nickson's assessment, another scholar Stephen Mikesell wrote:

"The London staff of the International Emergency Committee to defend the life of Abimael Guzman, the imprisoned leader of the Shining Path Guerillas of Peru, has been astounded by the volume of mail received from Nepal in support of him. From nowhere in the world has such a large number of letters been sent by so many members of a national legislature, to say nothing of common citizens.

Perhaps this support from a world away springs from ignorance of the less than complementary picture portrayed by the international press and western analysts of the Sendero Luminoso. Or does it derive from a naïve romance of Nepal's intellectuals with the revolutionary tradition? Or could the affinity for Comrade Gonzalo's ideology have deeper underpinning, based on similarity of certain underlying characteristics of Himalayan society with those of the Andean hinterland of Peru? If this were the case, could we then expect tendencies similarly violent to emerge in Nepal?"[4]

From what transpired, it was abundantly clear that their assessments went mostly un-noticed and unheeded. As a result, when the Maoist launched their insurrection by attacking remotely located police stations in several districts, it took the Nepali populace by surprise. Since the struggle for a

---

[3] Nickson, R.A., *"Democratization and growth of Communism in Nepal: A peruvia Secenario in the Making?"*, 1992, pp. 358 – 386.

[4] Mikesell Stephen, *"The paradoxical Support of Nepal's left for Comrade Gonzalo,"* Himal, March/April 1993.

democratic setting had already yielded positive results with the establishment of a multi party democratic system through the 1990 people's uprising, the reason to revolt again against a democratic set-up seemed completely irrational to most. Nevertheless, the Communist Party of Nepal (Maoists) formally launched their so-called "People's War" on February 13, 1996. The chief ideologue of the party – Dr. Baburam Bhattari, on fourth February 1996, had submitted a list of forty demands to then Prime Minister Sher Bahadur Deuba, and had demanded that they be fulfilled by 17 February. However, four days prior to the deadline, the Maoists launched their offensive by attacking isolated police posts in Rolpa, Rukum, Jajarkot, Gorkha and an eastern district of Sindhuli.[5]

The seeds of the armed conflict that suddenly seemed to erupt in 1996, however, were sown long before. In fact, the history of ideological Maoist movement can be traced back to the foundation of Communist party of Nepal in Calcutta in 1949.[6] When the late Monarch – King Mahendra, usurped State power in 1960 by dissolving the elected parliament and banned all political parties, two divergent factions had emerged in the communist party of Nepal. One faction preferred to collaboratively work with the King whereas the other demanded the restoration of the parliament.[7] Most communist groups opposed the King's hostile acquisition of power and continually sought to overturn the status-quo. In particular, two radical communist leaders, Mohan Bikram Singh and Nirmal Lama created a new party apparatus with a different approach. Unlike other communist leaders who continued to maintain cordial ties with other parties and work collaboratively to restore the parliament, Singh and Lama along with their supporters began plotting a strategy to begin people's movement through an armed revolt at an opportune moment. And most of the present day senior Maoist leadership emerged from this school of thought.

In 1983, Mohan Bikram Singh formed the Communist Party of Nepal (Masal). Singh essentially distanced himself from the mainstream of

---

[5] Thapa, Deepak and Sijapati, Bandita (eds), *A Kingdom Under Siege: Nepal's Maoists Insurgence, 1996 to 2003*, The Printhouse: Kathmandu, Nepal, 2003, pp. 85.

[6] *The Origins of the Nepali Maoist Insurgency*. Available at - http://www.raonline.ch/pages/story/np_mao14.html (Accessed on 16th May 2010).

[7] Ibid

Communists of the day to establish an ideologically pure Communist party. This very party that Singh formed became one of the founding members of the Revolutionary International Movement (RIM), a grouping of Maoist parties worldwide.[8] This party, however, was short-lived due to internal schism. Only two years following the birth of CPN (Masal), it split further into two groups: CPN (Masal) and CPN (Mashal). While the present Maoist chairman - Pushpa Kamal Dahal, who goes by the nom de guerre of Prachanda, was a part of CPN (Mashal) leadership, the second-in-command and ideologue of Maoist movement – Baburam Bhattarai, was with Singh's Masal faction.

There was a significant political transformation in the Nepali political landscape following a people's movement launched by a coalition of various political parties in 1990. The people's uprising ushered an era of multiparty democracy. This allowed for the emergence of numerous political parties. Amongst these political groups, there were four different communist groups in particular with similar ideologies; they opposed the foremost communist party of Nepal - United Marxist Leninist (UML). These four parties coalesced and formed a united front under the chairmanship of Pushpa Kamal Dahal. This front came to be known as the "Unity-Center." This group competed in the general election of 1991 and won nine seats in the House of Representatives. Beset by factionalism and personal and ideological difference, the Unity Centre too witnessed a split. While Dahal led one faction, the other one was led the Nirmal Lama. Only the Lama faction was recognized by Nepali Election Commission. Disgruntled by the Election commission's decision, Dahal's faction boycotted the mid- term elections in 1994.

That same year Dahal's faction espoused a different ideology and labeled their movement as "Maoism" and began to prepare for an armed people's uprising. Their agenda comprised of an armed revolutionary movement that sought to bring about a fundamental change in Nepal's political and social structure. It aimed to uproot the existing government to end feudalism, rewrite Nepal's constitution, abolish constitutional monarchy, and

---

[8] Ibid

establish Nepal as a republic. This faction also became the member of Revolutionary International Movement (RIM).

During the initial stages of the insurrection, the CPN(M) were easily dismissed as a small communist splinter group that could do no more than stir up trouble in a handful of remote regions. This bunch of ragtag insurgents with a puny organizational base and without any sophisticated weaponry, however, evolved into more organized and capable force in a matter of few years. Five years into insurgency, they had grown to be a formidable force capable of putting up a serious challenge against the State machinery.

In June 2001, a gory incident that shocked the entire world became a turning point in Nepal's history. The Crown Prince in Dipendra, in a drunken stupor, shot dead the King and Queen along with seven other members of the Royal family before killing himself. Following the Palace massacre, the dead King's brother was crowned as the new King. Immediately following the ascension to the throne, the new King – King Gyanendra seemed to take proactive steps in Stately affairs and in resolving the conflict. For the first time, there was direct peace talks held with the Maoists. This, however, did not yield any positive results. Rather, the armed conflict intensified exponentially as it took a vicious and bloody trajectory. Until 2001, the Maoists attacks on the State structures were limited. They had only sparred with the Police until then. On November 23, 2001, however, they brazenly attacked the Nepalese Army post in Dang. With this attack, they dragged the Army into the fray. Until then, the State had not employed the Army against the rebels. After the attack, a state of emergency was declared and the Army was formally deployed against the Maoists. With the deployment of the Army, military operations against the rebels only intensified. The rebels too stepped up their large scale offensives against the security forces and increased their other tactics such as strikes, lengthy blockades, use of landmines and other improvised devices and assassinations.

In May 2002, when the Prime Minister Sher Bahadur Deuba sought the King's approval to dissolve the Parliament and requested to postpone the polls for a year, the King intervened and dismissed the Prime Minister citing his incompetence. He was replaced by a loyalist (a former Prime Minister) – Lokendra Bahadur Chand, who too was shunted within a year. In June 2003, another former Prime Minister and loyalist Surya Bahadur

Thapa replaced Chand. Like the predecessors, Thapa's reign was short lived as well because he too was replaced by the former Prime Minister Sher Bahadur Deuba – whom the King had sacked back in 2002. On February 1st 2005, however, the King again sacked Prime Minister Deuba, declared a state of emergency invoking article 127 of the constitution[9] and took executive control.

The King's executive takeover in 2005 spawned new political dynamics. With the King usurping executive control through his personally appointed ministers, the political parties were completely sidelined. The Maoists were still battling the security forces to overwhelm the state and the international community was utterly miffed with the Monarch's move. With three different protagonists at three ends, Nepal's tri-polar conflict became more intense with one trying to retain power, the other vying to regain power and one trying to gain power through armed revolt. As the King with the security forces remained pitted against the Political parties and the Maoist rebels, the latter two decided to coalesce to counter the King. In November 2005, the Maoists and the Seven Party Alliance (SPA) signed the India-brokered 12 point agreement in New Delhi. The agreement called for the SPA and the Maoists to unite forces to go against the King. This culminated into a peaceful people's uprising in April 2006. In the face of mass protests, the King finally capitulated and re-instated the parliament that was dissolved in 2002. Subsequently, the Maoists and the SPA signed the Peace Accord in November of 2006. The signing of the accord marked the end of the Nepal's armed conflict.

Lame leadership and retarded response:

There have been numerous attempts to diagnose Nepal's armed conflict to pin-point the root causes. Conventional causality has generally hovered around

---

[9] Article 127 of the Constitution states: "Power to Remove Difficulties: If any difficulty arises in connection with the implementation of this Constitution, His Majesty may issue necessary orders to remove such difficulty and such orders shall be laid before parliament". The language is imprecise but the king has never laid any order before parliament. Rule without elections clearly goes against the spirit and language of the preamble of the Constitution that states (speaking in the royal voice): "We are convinced that the source of sovereign authority of the independent and sovereign Nepal is inherent in the people, and, therefore, we have from time to time, made known our desire to conduct the government of the country in consonance with the popular will"

the political and socio-economic grievances, marginalization, and lack of good governance. Certainly, there is more than a kernel of truth in the analyses that suggest that the underlying causes that fuelled the insurgency stemmed from increasing paucity felt by the poor, and the state's exclusionary practices. Although the assumption that armed conflict was a result of impoverishment, inequality, lack of development, and mal-governance has acquired much credence, this raison d'être is insufficient to validate the time-space manifestation of the conflict. First, the supposition that paucity, marginalization and under-development were the underlying factors why certain districts in the mid-western hills (Dang, Pyuthan, Rolpa, Rukum, and Salyan) became fertile ground for an armed insurrection is incomplete.[10] If these socio-economic inadequacies alone were responsible for the violent outbreak, there are other areas in Nepal that are in a far more deplorable and in wretched condition. In Nepal, the hilly districts of the far-western region surpass the wretchedness by almost all standards.[11] Had deprivation and difficult terrain been the underlying factors, then the remote far-western districts should have been prime candidates for such an insurrection. Second, the timing is salient. Following the political transformation of 1990, the Monarchy had already relinquished executive power to the democratic political forces. Therefore, the timing of the launch in 1996, six years following the re-establishment of multi-party democracy appears ill-timed because if the Maoists were truly fighting against feudal and reactionary elements, then pre-1990 Panchayat era would be more opportune.

Given the lack of confirmed unitary causality, there is a need to move beyond the simplistic socio-economic grievance causality and engage with the interplay of other variables. It is therefore imperative to explore other variables to rationalize the conflict's commencement. Amongst the myriad triggers and motives, the often ignored variable is the role of the leadership and their respective roles in delineating the contours of the armed conflict.

---

[10] Shah, Sauvagya, "*A Himalayan Red Herring? Maoist revolution in the shadows of the legacy Raj*," In Hutt, Michael, ed. Himalayan People's War: Nepal's Maoist rebellion, London, 2004.

[11] Gurung, Harka, "*Nepal Regional Strategy for Development*," June 2005. Available at - http://www.adb.org/Documents/Papers/NRM/wp3.pdf (Accessed on 22nd August 2011)

Political leaders with their hands on the levers of power are a key determinant in the progress or regress of any society. Those that are responsible for formulating objectives, convincing and mobilizing followers are pivotal in shaping the course of events. In accordance, in Nepal too, the political leadership that was calling the shots is worth examining because it elucidates how the conflict was also a result of mismanagement, malfeasance and self centered demeanor of various political personalities.

Amongst a slew of characters, Girija Prasad Koirala stands out. It is a remark made by a prominent communist leader Amik Sherchan (he was also a Member of the 1991 parliament and is currently a Maoist party member) that is quite telling. He had essentially blamed the Nepali Congress for the inception and proliferation of the Maoist led insurrection. In particular, however, he blamed Girija Prasad Koirala. He had once remarked: "If it had not been for the Girija Prasad Koirala and Khum Bahadur Khadka, there would perhaps have been no Maoist war.[12]

As charged by Sherchan, Koirala who had several stints as Prime Minister and later even served as the representative for mainstream political parties and signed the peace accord, remains a cardinal character in the inception, proliferation and termination of the Nepali armed conflict. To begin with, the Party which he was part of – Nepali Congress had a long-standing rivalry with the communist forces of Nepal since 1951.[13] Both the forces saw each other as opponents. The Congress' revulsion against the Communists stemmed from the fact that certain segments of the Communist factions were employed by the Monarchy during the Panchayat era to counter balance the Congress. As part of the NC hierarchy, Koirala naturally held antipathy towards the Communists. This antipathy, however, intensified after he was attacked by Masal supporters in Pyuthan district during 1991 election campaigning. As a result, when Koirala became Prime Minister, he exhibited his feeling of deep resentment towards communists by harassing communist activists in outlying districts by employing the local administration and local congress activists. As reported by Human rights year book of 1992 and

---

[12] Thapa and Sijapati, pp. 67.

[13] Ibid

1993 released by INSEC[14], that there had been serious misuse of authority by the state (mainly using the local administration and Police) to suppress opposition. Koirala with his well known aversion to the Communists, is believed to have actually instigated such actions in many instances and overlooked in others.

In the annals of modern day Nepali politics, not only is Koirala salient for his aversion to communists (which can certainly be listed as one of the factors that prodded Maoists to resort to arms as a result of the state repression), but also for his paramount role in destabilizing the political landscape through unprincipled opportunism.[15] Koirala has been held responsible for the failure of governance, institutionalization of rampant corruption and politicization of the administrative services. He was also chiefly responsible for the string of failed governments during the 1990s. The Nepali Congress had clearly acquired an outright majority in the 1991 parliamentary elections.[16] Since the forerunner for the Nepali Congress – Krishna Prasad Bhattarai had been defeated, Koirala as the Party General Secretary took charge as the Prime-Minister. There had always been factionalism with the Congress party but after Koirala became Prime Minister, he was accused by the other two senior leaders Krishna Prasad Bhattarai and Ganesh Man Singh of promoting cryonism and nurturing factionalism in the party. In fact, he was charged with practicing Bahunbad (favoring those that belonged to the Bahaun community to which Koirala belonged).[17]

Koirala became such a divisive character following his ascension to power that there emerged pro and anti-Koirala faction within the Congress party. In 1994, Koirala as the Prime Minister unilaterally dissolved the parliament after the anti-Koirala faction did not turn up in the parliament to motion a vote of thanks to the royal address. Koirala's move to dissolve a

---

[14] Informal Service Sector Center (INSEC) is a Non Governmental Organization working for the protection and promotion of human rights in Nepal. It has been operational since its foundation in 19988.

[15] Thapa, Sijapati, pp. 87.

[16] Out of 205 seats, Nepali Congress had won 110 seats in the 1991 elections. The Communist Party of Nepal (UML) had 69 seats and the United People's front Nepal (UPFN) had acquired 9 seats.

[17] Thapa, Sijapati, pp. 39.

parliament, in which his own party still had the majority of seats, would go on serve as the trigger to political chaos that ensued thereafter. From 2004 onwards, until the King dismissed the elected government and appointed a Prime Minister of his choice, Nepal had seen eight successive governments in a matter of eight years.[18] Interestingly, Koirala became Prime Minister twice during this period.

Another role Koirala had in the proliferation of the Maoist insurgency is brutal Police operations he authorized during his stint as Prime Minister in 1998. After realizing that influence of the Maoists posed a serious challenge to the State's authority, Koirala launched a Police operation to neutralize the Maoists. Only a month after he became Prime Minister for the second time, in May 1998, Koirala sanctioned a police operation code named – Kilo Sierra two. Kilo Sierra two was a "Search and Kill" operation that was launched with the objective of curbing Maoist influence and was spread out through most of Maoist affected areas. It was a ruthless campaign which targeted Maoists and their sympathizers. However, many innocent civilians succumbed to the police brutality. Consequently, these operations provided a vengeful motive for others to join the Maoists' crusade against the repressive state.

One can actually infer from Maoist rhetoric/slogans and actions that they regarded Koirala in particular to be the leader of their class enemy. Certainly, the Maoists had time and again projected the Monarchy as a feudal and regressive force and India as the expansionist and imperialist one. Besides that, however, both leaders and cadres from the Maoist camp throughout most of the insurgency have used derogatory language to depict Koirala. Maoist leaders had leveled the title of "fascist" frequently upon Koirala.[19] Not just the language, even certain actions reflected the Maoist antipathy towards Koirala. While training their new recruits at a camp

---

[18] Following were the Prime Ministers of Nepal following the 1994 mid-term elections until 2002: 1) Bharat Mohan Adhikari (30 Nov 94 – 12 Sep 95), 2) Sher Bahadur Deuba (12 Sep 95 – 12 Mar 97), 3) Lokendra Bahadur Chand (12 Mar 97 – 7 Oct 97), 4) Surya Bahadur Thapa (7 Oct 97 -15 Apr 98), 5) Girija Prasad Koirala (15Apr – 31 May 99), 6) Krishna Prasad Bhattarai (31 May 99 – 22 Mar 2000), 7) Girija Prasad Koirala (22 Mar 00 – 26 Jul 01) and 8) Sher Bahadur Deuba (26 Jul 01 – 4 Oct 02)

[19] Both Prachanda and Baburam Bhattarai along with the Maoist official statements labeled Girija as "Hitler" and "Fascist" on numerous occasions. Baburam's interview Available at - http://www.humanrights.de/doc_en/archiv/n/nepal/politics/130701 _interview_ baburam.html (Accessed on October 3rd, 2011)

somewhere in West Bengal, the Maoist commanders would apparently ask new conscripts to imagine Koirala as the target while they practiced lunging their bayonets into enemy dummies.[20]

There is further evidence that even down the line Koirala had played a huge role in stoking the conflict to accomplish his political objective. In a recent interview, the Maoist Chairman – Pushpa Kamal Dahal has revealed the wily and ruthless nature of Koirala. According to Dahal, the King's assumption of full control of state power had greatly weakened the mainstream political forces. Dahal goes further to claim that following the signing of the 12 point agreement, Koirala would call him to suggest different types of effective targets for their military operations to end the autocratic Monarchical system. [21]Dahal admits to having ordered his forces to attack the targets suggested by Koirala.

Apart from Koirala's role, the State's response as a whole to the Maoist problem was a hodgepodge affair. During the initial years of the conflict, the response was marked by ambivalence, apathy and confusion. Even a few years following the eruption of the conflict, the government in Kathmandu had not been able to define the nature of the threat. Official pronouncements continued to describe the armed conflict in Nepal simply as a simple law and order problem; as a socio-economic malaise; as terrorism; or as just another 'political issue.[22] In fact, when the Maoists first fired their salvo of "People's war" - the Prime Minister at the time – Mr. Sher Bahadur Deuba was so engrossed in safeguarding his position in the government, that his attention was barely drawn towards the Maoists' violent outburst.

The response the state put up against the Maoist morass amply depicts the mismanagement of intellectual, moral and physical resources of the state. When the state deployed its resources improperly, instead of curbing

---

[20] Dixit, Kanak Mani, "*Girija Prasad Koirala: Simple convictions*," March 21 2010. Available at http://www.himalmag.com/component/content/article/3415.html (Accessed on October 3rd 2011)

[21] Gateway Magazine, Vol 3, Issue 1, Oct-Nov 2011, pp.11.

[22] Shah, Sauvagya, "*A Himalayan Red Herring? Maoist revolution in the shadows of the legacy Raj*," In Hutt, Michael, ed. Himalayan People's War: Nepal's Maoist rebellion, London, 2004.

the insurgency, the ill-planned response only fanned the flames of the insurrection. The lack of conceptual clarity among the ruling political elites had rendered the State to fail in properly diagnosing the problem at hand, and envisaging befitting measures to mitigate the problem.

Although the response to the insurrection oscillated between two extremes – use of brute force and behind the scene negotiations, it was the political decision to indiscriminately apply brute force that served as a catalyst to inflame the revolutionary fire. The haphazard deployment of an ill-trained and ill-equipped Police force, (which had no prior experience or formal training in combating insurgency), to extinguish the Maoist threat was one blunder that would in later years prove costly to the entire nation. These police operations involved targeting of suspected Maoists. In the name of flushing out the Maoists, the Police ruthlessly employed tactics such as torture, rape, unauthorized detention and even outright murder in many cases. Many innocent civilians became victims of these indiscriminate police actions. The government should have immediately investigated the atrocities committed during the Police operations and penalized the culprits for their unlawful acts. By contrast, the government tried to emphatically justify the actions citing the Maoist menace. Eventually, these brutal police actions not only aggravated the festering grievances of those that had already joined the Maoist cause but it also alienated many who voluntarily joined the Maoists to exact revenge against the Police.

When the Police seemed incapable of surmounting the Maoist challenge, the government decided to erect a more capable and better equipped para-military force. The Armed Police force (APF) was established in October 2001 to counter the Maoist insurgency. However, after the Maoists mounted a daring attack on an Army base in Dang district on November 2001, the Army was deployed against the Maoists. As a result, the establishment of APF seemed pointless. The national Army that was larger in number and better trained and better equipped was deployed only a month following its formation.

Another response was the initiation of the Integrated Security and Development Program (ISDP). This plan was conceived by the Army prior to being deployed against the Maoists. The objective was to launch developmental projects under the security umbrella of the Army to win the hearts and minds of the public. This program, however, was abandoned. The State was not able to provide the security to the programs due to the increasing demand of security forces for other security operations. By abandoning this program, the State only allowed the Maoists to propagate the message that the government had simply abandoned its populace and that the Maoists were the only available alternatives.

In early 2003, a more holistic counter insurgency strategy encompassing all the national elements of power was conceived. This strategy came in the form of Civil-Military National Campaign Plan (CMNCP). The desired result of the CMNCP was the establishment of enduring peace and security under a multi party democracy and constitutional Monarchy. At the operational level, the CMNCP aimed at applying constant and intense pressure in order to compel the Maoists insurgents to seek for a peaceful alternative and abort all violent methods.

The fundamental element lacking in this strategy, however, was the support from the political parties. Primarily, the CMNCP was envisaged by the Army rather than through a joint collaborative effort with other national powers. The Army brass has consistently argued that it was the lack of political support for the campaign that rendered all the military operations futile. As one retired Army General put it - "All the burden of the resolving the conflict was dumped on the Army's shoulders. The Maoist problem was a political problem and the entire society was seeking a military solution. Everyone believed that the Army would wipe out the Maoists at one go."[23] The General's statement illustrates the flaw in the State's response. Those at the helm were essentially seeking a military solution to a problem that had both political and economic origins. The General further stated that – "the Army would conduct military operations to flush out the Maoists from certain areas and then leave. The objective was to provide space for other political parties to operate in. The political parties were supposed to fill that space. Unfortunately, major political parties chose to remain in safer central locations. Hence, after the Army left, the Maoists would come back to same area and revert back to their activities."

---

[23] Interview with a retired Lieutenant General of the Nepal Army on 02 August, 2011.

All in all, there was a disjointed effort in countering the Maoist problem. There was no unity amongst the various political forces in the country. Most political parties remained mired in political jockeying through the first half of the conflict. While the second half consisted of application of brute force coupled with conciliatory dialogue efforts. As it proved, both did not yield a propitious result.

Missed Opportunities:

There were some remarkable opportunities to put an end to Nepal's armed conflict. These opportunities, however, were neglected and no peaceful outcome resulted from these opportunities. Implementing the Dhami commission recommendation in 1997, the peace processes initiated in 2001 and in 2003 were such missed opportunities. Had there been genuine commitment from all sides involved, and the genuine will of the international community (particularly India), Nepal could have avoided the deaths, destruction and turmoil that ensued in the aftermath of these failed prospects.

Only a year after the inception of the armed insurrection, the government had formed a taskforce to investigate the Maoist activities and explore solutions. Under the leadership of CPN (UML) Member of Parliament (MP) – Prem Singh Dhami, the commission began its work in April 1997 and presented a 169 paged report in August 1997. It was the first document of its kind that had deeply analyzed the situation and recommended viable solutions during the early state of the conflict. The Dhami Commission report had – a) provided a comprehensive analysis of the growth of the Maoist organization, their military strategy, and future plans; b) made recommendations that prescribed socio-economic reforms as demanded by the Maoists; c) acknowledged that police operations against suspected Maoists were brutal and indiscriminate; and d) it called for the government to make a formal offer for talks to the insurgents. [24]

The state had expended significant resources on the Dhami commission. However, by shelving the Dhami commission report, and by totally neglecting the insightful recommendations of the commission, the government missed a golden opportunity to resolve the conflict at the initial stages. Had the

[24] Thapa, Sijapati, pp. 90

government begun to implement some of the commission's recommendations, the probability of resolving the conflict at the initial stages would have increased?

In 1999, Prime Minister Krishna Prasad Bhattarai formed another High-Level Committee to provide suggestions to solve the Maoist problem. The committee was headed by another former Nepali Congress Prime Minister - Sher Bahadur Deuba. This committee had come to a conclusion that the rise of the Maoists was not due to the failure of the democratic system but mainly due to the frequent changes in the government and mismanagement of the state's administrative services. It also affirmed that support for the Maoists was a by-product of the state's inability to assert itself. [25]

Although this effort to understand the Maoist problem appeared somewhat genuine, this too turned out to be duds. After all, no significant actions were taken in abidance to this committee's analysis and recommendation. Rather, in line with the committee's findings, the government led by Krishna Prasad Bhattarai was short lived as he was ousted in March 2000 by Girija Prasad Koirala. The political polarization between members of the Nepali Congress had soared to new heights and had resulted in the fall of the Bhattarai government. As those at the helm were enmeshed in political jockeying, they had once again missed another opportunity to put a lid on the Maoist problem.

Another such missed opportunity was the peace talks held in 2001. The government led by Sher Bahadur Deuba held direct peace talks in 2001 with the CPN (M) for the first time since the CPN(M) began their armed revolt. This took place almost immediately following the royal massacre. There were three main players in this equation: the Monarchy, the CPN (M) and the mainstream political forces represented in the parliament and government.

All protagonists involved failed to capitalize on this opportunity to resolve the differences through peaceful negotiation. Instead, all had their own personal motives and agendas. Upon ascension to the throne following the

---

[25] Thapa, Sijapati, pp. 73

grisly demise of most members of the Royal family, King Gyanendra direly needed to establish the legitimacy of the Monarchy. For that reason, the King had advised the Prime Minister to expedite efforts to resolve the conflict through peaceful negotiation. The Peace dialogue was an opening through which the Monarchy could consolidate the institution's standing in the Nepali society. By delivering the dividend of Peace – which the Nepali people had yearned for, the King wanted to replace his muddied image with a more glorified one.[26] The same longing for legitimacy also applied to the government of Sher Bahadur Deuba. Deuba too wanted to consolidate his fragile position within the party and in the national context. A peaceful solution to the conflict would have undoubtedly bolstered his standing to a great extent because none of his predecessors had been able to deliver the Peace dividend.

On the other hand, the CPN-M, took the peace talks to gain tactical advantage over the other protagonists more than anything else. The CPN (M) had already gained control of larger swathes of rural Nepal by then. Through their persistent onslaught on the State apparatus, the CPN(M) had compelled the state to abandon its presence in many parts of the country. When the peace talks were declared, they saw it as an opportunity to further consolidate their strength, increase pressure on the government and garner support for the abolition of the monarchy.[27] It also allowed them a moment of respite during a strenuous insurrection effort.

From the demands put forth by the CPN (M) and the preparations of the government side, it was abundantly clear that both sides were unwilling and unprepared to resolve the conflict. The ossified demands put forth by the CPN (M), made it clear that they were in no mood to compromise. They remained entrenched in their position to abrogate the constitution, dissolve the parliament and government to form a new interim government, abolish the Monarchy and establish a republic. Second, many have blamed

---

[26] ICG (2003) *Nepal: Obstacles to Peace*, International Crisis Group (ICG), Asia Report N° 57, 17 June 2003.

[27] Upreti, Bishnu Raj, and Daman Nath Dhungana. 2006. *"Peace Process and Negotiation: Revisiting the Past and Envisioning the Future."* In Shambu Ram Simkhada and Fabio Oliva, eds. *The Maoist Insurgency in Nepal: Causes, Impact, and Avenues of Resolution.* Geneva: Graduate Institute of International Studies, pp.214-252.

the government for its incompetence during the peace talk negotiation. There have been allegations that the government at the time did not care much for the peace talks and that it was merely lip-service to allay the peace aspirations of the public. Allegations against the government negotiating team's lack of aptitude to handle such crucial negotiations were also rife. Also, the government had entered the peace talks with clear mindset of not comprising with the Maoists. The two major parties – Nepali Congress and UML had stated that they would not accept the Maoist proposal for a constituent assembly. Third, there were spoilers that wanted to derail the process. People from within Deuba's party wanted him to fail in this endeavor. In fact, he was opposed by his own party. To make matters worse, neither could muster enough support from other parliamentary parties.

In a nut shell, the peace process of 2001 was not a genuine attempt by the protagonists to resolve the conflict but rather a circumstantial intersection of complementary short-term interests. Following the failure of the talks, both sides blamed each other for the failure. The mainstream parties argued that the peace dialogue was just a time-buying tactic of the Maoists while they surreptitiously made preparations for a full-blown confrontation with the Army. The Maoists, on the other hand argued that since the government imputed the talks as a sign of their weakness and did not make any concessions on the dialogue table, they had no available option but to resort to arms again.[28]

Immediately following the failed peace talks of 2001 and the exponential escalation of the armed conflict, another opportunity for resolution had availed itself in 2003. On 29 January 2003, a ceasefire between the government and CPN (M) was announced. A 22- point "code of conduct" was reached to essentially serve as military ground rules while peace negotiations were underway. This Peace process took place in a setting when the conflict between the political forces had peaked. By dissolving the parliament, dismissing the government and assuming full control, the King had sidelined the mainstream political parties. These political parties wanted to get back into power. Likewise, the CPN (M) too were strenuously battling against

---

[28] Dhakal, Amit, "*The people's liberation Army,*" In Bishnu Sapkota, eds. Nepali Security Sector: An almanac, Brambauer Publishers, Hungary, 2009. pp. 140

the state's security forces to acquire state power. Essentially, all three forces remained locked in a tri-polar struggle for public support and strategic position, each hoping to use the other in its bid to control the state.[29]

The renewed momentum for the Peace talks should be attributed to the King. Almost immediately after ousting Prime Minister Deuba accusing him of incompetence, the King appointed government officials discretely began dialogue with the Maoists. The Minister of Physical Planning, a former Colonel of the Army - Narayan Singh Pun, was tasked to reach out to Maoists. This initiative was kept secret from the political parties, and there have been credible suggestions that even India was left in the dark, a rather distinct departure from the past when New Delhi was kept closely informed about events that it viewed as central to its security concerns.

The flaw in this process, however, was obvious from the onset. Essentially, it was the King who keenly wanted to resolve the conflict and secure the mantle of Peace for himself. By resolving the conflict, the King sought to glorify his image as a peacemaker and further strengthen the position of the Monarchy. Hence, the mainstream political parties – who were integral part of this conflict, were not provided the seat at the negotiation rounds. This peace-process was strictly between the representatives appointed by the King and CPN (M). As a result, the mainstream political parties were in no way willing to allow these two protagonists to take credit for a peaceful solution. Hence, immediately after the first round of peace talks between the Royal government and CPN (M) on 27 April 2003, these mainstream parties began their agitation phase calling for the restoration of the Parliament and the formation of an all party government. In the wake of anti-government demonstrations, Lokendra Bahadur Chand ultimately resigned on May 30, 2003. Surya Bahadur Thapa was then appointed as the new Prime Minister on June 4th.

Unlike the previous 2001 round, the Maoist negotiating team consisted of senior most leaders of the CPN (M). Likewise, the members of the government were direct emissaries of the King. Yet despite several rounds

---

[29] ICG (2003:10)

of talks, it failed to yield any positive results. Rather, the conflict only intensified following the collapse of the peace talks.

There could have been multiple reasons behind the derailment of the 2003 peace talks between the government and CPN (M). For one, both sides on the opposite ends of the negotiating tables still stuck to their unwavering positions. Had there been some flexibility on both sides, perhaps a peaceful alternative to the conflict could have been engendered through dialogue. More importantly, however, incidents and interests managed to disrupt the process. First, the mainstream political parties, who were left out in the cold naturally had an interest in seeing the talks fail. It is difficult to substantiate that they had a direct hand in sabotaging the process but their agitation certainly intruded the process and triggered the resignation of the Prime Minister. A statement by Daman Nath Dhungana, one of the peace facilitators appointed by the Maoists in 2003, is telling. He claimed that the political parties were not interested to see the Maoists in the political mainstream because they feared that the Maoists would sweep the elections. Alongside, the Doramba incident in which the Army killed scores of CPN (M) cadres too had an adverse impact on the process. It was only a week or so after the Doramba killings that the Maoists unilaterally withdrew from the negotiating tables and returned to their violent spree.

Indian intercession

Throughout the conflict, there were various interpretations and speculations about India's role in Nepal's armed conflict. Overtly, India was providing a full throttled support to the Nepali government until King Gyanendra usurped power in February 2005. The Royal Nepalese Army was receiving Indian assistance (logistics, training and some intelligence) for its military operations. Likewise, India had assured the government and the Palace of full-fledged support to tackle the Maoist rebels. However, the rumors swirling around even during the initial stages of the conflict were that the Maoists rebels were actually incubated and mobilized by the Indian establishment. Many senior government officials at the time (including those in the security forces) privately admitted that India had a major hand behind the Maoist insurrection.

A prominent Nepali scholar – Sauvaghya Shah had written a compelling piece indicting India of complicity during the peak of the Maoist insurgency.

By extrapolating the historical patterns of India's role in Nepal, Shah had made an argument that India had been undertaking a range of diplomatic and covert maneuvers to mold the political evolution of Nepal in its own image and to establish some kind of de-facto protectorate.[30] He further argued that one of the most consistent features of this policy has been the covert and overt support India has provided to various oppositional outfits fighting the Nepali state, in order to exert leverage over the latter. In substantiating his argument Shah affirmed that without the blessing of the Indian government, opposition parties in Nepal had no sustenance capacity to mount any serious campaign against the government of Nepal. Some of the notable successes of Indian interventions he employs to make his argument are the dethronement of the Ranas in 1950s, and the fall of the absolute Monarchy in 1990 through a popular uprising that was clearly supported by Delhi. Likewise, the failed insurrections include Dr K. I. Singh's revolt against the agreement reached in New Delhi in 1950 between India, the Ranas, the Nepali Congress and King Tribhuvan and the violent campaign launched by the Marxist-Leninist faction of the Communist Party in Jhapa in the early seventies. Both of these uprisings lacked external backing. In K.I. Singh's case, Indian troops actually intervened to capture Singh from within Nepal. Shah had come to a conclusion that the Maoist insurgency provided a convenient leverage against the Nepali state to assist the Indian government in its pursuit of the strategic objectives contained in the treaty proposal of 1990.

Shah further hits at the Maoists' sinister duplicity to further his argument. From the 40-point demand which regards India as the "expansionist, imperialistic and reactionary" force to the persistent venomous rhetoric spewed against India, it seemed like India was the prime enemy of the Maoists. The Maoist chieftain had even gone to the extent of saying that the Maoists would ultimately fight the Indian Army in Nepal and eventually vanquish it. Shah, however, jeeringly points to the Maoists' double-speak by illustrating that anti-India rhetoric was in sharp contrast to their anti-India

---

[30] Shah, Saubhagya, "*A Himalayan red herring? Maoist revolution in the shadow of the legacy Raj*" In Michael Hutt eds. Himalayan People's war – Nepal's Maoist Rebellion, Hurst & Company, London, 2004, pp. 192-224.

activities. First, the Maoists were clearly residing comfortably in India and operating from bases in India. Second, while they systematically ravaged national infrastructure, they had not disrupted or damaged any substantial Indian economic interests in Nepal. Third, while they harassed Nepali citizens who wished to join Nepali military and police forces, they displayed a remarkable tolerance of the continued recruitment of Nepali youth into the armed forces of India.

Nepal, however, could not directly accuse the Indian side for stoking the conflict for numerous reasons. Although there were many on the Nepali side that claimed to have had irrefutable evidence proving India's support for the Maoist rebels, nothing substantive came forward. Moreover, the issue at stake was too sensitive for a land-locked Nepal to make such tall claims against a giant neighbor that surrounded it on three sides. It would appear even more preposterous for Nepal to allege that the Indian side had anything to do with the proliferation of Maoism in Nepal when India herself was battling the Maoist scourge within its territories. On top of that, it would be even more outlandish to accuse India of connivance and complicity when the Indian side had branded the Maoists as terrorists even before the Nepali sides had put a terrorist tag on them.

Following the signing of the Peace accord, however, many former unknowns about the Maoist-India linkage have come to the fore. The most interesting twist to argument about India's patronage of the Maoists comes in the sensational allegation made by a former Lieutenant General of the Royal Nepalese Army - Bibek Kumar Shah in his recently released memoir "Mailay Dekhayko Darbar (translated as – The Palace I saw)." In the book, Shah, who served as the former Principle Military Secretary at the Palace (later shunted by King Gyandera) has written about an incident involving an Inspector of the Nepal's Armed Police Force who had returned after receiving commando training in Chakrata in Dehradun. The Inspector had apparently submitted a report claiming that the Maoists had been trained at the same training facility a month prior to his training.[31] According to report filed by the Inspector, the sand models that the Maoists used in the attacks at Satbariya in Dang, Mangalsen in Achham and Chainpur in

---

[31] Available at - http://www.nepalitimes.com/issue/2010/12/31/FromtheNepaliPress/17792 (Accessed on 26th August, 2011)

Sankhuwasabha were exactly the same as the ones Armed Police Force officers were trained to build in Chakrata. A shopkeeper outside the training center had apparently informed him about the Maoist group that comprised of women that came to Chakrata from Nepal. And an instructor too had mentioned about India's role in training both warring sides of Nepal.

In his book Shah has also disclosed information about a former Senior Police Officer, Lal Bahadur Thapa, who was instructed to carry out a covert investigation on India's role in training the Maoists at Chakrata. Thapa, who apparently was very familiar with the Chakrata area, reportedly went missing and Shah was asked to resign from his post by King Gyanendra soon after the decision to investigate India's role in training the Maoists. Shah has further written about another incident involving a senior Nepali Police officer who had served in the United Nation Mission in Kosovo. Quoting the officer, Shah has written about a remark made by a senior Indian IPS officer. Allegedly, the IPS officer had told the Nepali Police officer who later told Shah that everything in Nepal transpired as per Indian intent. He was making a reference to the sacking of a senior Army officer in the Palace who had learnt about India providing training to the Maoists. According to Police officer, the IPS officer gloated about India's success in having so easily removed the Senior Army officer by mobilizing one of its trusted lackeys, Surya Bahadur Thapa, to influence the King.

Shah's allegations of India's covert role in Nepal's conflict are mostly anecdotal; however, they appear credible mainly due to its cardinal role in stitching an alliance between the CPN (M) and SPA. It was on November 22, 2005 the Indian establishment brought the Maoist rebels and the representatives of SPA to Delhi and forged an alliance between these protagonists. It was at the time when the CPN (M) were still declared as terrorists both by India and Nepal and many leaders that Interpol's red corner notices on their heads.

The fact is that India had not intervened in this manner before. There were several rounds of Peace talks between the members of the SPA alliance and the Maoists previously. India had not twisted arms of either side to yield a peaceful solution to the conflict. India's role in the conflict became overtly intrusive only after King Gyanendra became more of a liability to the Indian side than the other protagonists. First, the Nepali Monarch had dismissed the political parties and taken up executive authority and had begun to rule claiming that he would institutionalize peace in the country. Second, he had time and again snubbed India's call to accommodate the political parties. The King's proposal to confer China with an observer status during the 13th SAARC summit too seems to have miffed India. Hence, it was not a mere coincidence that the 12 point agreement was hammered out in Delhi (where the Maoists were still officially declared as terrorists) only a week after the SAARC summit where Nepal has proposed an observer status for China. India clearly sought to emasculate an unheeding and straying Monarch primarily for his haughtiness and his sino-inclination. If India were really intent on institutionalizing peace, could it not have used its leverage during the previous rounds of peace talks? Given the expediency and finesse with which the 12 point agreement was contrived, it illustrates how effortlessly India could have arm-twisted the Maoists.

The fact that the Maoists themselves have revealed that they lived in India for most of the ten year insurgency period, however, has become damning for India. Much of the Maoist senior leadership had used Northern India as a staging area and refuge, particularly the states of Bihar and Uttar Pradesh.[32] Certifying that claim, many senior political leaders of other parties have constantly talked about how they had held meetings with the Maoists at various Indian cities. It would be hard for the Indian establishment to justify how Nepali leaders could reach out to the Maoists leadership who were on the Interpol's most wanted list with such ease without the Indian intelligence agencies knowing about it. Either India had knowingly avoided apprehending the senior CPN (M) members because they were using them as strategic pawns or that the Indian Intelligence agencies were incapable of tracing them. The later proposition appears highly improbable because when Nepali leaders had easy access to the Maoists, it is unfathomable to presume that Indian intelligence agencies were in the dark.

Regardless of the India's role and its subsequent maneuverings, to heap all the blame on India would be naïve and unjustified. It was more the

---

[32] ICG (2003:24)

ineptness of Nepalis at the helm. Certainly, they had failed to govern the country well. They also have failed to convince and persuade the Indian side to elicit propitious conditions and assistance in dealing with the situation. First and foremost, it was the Monarch who had failed abysmally in convincing and persuading India. Instead of accommodating the political parties as suggested by India, his decision to take executive control was taken as a slap in the face to India. India was shocked that the Monarch had snubbed its advice so openly and undiplomatically by usurping power in February 2005. India was seething following the King's move. According to one senior Indian analyst, "People in Dehli are angry, very, very angry. The last time Nepal went against India so openly was the Ranas in 1950s and look what happened to them...the King has deliberately gone against clear advice. By doing this he has made India, if not an enemy, then an opponent." [33] Second, even the parliamentary parties employed the Indian leverage only for personal political gains rather than genuinely seeking assistance against the Maoists. They too had collectively failed in generating positive resolution in the earlier period of the conflict.

One can also infer from the language in the 12 point agreement and the above mentioned analyst's remarks that it was the resentment against the Monarch that actually precipitated the momentum towards a peaceful resolution. Without India's role in stitching an alliance between the two protagonists of a tri-polar conflict, a sustainable solution was very unlikely.

Emerging Challenges

Following the signing of the CPA in 2006, the ten year long armed conflict in Nepal came to an end. A constituent assembly election was held smoothly without major hiccups in 2008. The former Maoist rebels astonishingly pulled off a remarkable victory. They won majority of the contested seats and emerged as the largest political party in the CA but fell short of securing the majority. The members of the newly established CA during its first sitting voted overwhelmingly to abolish the monarchy. With the abolition of the Monarchy, Nepal transformed into a federal Democratic Republic.

---

[33] ICG (2005) *Nepal's Royal Coup:Making a bad situation worsee*, International Crisis Group (ICG), Asia Report N° 91, 09 February 2005, pp. 11.

Since then, significant achievements have been made to transform the polity from conflict to sustainable peace. The transfer of power to the Maoists and the transformation of a country from a Kingdom to a federal Democratic Republic went smoothly. The NA has remained confined to barracks. Likewise, the Maoist combatants have been housed in cantonments. With a few exceptions aside, both the warring sides have not flagrantly violated the terms and conditions of CPA. Most importantly, there has been no armed confrontation between the former protagonists. Political Parties have continued to settle their differences through dialogue rather than resorting to arms.

These achievements, however, pale in comparison to the unsavory trends that have cropped up during the same time period. The cardinal tasks stipulated in the CPA are yet to be implemented. Although the latest political developments indicate that the impending tasks could be completed in the future, uncertainty over the commitments of the actors and the progression of tasks still lurk. The constitution is yet to be drafted. It has already been extended four times. The task of integrating/ rehabilitating the Maoist combatants languishing in various cantonments is still on hold. The process of returning of properties seized by the Maoists during the time of conflict as stipulated in the peace accord has not begun. Formation of a Disappearance and Truth & Reconciliation Commission to address impunity for abuses committed during the conflict still has not seen the light of day. And the major political actors remain undecided on how the restructuring of the State will progress.

Throughout the political transition, due to political mismanagement and malfeasance, many new intractable challenges have emerged and existing ones exacerbated. Reports of insecurity and rampant lawlessness persist. Although serious incidents like killings and explosions – have decreased relatively in recent times, other forms of insecurities such as intimidation, extortion, abduction, and targeted assassinations have spiked. This is mainly due to the proliferation of armed groups throughout the country, criminalization of politics and politicization of crime and increasing impunity. Combined together, all these security shortcomings have instilled a strong sense of vulnerability in the general public mainly because the state has been incapable and unwilling in numerous cases to curb these unlawful elements and activities. Overall, the Nepali Sate has weakened tremendously after 2006 owing mainly due to the muddled maneuverings and mishandling by the major political actors.

Proliferation of Armed Groups:

An ironic and alarming trend in the Nepal's post-conflict situation has been the surge in the number of armed groups. The objective of any peace process following an armed conflict is to reduce violence and foster sustainable peace. By contrast, Nepal's peace process has inadvertently encouraged more violence. Prior to the peace accord, the CPN(M) was the only significant armed group in the country. Since the signing of the CPA, however, the number of armed groups has surged exponentially. According reports, there are now more are dozens of known armed groups operating in Nepal. As of February 2010, 117 armed groups were operating in Nepal.[34] According to the Nepal Police, however, this number has decreased significantly since then.[35]

Initially, it was difficult to validate the reasons behind the proliferation and the exact motive and characteristics of these groups. Today, however, it has become quite apparent that most of these groups were created with a criminal intent. A majority of them are criminal groups seeking to make a financial profit by exploiting the post-conflict instability and a weakened state. The criminal activity that these groups are involved in range from simple extortion to operating as hired assassins.

Many interpretations have been proffered to explain the proliferation of armed groups in the post conflict period. Some have attributed the surge as a consequence of the failure to make progress on key provisions of the CPA, a high level of impunity, and even unemployment for this upsurge. Given the criminal nature of most of these groups, such reasoning sounds sensible. However, along with these reasons, the fact that Nepal's peace process seems to have propagated the wrong message cannot be overlooked.

---

[34] Bhattarai, Binod, *Impunity in Nepal: A study of excesses during the transition*, Center for Investigative Journalism (CIJ), The Asia Foundation (TAF), Kathmandu, Nepal. 2010, pp.5.

[35] According to the Nepal Police HQ, the number has almost halved.

Instead of spreading the message of peace and harmony, the peace process has strangely encouraged the rise of more violent groups. This can be directly attributed to acceptance and the ascendancy of the Maoists. The Maoists' rise to power employing the instrument of violence has set a benchmark in the Nepali society. The fact they have not completely eschewed violence even after coming to power, has only worsened the trend. Others grievous groups have taken a lesson from their rise and followed suit hoping to replicate their success story. Also, to a great extent, the proliferation of small arms in the last three years has only exacerbated the situation.

Criminalization and Militarization of politics and politicization of Crime:

Alongside the surge in the number of armed groups, another very unsettling trend is taking root in the Nepali society. The United Nations Office of the High Commissioner for Human Rights in Nepal (OHCHR-Nepal) Representative Jyoti Sanghera recently expressed her serious concern towards the political crimes in the country.[36] Her concerns are valid because following the peace accord, the insatiable desire of political leaders to attain state power and retain it through all means possible is fostering a culture of "criminalization and militarization of politics and politicization of crime." The parties that are part of the government and the CA have established militia like outfits, condoned and unwaveringly defended the unlawful activities of these groups, openly obstructed and flouted the law of the land and at numerous instances even challenged law enforcement.

Today, contemporary Nepali politics has been inundated by cases of criminals-politicians nexus. The relationships between criminals and politicians are becoming more entrenched. Both the upper echelons of the political parties and the district level leadership are increasingly becoming linked to criminal elements on whose strength they thrive and whom they use to enhance their influence and their affluence. An emblematic case is illustrated in an editorial in the Rebublica. "The attempt by Youth Force goons to murder of Republica's Biratnagar reporter Khila Nath Dhakal is the latest example

---

[36] See MyRepublica, August 25, 2011. Available at - http://www.myrepublica.com/portal/index.php?action=news_details&news_id=35208 (Accessed on 26th August, 2011)

of how Nepali politics is becoming increasingly criminalized. And the state's failure to nab the goons and the UML party's continued protection of the assailants only demonstrate how this criminalization is encouraged by top-level politicians. Just a brief background to explain the seriousness of this case: Youth Force, the UML's sister wing, attacked and tried to kill Avishek Giri at the premises of the district court in Biratnagar."[37]

In addition, criminal activities are gaining political color. Many notorious criminals are becoming affiliated to political parties. Some have acquired party membership while others remain closely affiliated. Whenever they are apprehended for any crimes, politicians have come to their rescue by employing undue influence to extricate these criminals from the grasp of the law. Claiming that these individuals are members of their respective parties, and providing a political hue to the crime committed, Political parties are playing a role in exonerating these criminals.

The political parties are not only becoming a haven for criminals but are also inching towards militarization. As can be seen from the table below, many large political parties are erecting militia like outfits. Many view this trend as a result of compulsion. Following the formation of Young Communist League (YCL) by the Maoists, many other parties saw a need to erect a similar outfit to gain/retain/ political influence. These outfits are operating as the brawn of the political party as they are being employed to attain political objectives through the use of force. Violent clashes between these different outfits have also become a matter of great concern.

---

[37] Available at - http://www.myrepublica.com/portal/index.php?action= news _details &news_id=32149 (Accessed on October 15, 2011)

Political Militia	Affiliated Party	Network
Young Communist League (YCL)	UCPN-Maoist	Countrywide
Youth Force	CPN-UML	Countrywide
Madeshi Youth Force	Madhesi Janadhikar Forum	East to Midwest
Chure-Bhawar Santi Sena	Chure-Bhawar Ekta Samaj Party	Central & Midwest
Rakshya Bahini	Nepal Sadbhawana Party-Rajendra Mahato	Central & Midwest
Madhesi Commando	Nepal Sadbhawana Party	Central & Western
Terai-Madesh Sewa Surakshya Sangh	Terai Madhes Loktantrik Party	West and Farwest
Tharu Army	Tharuhat Autonomous Council	West and Farwest
Akhil Nepal Democratic Youth Organization	Rastriya Janamorcha Party	West and Farwest
OBC Regiment	Organization of Backward Class	Middle Terai
Limbuwan Volunteers and Liberation Army	Limbuwan State Council	Eastern Region
Kirat Limbuwan Volunteers	Pall Kirat Limbuan National Forum	Eastern Region
Jana Surakshya Bal	CPN-Maoist (Matrika Yadav)	Some districts
Madheshi Raksya Bahini	Sadbhavana Party	Terai
Khas Chettri Ekta Samaj	Khas Chettri Ekta Samaj	Some Areas
Tarun Dasta	Nepali Congress	Proposed

Source: Nepal National Weekly, August 22, 2010, pp 29.

Impunity:

Criminalization of politics and politicization of crimes has led to institutionalization of a culture of violence and impunity. Today, one of the foremost challenges plaguing the Nepali society has been the widespread impunity. As per the 2006 CPA, the major political parties committed to establish transnational justice mechanisms to address the crimes and human rights violations perpetrated during the armed conflict. Almost four years have passed since the signing of the CPA and yet no process is underway to prosecute those guilty of such criminal acts.

A 2010 study highlights how impunity has become a critical problem in Nepal.[38] The report enumerates several major reasons that have contributed to the rising impunity. First, the report lists the compromises made by the political actors to secure and consolidate peace that have included granting immunity to people accused of criminal offenses as one of the primary factors leading to impunity. Second is the government's withdrawal of cases involving murder, abduction, and rape. As a result, politicization of crime and criminalization of politics is rife and both have gone unpunished. Third, a lack of effective justice delivery system which is further beset by political interference and corruption is abetting impunity. Fourth, the inability of watchdog institutions to monitor the transgressions and the failure of the successive governments to take legal actions has also led to growing impunity. Finally, the post-2006 political setup has seen governments formed through unwieldy coalitions. To keep these coalitions intact and remain in power, it had compelled the Prime Minister and other members of the cabinet to overlook the transgressions of political actors.

Impunity has been detrimental to the State's authority as it has critically undermined the trust of people in the State's ability to enforce its writ in accordance to the law. Preferential treatment for those with political influence that are violating the law, is ominously eroding the public's faith and trust in the state structures. Furthermore, as impunity and lawlessness become the norm, it is critically blunting the credibility of the government due to its laxity

---

[38] Bhattarai, Binod, *Impunity in Nepal: A study of excesses during the transition*, Center for Investigative Journalism (CIJ), The Asia Foundation (TAF), Kathmandu, Nepal. 2010.

in enforcing the law strictly and perpetuating conflict in the society.

Conclusion

Nepal's armed conflict is a poignant narrative of political bungles and missed opportunities. Although general narratives of grievances characterize Nepal's conflict, a sober evaluation would reveal the malfeasance, mal-administration and acute corruption played a significant role in stoking and inflaming the conflict. The lack of public accountability of those elected by the people had enormously disenchanted the public. This disillusionment only served as a rallying call to motivate people to join the Maoists in their so called emancipation crusade. Had those at the helm mainly the prominent leaders of the major political parties, the Monarch with the Palace officials, and the officials from the security sector genuinely acted responsibly and coordinated their efforts, the conflict could have probably been nipped at the bud. A collaborative and coordinated effort of all major national actors along with the assistance of the international community should have been able to prevent the conflict from taking a vicious trajectory. As prominent political personalities remained mired in political jockeying and mantle of peace became an object of contention, Nepali people's earnest desire of peace, stability and prosperity floundered. Ultimately, an international machination fuelled mostly the convergence of vengeful motives precipitated an alliance between two protagonists of a tri-polar conflict. This alliance would go on to oust the third protagonist and later smoke the peace –pipe.

Since then, in the process of consolidating peace, significant achievements have been made. The constituent Assembly election was held and the first sitting of the assembly overwhelmingly declared Nepal as a "Federal Democratic Republic." Nepal's transition from a monarchical setup to a Republic went quite smoothly. Both the Monarch and the Army acquiesced and embraced the CA's verdict. The Maoist combatants were verified by the UN and housed in cantonments while the Army went back to its barracks. No confrontation between these warring factions has occurred since then.

These remarkable achievements, however, have been dwarfed by the other unsettling prospects. Today, the euphoria and the glimmer of hope the Nepali people had following the signing of the Peace accord has been supplanted by gloom and disenchantment. This is primarily because of recidivist tendencies of the political actors to wrangle unabashedly for political power and the glacial pace of the peace process. The wrangling is not just between the top political leaders of different political parties but there are vicious tussles even between top leaders of the same party. Such squabbles are more or less endemic in all major political parties. Many of the agreements made in the peace agreement are still impending. The constitution has not been drafted, the Maoist combatants have not been integrated or rehabilitated, and the process of delivering truth, justice and reparations for violations committed during the conflict has not progressed. This has been further exacerbated by rise of unsavory trends such as impunity, criminalization of politics and politicization of crime, entrenched corruption, and spike in armed groups.

Nepal's peace process is not only faulty but is fragile as well.[39] Today, there is an exigent need for those at the helm to act responsibly and dedicate their efforts towards genuinely redressing the various grievances afflicting the Nepali populace. Above all, the unity amongst all the political forces in Nepal and their unwavering commitment to institutionalize peace is paramount. Only if the power lust of leaders at top is tempered and grievances at grassroots are tended to, can there be sustainable peace in Nepal. Sans such pursuit, the prospect of relapse into armed conflict will continue to lurk around.

---

[39] Thapa, Chiran Jung, "*A faulty peace process.*" Available at http://www.nepalnews.com/home/index.php/guest-column/5064-a-faulty-peace-process.html

8

Ethnicity in Post-war Sri Lanka

Kalinga Tudor Silva

Examining the nature of ethnicity in post-LTTE Sri Lanka is important from a number of angles. Given the fact that the primary axis of political conflict in Sri Lanka has been identified as an ethnic conflict between a hegemonic ethnic majority seeking to entrench its power within a multiethnic polity and an astute and articulate Tamil minority contesting and resisting this state power[1], it would be useful to know what is the nature of ethnic relations in post-war Sri Lanka where Tamil militancy within the country has been militarily suppressed by a majoritarian state. Here we need to consider Sinhala and Tamil politics in Sri Lanka within the changing balance of power as well as the role of the Tamil diaspora in the international arena. On the other hand, ethnic politics over-determined the Sri Lankan polity to the neglect of other forms of collective politics whether they be class politics, caste politics or even gender politics ever since independence if not before and how far this will continue in the post-war era is yet to be discovered. Ethnicization of all political parties in the country, including reorientation and reconfiguration of Marxist left and mainstream national political parties and the emergence of Tamil, Muslim and Sinhala Buddhist political parties with pro-ethnic political agendas is one manifestation of this ethnic over-determination of politics evident from the 1950s. This in turn poses the question how far Sri Lanka will progress towards a post-ethnic society where ethnicity ceases to be the primary axis of identity and political mobilization and has to progressively compete with numerous other social

---

[1] Jayadeva Uyangoda, Questions of Sri Lanka's minority rights. (Colombo: ICES, 2001)

forces and processes emanating from class, gender, consumerism, and other global dynamics.[2] Finally there are specific issues related to reconciliation and re-integration of war-affected communities with bitter histories of mutual annihilation, ethnic attacks, militarization and multiple episodes of violence and counter-violence. Promoting mutual trust among such communities is a major challenge in any post-war society.

Politics of Ethnic Reconciliation?

Post-war politics in Sri Lanka has been characterized by concentration of power in the centre on the one hand and increased militarization of northern and eastern provinces of Sri Lanka on the other hand. In 2010 18th amendment to the constitution was introduced in order to remove the bar on the incumbent president to hold the presidency beyond two terms enabling him to prolong his power.[3] Since 2005 Sinhala Buddhist nationalism was successfully articulated and mobilized by the Rajapaksa regime for achieving electoral success and organizing a strong majoritarian rule initially and marshalling armed forces against the LTTE from 2006 to 2009. After the government's successful military victory against the LTTE, the political forces that stood behind this military victory made it difficult for the government to make any reasonable political concessions to the minorities or recognize and deal with the adverse impact of the war on affected communities. After the military victory, President Rajapaksa stated perhaps with good intention that everyone is a Sri Lankan citizen irrespective of his or her ethnicity and that the term 'minority' should be taken away from the political lexicon, but this removed any possibility for creating space of ethnic reconciliation or recognizing and responding to minority rights as such. Presently there is a complex variation in positions within the ruling political elite some claiming that the elimination of the LTTE saw the end to the terrorist problem that was the only problem that prevailed while others arguing that the elimination of the LTTE created a new opportunity for dealing with the Tamil problem within a united Sri Lanka. As of now the former view has prevailed over the latter.

---

[2] David A.Hollinger, From identity to solidarity. *Daedalus* (Fall) 2006: 26-31.

[3] Parkyasorthy Saravanamttu, "Centralization and dynastic rule" and J C Weliamuna, "Empowering an already all-powerful executive: the impact of the 18th amendment" in Sri Lanka Governance Report, (Colombo: Transparency International, 2011)

The militarization of the state has continued unabated after the end of war. The defense expenditure accounted for 6 and 7 percent of the GDP in 2010 and 2011 respectively. The military bases in the north and the east were strengthened and further expanded giving the character of an occupied army particularly in the predominantly Tamil areas in the Northern Province where a more or less exclusive Sinhala army continues its consolidation of power and search operations for suspected Tamil Tigers and their hidden armories of weapons and explosives. The state has been heavily involved in the celebration of the war victories and honouring of war heroes. On the other hand the military has been engaged in the establishment of military monuments, Buddha statues, renaming of roads and landmarks in the Wanni in particular in ways that enhances the suspicion and resentment of the Tamil civilians returning to the areas after long periods of displacement during the war. The governors of the Northern and Eastern Provinces are former military personnel with scant regard for minority grievances and human rights. The military is increasingly engaged in civilian activities, including road construction, running of state farms, retail trade, control of land resources and certain reconstruction and rehabilitation operations. In some areas civilians are dependent on the military for access to services of the state, including electricity and water supplies.

The ruling regimes have had a number of state-sponsored initiatives for addressing minority problem in Sri Lanka and enhancing minority participation in governance. The 13th Amendment to the Constitution implemented under the Indo-Lanka Accord reached in July 1987 resulted in the formation of Provincial Councils as a means of devolving power to the Provinces. In spite of its limitations and incomplete implementation, the 13th amendment remains the only piece of legislation responding to the demand for recognition of political rights of minorities in Sri Lanka in recent times. The All Party Representatives Committee (APRC) had deliberations for over 5 years and came up with a number of recommendations for addressing the minority question but the government opted to not to act on these recommendations in spite of taking leadership for the process. A similar fate seems to be awaiting the recommendations of the Lessons Learnt and Reconciliation Commission (LLRC) published in November 2011 even though the implementation of some of its recommendation is still on the cards.

Present discussions centre around utilizing a Parliament Select Committee for dealing with the issue but judging by past practices not much can be expected from this process. On the other hand post-war reconstruction of war-affected regions has been conceptualized in terms of two government implemented development programmes, Nagenahira Navodaya (Awakening of the East) and Uturu Wsanthaya (Northern Spring), that focus on rebuilding war-devastated physical infrastructure such as roads, houses, railway lines, hospitals and irrigation systems and the like, participation has not been obtained from the affected minority communities for the development and implementation of these programmes designed from the top. How far this new discourse of development can respond to the actual needs of the war-affected minority populations being resettled after periods of multiple displacements is problematic in so far as it is not accompanied by creation of a viable political space for articulation and resolution of minority concerns. A Ministry of National Languages and Social Integration has been established for the purpose of promoting social harmony through implementation of official language policies. In addition, a presidential task force has recently embarked on a campaign for development of a trilingual Sri Lanka as a policy towards promoting mutual understanding among ethnic groups.[4] These policies, however, have had limited shelf life and limited actual impact on ethnic relations in the country.

Ethnicity and Clientalistic Politics

In terms of real politics, the Sri Lankan ruling elites increasingly dominated by the Sinhalese evolved a pattern of clientalistic politics in the post-independence era. The foundation of this clientalistic politics was that those who are in power use that power to create and sustain followers across caste, class and ethnic divides. The clientalistic politics serves to suppress mass political mobilization of people along class, caste or ethnic lines but rather create political machines that serve the ruling elites and keep the limited numbers who are within the patronage networks happy while making socially and politically excluded large numbers discontented and unconnected or only loosely connected to the state. The outcomes have been JVP-led

---

[4] Sunimal Fernado, *Ten Year Master Plan for a Trilingual Sri Lanka, 2011-2020*. Colombo: Presidential Secretariat, 2011.

political insurgencies in the south and LTTE-led uprisings in the north and east. Since the victory of the government military campaign against the LTTE in May 2009, the Rajapaksa regime tends to continue the same clientalistic politics bringing some benefits to the majority ethnic group, but only marginal relief to those in minority ethnic groups severely affected by the war and seriously disadvantaged by majoritarian politics and policies of the ruling regime. Caste and class tensions seem to have largely dissipated and diverted at least in part through the operation of clientalistic politics but its biggest failure has been in relation to addressing Tamil grievances in the north and east. The clientalistic networks extending to those outside the ruling clique via selected minority politicians do provide some relief to those who are close to such politicians including some former LTTE activists, but it tends to fuel minority grievances rather than addressing the root causes of their grievances satisfactorily.

State-sponsored Clientalistic Politics in the South

The state-sponsored patronage politics in the South has served to distribute resources at the control of the state, including public sector employment, crown land and permits for business activities, among core political supporters and known contacts. To a considerable extent, patronage politics has been informed and shaped by the Sinhala nationalist ideology driving state policies and programmes. In spite of the programme of economic liberalization introduced in 1977, there has been an expansion of the role of the state in many of the sectors. For instance, the expansion of the military and civil defense forces since 1980s served to create employment opportunities for unemployed rural youth in the Sinhala south in particular.[5] State land policies too have played an important role in keeping clientalistic networks going among the land hungry Sinhala peasants. [6]

As an outcome of the successful appropriation of the Sinhala nationalist ideology by the state, leftist and JVP vote bases have been gradually reduced in the South. Parallelly, the decline of the trade union movement too represents

---

[5] Rajesh Venugopal, *Cosmopolitan capitalism and sectarian socialism: conflict, development, and the liberal peace in Sri Lanka*. (PhD thesis, Oxford University, 2009).

[6] Mick Moor, *The state and the peasant politics in Sri Lanka*. (Cambridge: CUP, 1985).

a decline of class politics in the South. For the most part, low caste constituencies in the South have been gradually absorbed and won over by Sinhala nationalist forces. On the whole, the pro-Sinhala JVP actors who rebelled against the governments in 1971 and 1978-1979 have been successfully brought into the democratic processes including the fold of clientalistic politics of the state in some instances.

On the other hand criticisms against the state in the North and the South have been handled by intimidation and use of violence. Politicians at various levels have increasingly relied on illegal means to fund their expensive election campaigns, silence political enemies and media and recruit army deserters, drug lords and underworld elements in general during their election and other political campaigns. Political violence has been used not only in inter-party rivalries but also in factional conflicts within political parties, revealing the increasingly fractured nature of the Sri Lankan polity in spite of the apparent unity of the ruling classes. The weakness of the opposition parties to mobilize successful protest against the ruling regime or to prevent misuse of power by the ruling regime is another important manifestation of the failure of the democratic process against the background of armed conflict and tyranny of the ruling elites.

Patronage for some on the part of the state often existed side by side with discrimination for others in matters such as recruitment to government employment, and this appears to be the essence and a primary attraction of Sinhala nationalism for the electorate in the South. On the other hand, clientalistic politics of the state has so far failed to provide a successful solution to the ethnic problem or satisfactorily incorporate the Tamil minority into the Sri Lankan polity.

Ethnicity and Clientalistic Politics in the North

Even though Muslims have had many grievances against the Sri Lankan state from time to time, they have always been included in clientalistic politics in post independent Sri Lanka. As at present, most Muslim political groups including the Sri Lanka Muslim Congress and its breakaway groups have joined the government having accepted cabinet portfolios and other positions. This in turn has given them access to state-owned land resources, state sector employment opportunities, and opportunities for legitimate and illegal business activities. This also applies to the Ceylon Workers Congress representing plantation workers even though the extent to which this has actually benefitted the structurally marginalized Indian Tamil resident labour in the plantations cannot be over exaggerated.

The successive Sinhala regimes in the South identified and worked with Douglas Devananda faction with roots in islands off Jaffna Peninsula in its efforts to eliminate the LTTE and extend clientalistics networks over the ethnic divide. Later Karuna and Pilleyan factions were mobilized by the state for the same purposes in Eastern Sri Lanka. These Tamil politicians have derived considerable benefits for themselves and for their immediate supporters from their presence within the ruling government and from their alliances with the security forces. For the most part, they have received some positions within the state and used their power and alliances with the ruling regimes including the military to continue some shady activities, including certain aspects of the war economy in northern and eastern Sri Lanka in spite of the end of war. Even though they have established their own followings and political machines among some Tamil civilians and armed groups, for the most part these Tamil politicians who cooperate with the government are seen as black legs and traitors to the cause of Tamils.

The two mainstream Tamil political parties, Tamil National Alliance (TNA) and Tamil United Liberation Front (TULF), have remained outside and critical of the state in spite of various efforts by the Rajapaksa regime to co-opt them to the government by offering them cabinet portfolios and other benefits. As a result, the development of an UMNO type political solution to the ethnic problem evolved in Malaysia has so far been averted in Sri Lanka. The failure of the political leadership in the South to evolve a formula acceptable to the Tamil population emerging from three decades of war and the intransigence of the Tamil political leadership to move away from ethnic politics evolved over the years have created a stalemate in potential re-integration of the Tamil community to the Sri Lankan polity. The parliamentary, presidential and local government elections in the North in 2010 and 2011 have consistently shown an anti-government vote in the North, while the Rajapaksa regime has comfortably won all these elections due to a nationalist Sinhala block vote in the South and East also helped by Muslim vote in most areas. The precarious position of the state in the North is also reflected in its failure to conduct elections for the Northern Provincial Council so far even though government and pro-government political groups have won all other Provincial Councils in the country including the Eastern Provincial Council. It is interesting that while the government won most of the local government elections held recently, the opposition won the Colombo Municipal Council elections. The significant presence of ethnic minorities in Colombo Municipal Council area, Muslims and Tamils together comprising nearly 50 percent of the constituency in the Colombo Municipal Council area, may be seen as an important factor in the government's marginal loss in the CMC elections. This, in turn, indicates that the government has failed to address the minority grievances through its clientalistic politics or through the piecemeal measures already described.

Ethnic Relations during the War

In the same way that preexisting ethnic tensions in the country fueled the war in Sri Lanka, the war itself added to ethnic tensions in the country. The July 1983 ethnic riots marked a watershed in ethnic relations in the country in that the Tamil civilians living in the South and their properties and businesses were attacked by Sinhala mobs with the backing and even interventions of sections of the Sinhala nationalist political elite and the security forces. Even though this was not the first time such ethnic riots occurred in southern Sri Lanka, it produced widespread devastation and resentment among the Tamil minority that, in turn, fueled the Tamil separatist struggle and the violent and brutal form it took under the LTTE leadership in the years that followed. The resulting armed conflict driven by a militant Sinhala nationalism held by the state and an equally if not more militant Tamil nationalism and a corresponding Tamil liberation struggle led by the LTTE, contributed to further polarization of the two communities. Even though the LTTE had initially identified and worked with Tamil speaking Muslims particularly in Northern and Eastern Provinces as co-ethnics and potential partners of the Eelam campaign, this proved to be unsuccessful and by 1990 the LTTE identified Muslims as informants and collaborators of the government security forces and started a campaign of terror against Muslims communities in the Eastern Province and a campaign of ethnic cleansing against Muslim communities living side by side with Tamil communities in the Northern Province. This, in turn, led to a large scale displacement of Muslim communities interspersed among Tamil populations in the Northern Province and their involuntary movement to the South with Puttalam as their new place of congregation. The brutal LTTE attacks on Muslim communities in the Eastern Province illustrated by the Kaththankudi massacre on August 3, 1990, led to Muslim backlashes against nearby Tamil communities with whom they have had peaceful co-existence for generations. The resulting population movements in the Northern and Eastern Provinces enhanced ethnic segregation that in turn reflected growing ethnic polarization in the country and fueled resentment and mutual suspicion not only between Sinhalese and Tamils but also between Tamils and Muslims on the one hand and Sinhalese and Muslims on the other.

The war between the government security forces and the LTTE directly impacted on Sinhala-Tamil relations in the country in a number of ways. In its military operations the Sinhala-speaking government security forces often found it difficult to distinguish between Tamil Tigers and Tamil civilians, particularly in a situation where the Tamil Tigers tended to use Tamil civilians as a human shield in their operations. This, in turn, provoked army reprisals against Tamil civilians causing death, disability and displacement. The establishment of high security zones particularly in the land scarce Jaffna Peninsula added to the misery of civilians living in those areas as they became more or less permanently displaced. The richer civilians in the war-affected Northern and Eastern Provinces were able to move to safety in Colombo or overseas destinations using their contacts, marketable skills and language proficiency, leaving behind the poorer Tamils to eke out a vulnerable existence in LTTE or government controlled areas.

On the other hand, the LTTE carried out a brutal campaign of terror in Sinhala border villages whether they are state-sponsored colonization schemes or villages naturally evolved in these areas in an all out effort to push back the Sinhala frontier and expand the territory under the so-called Tamil Eelam. This, in turn, led to the formation of "home guard" service, later christened as "civil defence force" under the regular security forces in Sinhala and Muslim border villages with resulting penetration of the armed conflict into civilian populations. In spite of these developments, Sinhala and Muslim civilians in many of the border villages were either displaced to mainstream Sinhala or Muslim areas respectively or spent the night in nearby jungle areas in order to avoid potential pre-dawn LTTE massacres. Thus the war clearly engulfed not only armed combatants of either side with the battle lines clearly drawn on ethnic lines, but also Tamil, Muslim and Sinhala civilians occupying the war zone or war-affected regions.

It is, however, wrong to over generalize the ethnic divide and characterize the ethnic relations in the country during the war purely in adversarial terms. After each ethnic riot there has been a cooling off period where relations have gradually improved and mutual mistrust declined over the years. For instance, after the 1983 ethnic riots there has been no repetition of widespread Sinhala civilian mobilization and mob violence against Tamil civilians in the South in spite of many potential provocations by the LTTE such as attacks on sacred Bodhi Tree in Anuradhapura on the Vesak day of 1985, massacre of 33 Buddhist monks in Arantalawa in 1987 and brutal attack on Temple of the Tooth in Kandy in 1998. Moreover, the Buddhist monks and civilians in Ampara town in eastern Sri Lanka played an active role in providing accommodation and relief to Tamil and Muslim civilians who survived the December 2004 tsunami and who were displaced from their coastal settlements to interior areas clearly trespassing the ethnic boundaries evolved during the war. Research in selected Sinhala border villages in the Northern Province such as Varikuttiuruwa in Vavuniya South and Pollebadda in Mahaoya DS Division in the Ampara district reveal that the older generations of Sinhalese had established good social relations and economic ties with their Tamil counterparts in the areas and had even mastered Tamil language to a considerable extent while this pattern ceased to penetrate to the younger generations due to increased ethnic polarization in the years that followed.[7]

In an interesting field research conducted in Kottiyar Pattu, Trincomale, from 2003 to 2008 Gassbeek[8] found that everyday interethnic interaction continued among the Tamils, Muslims and Sinhalese in this volatile area in

---

[7] Report on the baseline survey on social integration in selected districts in Sri Lanka. (Colombo: ICES, 2011) Also see, Upali Weerakoon, *The role of kinship in resettlement of Sinhala IDP communities in Sri Lanka.* (PhD thesis, University of Peradeniya, 2012).

[8] Timmo Gaasbeek, *Bridging troubled waters? Everyday inter-ethnic interaction in a context of violent conflict in Kottiyar Pattu, Trincomalee, Sri Lanka.* (PhD thesis, Wagenningen University, 2010).

spite of violent conflict. The everyday interethnic interaction included economic interaction, shared use of irrigation water, marketing channels and settlement of interpersonal conflicts and even interethnic marriages. Ethnicity was not the only or even most important basis of identity employed or mobilized in given situations facilitating social interaction across the ethnic divide. While sources of interethnic tensions were many and ethnic entrepreneurs often mobilized them to their advantage, a practical logic prevailed in most circumstances and vital lines of communication were preserved among the different ethnic groups using a range of intermediaries and cultural brokers.

Ethnic Relations in the Post-war Era

In many ways ethnic configurations and relations evolved during the war continued in the post-war era which began in 2007 in Eastern Sri Lanka and May 2009 in the Northern Province. As for some new developments, wherever possible the internally displaced persons returned to their original places, established temporary shelter and started their livelihoods. Many of the IDPs from Jaffna Peninsula who were displaced in Vanni have now returned to the Jaffna Peninsula. Similarly Muslims IDPs in Puttalam have begun to return to their original places in Mannar and other districts in Northern Province and Sinhala IDPs from border villages in Northern and Eastern Provinces have commenced their return to original places. In many instances the older generations have returned first, leaving behind the younger generations in places where they were brought up during the war. This pattern is evident among Muslim IDPs in Puttalam, Tamil IDPs in Vanni as well as among Sinhala IDPs from Vavuniya South who were displaced to predominantly Sinhala Rambawa DS Division in the Anuradhapura District. It is likely that branches of their families will continue in both locations at least until they are firmly established in one location or the other. While a smaller section of Tamil IDPs in Northern Province is yet to be resettled due to the continuation of high security zones and incomplete clearance of land mines in some areas, the progress achieved in resettlement since the end of war has been substantial. Similarly opening of A9 road and development of the road network linking the Northern and Eastern Provinces to the rest of Sri Lanka have facilitated the flow of goods and services stimulating economic recovery in the war-affected areas and their market integration with the larger economy of Sri Lanka.

There are, however, a number of continuing obstacles to promoting mutual trust among the three ethnic groups increasingly polarized from each other during three decades of armed conflict. First and foremost, there is heavy military presence among civilian communities in Northern Province and, to a lesser extent, in Eastern Province. The government has been extremely cautious about potential security risks in withdrawal of military from the conflict affected areas, viewing a remobilization and regrouping of LTTE as a real potential in the post war Tamil society. On the other hand, the heavy presence of the predominantly Sinhala security forces mainly conversing in Sinhala among Tamil civilians has the potential to sustain mutual mistrust or even mutual resentment. The demographic deficit of males in Tamil civilian populations in the affected areas due to war related deaths and disappearances and outmigration has added to the insecurity generated by heavy military presence in such areas. The civilian engagements of the security forces including control of land resources have given rise to many unsubstantiated suspicions and rumours in the civilian populations belonging to different ethnic groups. On the other hand development of democratic institutions with active participation of local communities has been hampered by the need to secure military approval and even participation in any public gathering. Only some NGOs have so far been allowed to initiate their activities among the civilians in the Northern Province. In the elections held so far in the Northern Province, voter participation has been low and the conduct of free and fair elections has been difficult to achieve due to interference by pro-government Tamil political factions, episodes of violence and restrictions imposed on mainstream Tamil political parties. The delay in establishment of the Northern Provincial Council has further contributed to the political vacuum prevailing in the Northern Province.

Feelings of insecurity among the ethnic minorities, in particular, were evident in the Grease Bhutam or Grease Yaka (grease demon) phenomenon that became a political issue and security concern in various parts of Sri Lanka, including North and East during the latter part of 2011. The unknown grease demons were known to hover around houses at night looking for female companions or simply as peeping toms. Also some indiscriminate night-time killings of lonely women in some households in some Sinhala predominant Southern areas were attributed to grease demons. Where groups of vigilant civilians found suspected grease yakas, often people took the law into their own hands and started attacking them violently resulting in a number of deaths of innocent strangers. In many instances these strangers happened to be persons connected to security forces leading to open confrontation between civilians and security forces in some instances. Even though the fear of grease yakas prevailed in all ethnic groups, among the ethnic minorities the phenomenon reflected strong mistrust towards the security forces in particular. The demographic imbalance in the civilian populations in the former conflict zone with a high proportion of female headed families and relative absence of adult males in many households added a further dimension to the fear and moral panic surrounding grease demons.

Manifestations of Religious Intolerance

Even though Sri Lanka is home to four world religions, including Buddhism, Hinduism, Christianity and Islamism, actual religious practices have been eclectic in popular religious sites such as Kandy and Katharagama.[9] The efforts to purify religions however emerged in the effort at religious revival that began in the colonial era.[10] The animal sacrifice for Kali in Munneswaram shrine located in Putlam district has continued for generations with the participation of Hindus, Buddhists and followers of other religions in the country. In 2010, a militant Buddhist movement decided that animal sacrifice is bad and un-Buddhist and publicly campaigned against the Munneswaram cult by organizing a protest march in front of the shrine. The police intervened and prevented disruption of the cult including animal sacrifice on that occasion. In 2011 the campaign once again started and the protesters obtained a court injunction against the practice also helped by some Sinhala nationalist politicians at the Colombo level. This prevented the performance of the ritual, pointing to how political power of the Sinhala nationalists was used

---

[9] Jonathan Walters, "Multireligion on the Bus in Sri Lanka: Beyond 'Influence' and 'Syncretism' in the Study of Religious Meetings," delivered at the Institute for the Advanced Study of Religion, The University of Chicago Divinity School, November 1991

[10] Gananath Obeyesekere, "Religious Symbolism and Political Change in Ceylon." *Modern Ceylon Studies: Journal of the Social Sciences* I:1., pp. 43-63. 1970

side by side with legal sanctions against the long-established pattern of religious freedom and diversity in Sri Lanka.

Another similar example is the Deegavapi land issue where an ancient Buddhist shrine discovered in 1915 had the effect of the Muslim residents in the area having to surrender in 2009 some of the land they occupied and cultivated for generations as part of the historical property claimed by militant Sinhala nationalist from Colombo on behalf of the temple. In this instance, a clause in the Urban Development Ordinance that permitted the state to declare certain land as sacred sites was used to acquire and annex the land held by the Muslim peasants as part of temple property. The legal provision for sacred sites disregarded the well established cultural practice of religious syncretism in principal pilgrimage sites in Sri Lanka including Kataragama, Kandy, Mahiyangana and Adams Peak.

In April-May 2012, a mosque erected many years earlier in Dambulla in close proximity to the Buddhist sites in the town was ordered to close down due to the pressured from Sinhala Buddhist leaders in the area and from Colombo. These events indicate that the ethnic tensions in the country are continuing under the radar in spite of the end of war and the refusal on the part of the state to recognize and deal with possible sources of ethnic tension in post-war Sri Lanka.

Ethnic Relations outside the War Zone

On the other hand, there is evidence that ethnic relations outside the war zone have gradually become stabilized over the years. In a research study conducted by the International Centre for Ethnic Studies in a number of Districts in Southern Sri Lanka in 2011indicated that Tamil and Muslim minorities in Sinhala-predominant areas tended to learn Sinhala language and, moreover, had many close friends within the Sinhala community. [11]

---

[11] Report on the baseline survey on social integration in selected districts in Sri Lanka. (Colombo: ICES, 2011)

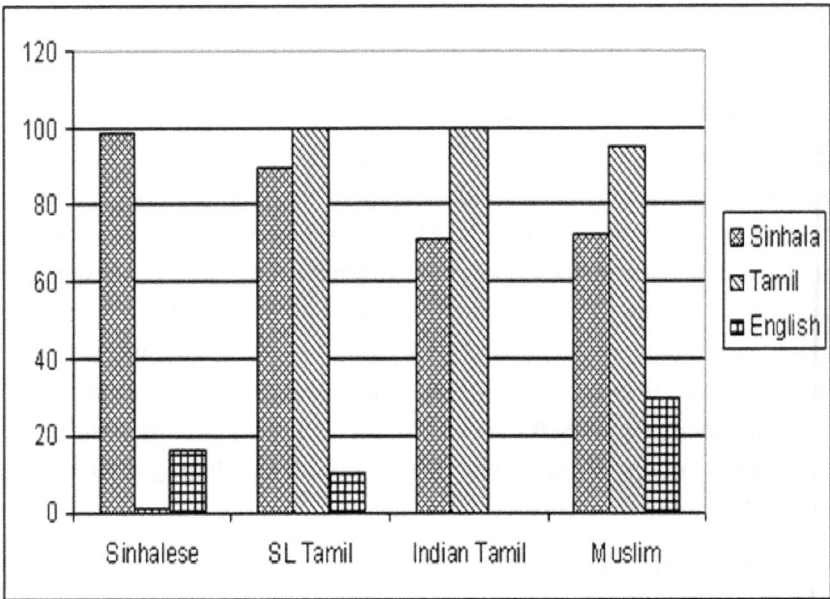

Figure 1: Percentage of People Speaking Fluently Each of the Three National Languages by Ethnicity in Selected locations in Bope Poddala DS Division, 2011

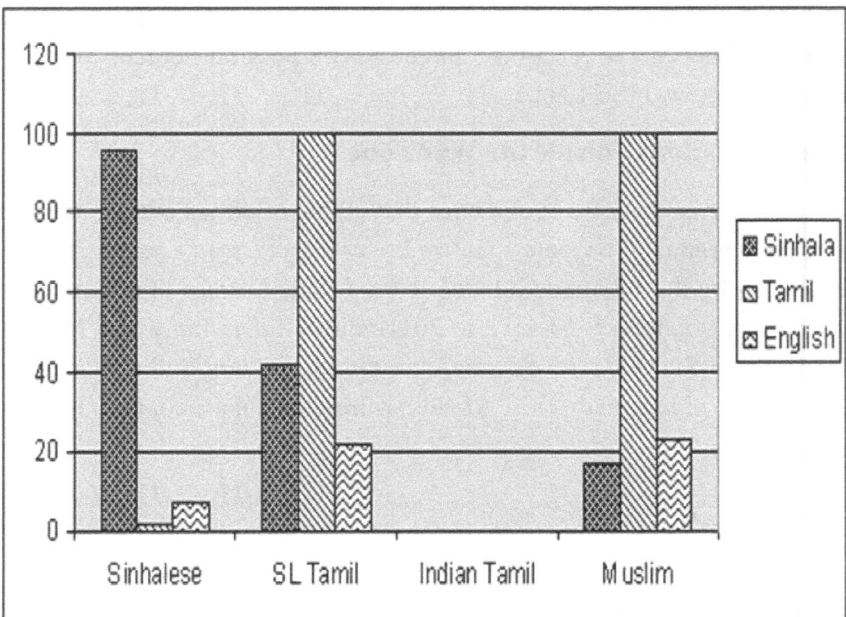

Figure 2: Percentage of People Speaking Fluently Each of the Three National Languages by Ethnicity in Selected locations in Puttalam DS Division, 2011

Data presented in Figure 1 and 2 indicate that while the ethnic minorities in the Sinhala predominant area of Pope Poddala speak Sinhala besides their Tamil mother tongue more widely compared to Puttalam where minority presence is more widespread and, therefore, the need to learn Sinhala does not appear to be that important for ethnic minorities. On the other hand, the Sinhalese in both locations have not felt compelled to learn or acquire Tamil given the fact that Sinhala is widely spoken in these areas with the Sinhala language belt.

The same study also examined the number of close friends within one own ethnic group and outside. This was in order to determine the extent to which social networks extend outside one's own ethnic group.

Table 1: The mean number of close friends within and outside one's own ethnic group by ethnicity, selected locations in Galle, Puttalam and Badulla Districts in Sri Lanka, 2011

Ethnicity			No of close friends within the ethnic group	No of close friends outside the ethnic group
Sinhala		Mean	3.76	0.93
		N	241	242
		Std. Deviation	5.470	2.820
SLTamil		Mean	33.79	34.33
		N	33	33
		Std. Deviation	89.410	93.973
Indian Tamil		Mean	20.68	10.19
		N	31	31
		Std. Deviation	49.844	32.426
Muslim		Mean	103.37	18.69
		N	59	59
		Std. Deviation	273.402	66.733
Total		Mean	23.91	7.55
		N	367	368
		Std. Deviation	118.598	40.980

These data suggests that in the case of minority ethnic groups a substantial number of their close friends come from outside their ethnic group while the Sinhalese, whose close personal friends were much smaller in number compared to the Tamils and Muslims, tend to have most of their close friends within their own ethnic group. This, in turn, is in keeping with greater prevalence of monolingualism in the Sinhala community. These data contradicts the stereotypical view that ethnic minorities in the South are limited in their social networks to those from within their own ethnic groups. On the contrary, this appears to be more the case among the ethnic majority perhaps due to the increased penetration of Sinhala nationalism in their world view, and day-to-day social relations.

Conclusions and Recommendations

On the whole, the analysis pursued in this essay suggests that while a process of ethnic reconciliation may be at work in post-war Sri Lanka society, the state policies and programmes as well as the mainstream Tamil political parties have served to arrest these trends and prevent progression of ethnic reconciliation as such. Primarily influenced by Sinhala nationalism, state policies have increasingly moved away from recognizing and fostering cultural diversity in the country's population and devolution of power as a prerequisite for re-integrating politically alienated ethnic minorities to the Sri Lankan polity. The clientalistic politics of the Sri Lankan state has had some success in averting or diverting class and caste tensions but failed to respond satisfactorily to the ethnic based loyalties and grievances in minority communities. The mainstream Tamil political parties too have contributed to this situation by overplaying the Tamil card and ignoring the political reality and processes of ethnic reconciliation actually in operation in society.

In order to promote minority participation in the democratic process and gradually eliminate their mistrust towards the Sri Lankan state, the following measures can be recommended.

1. Establish the Northern Provincial Council, conduct free and fair elections and enable a democratically elected Tamil political leadership to guide, influence and contribute towards the ongoing development and human resettlement processes, while making sure that they are in keeping with overall plans of the political centre.

2. Gradually withdraw military from the Northern and Eastern Provinces and increase minority presence in the security forces as an interim measure towards building trust among civilians in the war zone.

3. The discourse of development with a focus on infrastructural development alone cannot   satisfactorily respond to the demands of post war Sri Lanka society with structural problems characterized by issues relating to social justice, governance and social inclusion. Such problems require explicit recognition and innovative ways of addressing them through required political reform.

4. Identify and build upon the ongoing processes of ethnic reconciliation in the country while ensuring that religious and cultural diversity fostered and preserved in the country over centuries is recognized and duly respected.

5. Efforts must be made to foster a broader Sri Lankan identity that transcends narrow ethnic loyalties as an overarching goal of nation building in post-war Sri Lanka. Among other things education, cultural and development policies of the state must strive to develop a more inclusive Sri Lankan consciousness as a corrective measure against ethnic over determination in the country.

9

Sri Lanka's Ethnic Conflict: Role of the State

Jayadeva Uyangoda

Introduction

Sri Lanka's conflict has been identified in scholarly as well as policy literature as an ethnic conflict.[1] The conflict has highlighted a variety of themes such as minority rights, majority-minority relations, devolution of political power, and state security under conditions of a protracted ethnic insurgency. During 2005 - 2009, issues of terrorism and state security dominated the policy discourse about the conflict. The period after end of war in May 2009, the question of reconciliation and minority rights has come back to the policy debate in a context where state security and minority rights are seen in Sri Lanka's official policy ideology as mutually non-inclusivist goals. The policy debate in the post-civil war era has once again been polarized along these two seemingly irreconcilable perspectives, national security vs. minority rights. Why do such irreconcilable perspectives continue to exist in Sri Lanka with regard to the politics of inter-ethnic relations? How have they defined Sri Lanka's conflict? What does it tell us about the nature, dynamics and future possibilities of Sri Lanka's conflict? This paper reflects on these questions.

The central argument offered in this paper can be summarized as follows: Sri Lanka's ethnic conflict has essentially been a contestation for state power, although issues of nation-building, state-building, claims for and denials of minority rights have been at the center of the processes that produced and re-produced the conflict. When the Sinhalese majoritarian and Tamil minoritarian nationalist projects engaged themselves in a hostile

---

[1] Some of the key writings on Sri Lanka's ethnic conflict are Wriggins (1960), Kearney (1967), Roberts (1978), Tambiah (1986), Wilson (1988 and 2000), De Silva (1998), DeVotta (2004).

and protracted struggle for domination and resistance, war and state power became main sites of contestation. When the ethnic conflict became militarized, it was the outcome of the war, and not of politics, that parties to the conflict viewed as central to determine the outcome of the conflict. Therefore, to adequately understand Sri Lanka's ethnic conflict, one must not confine one's attention to the original, or root, causes of the conflict. While understanding root causes may shed important light on the original conditions against which the conflict formed itself developed in its early phases, what has happened in the process of conflict's development are also important to understand why the conflict has protracted over long periods of time. This invites us to think about how consequences of the conflict may have also contributed to shaping the new dynamics of the conflict.

This chapter is organized as follows: Initial section of the chapter will set out the analytical focus of the chapter, arguing that Sri Lanka's ethnic conflict could be seen, and better treated, as a state formation conflict. It will also suggest a framework of periodization as a heuristic devise to map out and interpret, from a perspective of retrospection, the ways in which the ethnic conflict and the question of state power have unfolded in post-colonial Sri Lanka. Next section will elaborate how the question of state power became intertwined with ethnic politics during the first phase of conflict formation. Thereafter focus is on the ways in which contestation for state power took new turns with the consequence of ethnic conflict escalation in Sri Lanka in the 1970s. This is followed by discussion on the context in which Sri Lanka's ethnic conflict became militarized, highlighting the consequences for the argument for state reform and a political solution to the ethnic conflict. The author will take this discussion further by examining the consequences of the protracted civil war in re-shaping the dynamics of the conflict. Finally, the author examines the relationship between the types of government in Sri Lanka – parliamentary and presidential – and conflict trajectories, showing how both forms of governance have contributed to making the conflict resolution process difficult and complex.

Ethnic Conflict as State Formation Conflict

One useful way to understand why Sri Lanka's ethnic conflict became a violent, protracted and relatively intractable civil war, ending in a one-sided military victory to the state, is to view it as a complex 'state formation conflict'.[2] Reluctance to acknowledge the state formation dimension in intra-state ethno-political civil wars is one of the lacunae in the scholarly literature on the subject. The literature is generally preoccupied with such issues as (i) the causes that produce the conflict, framed in terms of identity needs vs. economic determinants, (ii) the role of negotiation, mediation and reconciliation in peace-building, and (iii) the adequacy and inadequacy of peace agreements to manage the conflict in its post-peace deal processes, and (iv) factors that lead to the breakdown of peace agreements and the relapse to war and violence. Wallensteen's[3] characterisation of intra-state ethnic conflicts as 'state-formation conflicts' is one of those rare occasions to acknowledge the centrality of disputes and contestations on the construction, or the reconstruction, of the state in defining the specificity of ethno-political civil war. Extrapolating on Wallensteen's theorising of state formation conflict, the claim can be made that the dimensions of Sri Lanka's ethnic conflict as surfaced in the course of, and after, the civil war cannot be adequately understood if they are framed solely in the language of 'identity politics', 'identity needs,' 'grievance-based politics,' 'politics of minority rights' or a 'majority –minority conflict.' despite the fact that all these dimensions were present in the conflict at some level. Sri Lanka's ethnic conflict is about all those dimensions plus something more fundamental than all of them; it is about the non-negotiable contestation for state power. In parallel, the military dimension of the conflict has effectively displaced the politics of minority grievances and rights. Thus, the war, from the point of view of the Sri Lankan state and the LTTE, became a process autonomous of the original political causes of the conflict.[4] During the civil war, Sri Lanka's ethnic conflict became relatively independent of its original causes – minority grievances – despite the fact that those grievances continued to define the basic character of the conflict. Rather, the conflict came to be propelled

---

[2] Jayadeva Uyangoda, *Ethnic Conflict in Sri Lanka: Changing Dynamics*, (Washington D.C.: East-West Centre, 2007)

[3] P Wallensteen, *Understanding Conflict Resolution: War, Peace and the Global System*, (London: Sage, 2007)

[4] Rajasingham-Senanayake (1999) has argued in a slightly similar vein that the Sri Lankan conflict has ceased to be an 'ethnic' conflict as such. According to her, the war has created a specific culture and political economy of war, providing the conflict a possibility of existence outside the framework of ethnic grievances.

forward by the competing and adversarial imperatives of state formation in the Sinhalese and Tamil ethnic projects.

Trajectories of Sri Lanka's ethnic conflict during the twentieth century can be roughly periodized into three phases, namely, (i) conflict formation, (ii) conflict escalation, and (iii) conflict intensification. The phase of conflict formation covers the immediate pre-independence decades and the two decades after independence. This is the period in which Sinhalese and Tamil political elites in Sri Lanka found themselves having competing political interests under both the colonial and post-colonial political orders. This was also the phase in which Sinhalese and Tamil nationalisms as ideological and political projects began to take initial shape. During the second phase, starting in early 1970s, these political elites found their political interests and projects not only competing with each other, but also irreconcilable and beyond the realm of compromise within the framework of even constitutional reform. Parliamentary competition, debate and coalition experiments for accommodation thus gave way to open hostility during this second phase of the conflict formation. During the second phase, Sinhalese and Tamil nationalist projects also entered a state of maturity in the sense of adversity, enmity and dialectically in need of each other for the sustenance of one another. In the third phase of its intensification, Sri Lanka's ethnic conflict developed itself into a civil war between the state and Tamil insurgents who sought secession through armed struggle as the means to achieving political goals of Tamil nationalism.

How does one treat the question of 'governance' in relation to these three phases of conflict formation, escalation and intensification in Sri Lanka? We will examine this question in the next three sections of the Chapter.

Question of the State during Formative Years of the Conflict

The competition among ethnic elites for representation in the colonial legislation under conditions of electoral and representative democracy was the main aspect of the earliest phase of the formation of ethnic conflict in Sri Lanka. This inter-elite competition began to shape itself in the 1920s on the question of sharing of political power in the colonial legislature through representation. After the Donoughmore Constitutional Reforms of 1931, which brought to Sri Lanka universal adult franchise and a prototype of

Cabinet government through the Executive Committee system in the Legislative Council, this competition took a sharper turn, contributing to the consolidation of ethnic politics in terms of Sinhalese, Tamil and Muslim identities. Thus, the operation of electoral democracy and representative government in the pre-independence years facilitated the shaping of ethnic identity politics as the organizing framework of political competition and state power for the post-independence, post-colonial contexts as well. When Sri Lanka received political independence from the British in 1948, the transition was peaceful whereas in India and Pakistan, in the context of ethnic identity-based partition of British India, the setting-up of post-colonial states was defined by extreme violence among Hindu and Muslim communities. Whereas in the sub-continental South Asia, the emergence of the post-colonial nation-state was marked by mass scale ethnic violence, Sri Lanka's experience was totally devoid of ethnic violence. However, beneath the peaceful, legal and painless establishment of the foundations for a post-colonial nation-state in Sri Lanka were serious differences on questions such as the nature of the new state, who its citizens should be and who should constitute the nation, how should political power be distributed. These differences came to the open when the Sinhalese political elite used the newly gained state power to exclude from Sri Lanka's citizenship large numbers of Indian immigrant workers employed in the tea plantations and later to deprive then their franchise rights as well.[5]

At the time of independence, there were three broad perspectives on these questions, one informed by class analysis, the other derived from liberal democratic constitutionalism and the third defined by ethnic identity politics. The class analysis, associated with the Left parties, offered a non-ethnic vision for organizing the post-colonial political order, which emphasized equality and class-centric, not ethnicity-centric, egalitarianism as the guiding principles of public policy. The liberal-democratic constitutionalism was essentially enshrined in the Constitution of Sri Lanka, which was drafted by a team of British liberal lawyers and officials. Sri Lanka's political elite shared liberal constitutionalism to some extent, but their abiding political

---

[5] Wriggins (1960) and Kearney (1967) provide detailed accounts of these inter-ethnic elite differences and their political consequences during the immediately post-independence years.

worldview was shaped by the third perspective – ethnic identity politics. Both Sinhalese and Tamil political elites had their own ethnic ideologies and political visions. Their approaches to issues of nation, state, citizenship, and public policy were shaped by an emerging, ethnic zero-sum logic which privileged sectional interests.

This was also the period in which specifically ethnic majoritarian and ethnic minoritarian approaches to democracy and governance, mediated by ethnic ideologies, began to take a concrete shape. Consequences of this inter-phase between ethnic nationalisms and political democracy are quite crucial to understanding how a specific mode of governance emerged in the immediate post-independence years in Sri Lanka. Borrowing a concept from Lijphart, we may call this mode of democratic governance 'majoritarian democracy' in which representatives of the majority ethnic community had a near monopoly in controlling the state, government and public policy through their majority-control of parliament. DeVotta calls it 'control democracy' - a democracy in which the ethnic majority solely controls the levers of power. The Westminster system of parliamentary democracy, on which the Soulbury Constitution was essentially modelled, historically better suited to ethnically homogenous societies in which competition for state power had greater orientation towards social class than ethno-nationalist interests. What it meant was that in Sri Lanka in which social class and ethnic identity had become parallel sources of competition for political power, parliamentary democracy and cabinet government could have worked better in an altered model of the unitary state. As an emerging nation-state in the post-War II post-colonial world, Sri Lanka could have followed the Indian example of federalization in recognition of the ethnically, linguistically and culturally pluralistic nature of society. Quite interestingly, the demand for the recognition of that pluralism emerged from the Tamil ethnic minority when, in the early 1950s, a major faction of Tamil political elite formulated a demand for federalist reconstitution of the Sri Lankan state. However, the very fact that the federalization argument was put forward by an ethnic minority party and it was the key goal of a minority political project, it became politically unacceptable to the elites of the majority Sinhalese community. In fact, while the federalist demand became the centre of the political programme of the Tamil nationalists, resistance to federalism and protection of the unitary state was the main mobilizing agenda of the Sinhalese nationalists. Thus, the post-colonial nationalisms of the Sinhalese and Tamils evolved since the early 1950s primarily on two competing perspectives on the character which the post-colonial Sri Lankan state should take, unitarist or federalist. Two attempts at finding a compromise between these two competing visions of the state – unitarist and federalist - made in 1958 and 1966 by government and Tamil leaders failed in the face of Sinhalese nationalist mobilization. The attempt of 1958 was made by Prime Minister S.W.R.D Bandaranaike and the Federal Party Leader S.J.V Chelvanayakam and the second was by Prime Minister Dudley Senanayake and Chelvanayakam, the Federal Party Leader. Both attempts had led to agreements - or as 'pacts' as they are known in the Sri Lankan political lexicon – between a Prime Ministers who had given leadership to the Sinhalese nationalist project of the unitary state and a Tamil leader who gave leadership to the federalist project, promising the Tamils a limited measure of regional autonomy in the form of 'regional councils.' They were significant state reform measures that had the potential to broaden the ethnic foundations of the Sri Lankan state and make the mode of distribution of state power more democratic to suit a multi-ethnic society.

Question of the State during Conflict Escalation in the 1970s

The decade of 1970s can be retrospectively seen as the period of escalation of Sri Lanka's ethnic conflict. This was also the decade during which struggles over the state and state power defined the entire political trajectory of the country. The first such struggle was the armed uprising occurred in April 1971 in the Sinhalese society of Sri Lanka. It was a serious challenge to the state power held by the dominant Sinhalese elites and the first attempt in post-colonial Sri Lanka to wrest control of state power by subordinate social classes by means of an armed insurgency. Though the insurgency failed, it highlighted, in a rather dramatic fashion, how the question of who controls the state power in Sri Lanka and the social resistance to the elite's hold of the state had remained a major issue of concern among subordinate social classes in Sri Lanka's Sinhalese society in an astonishingly subterranean fashion. Although the United Front (UF) coalition of the Sri Lanka Freedom Party, Lanka Sama Samaja Party and the Communist Party managed to putdown the JVP's armed insurrection to capture state power, the question of state power had already appeared in Sri Lanka's political struggles in a different form and with qualitatively harsher consequences. This particular development was linked to the UF government's project of altering the constitutional foundations of the Sri Lankan state, within a republican framework.

One major criticism that had emerged against the Soulbury Constitution of 1947, which had provided the juridical and institutional framework for Sri Lanka's post-colonial state, was that it did not affect a total break from the colonial rule and therefore it marked only a partial and incomplete political independence. Both the Sinhalese nationalists and Sri Lankan Left parties alike shared this critique. The United Front Regime of 1970 in fact was an ideological and programmatic coalition of both Sinhalese nationalists and the Left parties who were committed to 'completing' Sri Lanka's political independence from the British and transforming the Sri Lankan state to be the institutional embodiment of that 'complete independence' (*purna swadhinathvaya*, in Sinhalese). Quite importantly, this discourse of 'complete independence' was essentially a part of Sinhalese nationalist political project, supported by the Left parties, and not an inclusive one which could have accommodated even to a limited degree the Tamil nationalist goals of 'independence' as well. In fact, by the early 1970s, there had developed two discourses of post-colonial independence in Sri Lanka along ethno-nationalist lines. The Sinhalese nationalist discourse of post-colonial independence, which had already informed the public policy regimes of Sri Lankan governments since 1948, envisaged further entrenchment of the unitary and centralized state, inherited from the British colonial rule, as the ultimate embodiment of the political will of the majority Sinhalese-Buddhist community. In contrast, the Tamil nationalist discourse of post-colonial independence sought regional autonomy to the Tamil minority within an altered, federalist framework of the state. When the UF regime started its constitutional reform initiative immediately after the electoral victory in July 1970, it only provided a new political space for these discursive divisions to crystallize further and eventually transform themselves into antagonistic projects. The high point of the antagonistic engagement between these two projects of post-colonial independence was the Republican Constitution of 1972 which gave concrete expression to the Sinhalese nationalist vision of a centralized, unitary state. In fact, the makers of the 1972 Constitution, who were ardently committed to the doctrine of 'autochthonous constitutionalism,' totally rejected the Federal Party's plea to consider a federal constitution on the premise that a federalist reform would be harmful to the unity of the nation and the state.[6]

The First Republican Constitution of 1972 in fact marked a turning point – highly problematic though, as the subsequent events were to prove - in the process of post-colonial state formation in Sri Lanka. It gave juridical and institutional recognition to a number of key elements of the dominant Sinhalese nationalist – Left political ideology concerning the post-colonial Sri Lankan state. The Constitution was conceived within the ideological framework of constitutional monism, which both Sinhalese nationalists and socialists shared with equal vigour, and established a unitary and highly centralized state. The constitution also gave expression to what one may call the ideology of 'populist constitutionalism.' The idea of the 'Republic' had its roots in this populist doctrine constitutionalism shared by Sinhalese nationalists as well as the Left. Their concept of the 'Republic' had two basic doctrinal elements, as reflected in the 1972 constitution. The first was the notion that people's sovereignty should be exercised by a 'sovereign legislature' which should be unicameral in its composition and whose legislative power should not be subjected to any institutional or procedural checks and balances, except the will of the leaders in the ruling party or the coalition. The second was the use of the state as an instrument to achieve an ideological goal as set out by the framers of the Constitution. That goal in 1972 happened to be what was understood at that time as socialism, which was to be achieved through the parliamentary path. This we may refer to as the instrumentalist approach to constitution-making. The Republican model in any case does treat the constitution from an instrumentalist perspective; yet it usually derives its sanctity from a commitment to a set of normative goals such as liberty, equality, justice and pluralism. In contrast, Sri Lanka's Republican Constitution of 1972 was devoid of the republican spirit in a number of vital areas. The Republic was not to be a pluralistic polity. Its

---

[6] Literature that covers the constitutional debates and positions among Tamil and Sinhalese political elites in the early 1970s include Uyangoda (2001), Wilson (1988), Coomaraswamy (1996).

citizens were not to enjoy justiciable fundamental rights. Nor were they expected to be 'active citizens' as envisaged in all republican models of the state. Citizens could be politically active primarily within the constituent parties of the ruling coalition or the 'popular' organizations linked to the ruling coalition. In a dialectical sense, consolidation of this particular type of the state also completed another process, the power struggle between Sinhalese and Tamil political elites. The Sinhalese political elites found satisfaction in their 'victory' of excluding the Tamil political elites from the realm of state power while Tamil political elites saw in it the culmination of a political process of their exclusion from political power. Thus, in a few years after the enactment of the Republican Constitution of 1972, the stage was set for the escalation of the ethnic conflict. The conflict did escalate in the latter part of the 1970s when the Tamil leaders opted for a secessionist goal, abandoning the strategy of campaigning for regional autonomy. The formation of the Tamil Liberation Front in 1976 and its decision to launch a campaign for secession set in motion a new process of direct confrontation between the state and the Tamil minority, which within two to three years led to the beginning of an armed struggle for separation. Once secession began to define the nature and dynamics of the ethnic conflict, state reforms for the constructive management of the conflict became both irrelevant and implausible. We will discuss this theme in the next section of the paper.

The implausibility of substantial political reforms in Sri Lanka even to arrest the impending threat of secessionist civil war became starkly clear in 1981 when the government of President J.R Jayewardene proposed and then implemented a new administrative scheme called District Development Councils (DDCs). This scheme was based on a set of proposals made by a Committee appointed by the government in 1979 to make recommendations regarding a scheme of devolution and decentralization. However, the legislation passed by parliament to establish DDCs envisaged only an extremely limited measure of administrative decentralization, which did not go beyond the existing local government system. In fact, powers, duties and functions of the DDCs were to approximate those of the Town Councils and Village Councils. Even then, the DDCs were to be politically controlled by the ruling party through its MPs and Ministers in districts within which the Councils are formed. While the DDCs were "not involved in any of the important Central Government affairs at the district level," they had "too much influence from the centre".[7] The important point highlighted in the failed DDC scheme was the extreme reluctance of the government, and the Sinhalese political elites, to view Tamil political demands as warranting a political solution within a framework of sharing political power beyond minimalist administrative decentralization.

Conflict Intensification, Civil War and the Impossibility of State Reform

After the anti-Tamil riots occurred in Sri Lanka in July-August1983, the ethnic conflict entered a qualitatively new phase in which the armed rebellion launched by Tamil militant groups for secession dominated the dynamics of the conflict. Militant groups committed to secession by means of armed struggle replaced the traditional Tamil political actors who had earlier radicalized the Tamil nationalist political project through their campaign of mass mobilization for 'independence.' The Sri Lankan government responded to the new development militarily. Thus began the period of total militarization of Sri Lanka's ethnic conflict, which in fact foreclosed any possibilities for non-military solutions to the conflict, although there were many efforts made to resolve the conflict politically and through negotiation. [8]

It is necessary to note that during the protracted civil war that began in the early 1980s, the option for a negotiated political solution had not been totally abandoned by either the Sri Lankan government or the Tamil nationalist rebels, at least for strategic, partisan and purely opportunistic reasons. The Thimpu Talks of 1984, the Indo-Lanka Accord of 1987, peace talks in 1989, 1994, and 2002 were key events that marked the periods of pause in the trajectory of civil war. However, none of these attempts at a negotiated solution to the conflict could produce a compromise to provide the basis for a sustainable peace agreement leading to the termination of civil war and solving the conflict. In this section, we will briefly outline how the question

---

[7] Shirani Bandaranayake, "The Development Councils Act of 1980: The Decentralization of Administration and Devolution of Authority," The Colombo Law Review, Volume 6, 102-119, 1987.

[8] There is a significant body of literature on negotiation attempts in Sri Lanka during the civil war for a political settlement to the ethnic conflict. Notable among them are Dixit (1998), Loganathan (1996), Muni (1993), Rupesinghe (2006)

of state power has been present in these events of negotiation and also how it made the goal of a political solution to the conflict unachievable.

The Thimpu Talks of 1984 were the first attempt at a negotiated settlement to the conflict made after the conflict entered the phase of civil war. The Indian government facilitated these talks. The key issues emerged in the Thimpu negotiations were about the political framework within which the Sri Lankan government and the Tamil nationalist groups could agree on a solution to the conflict. The government's approach was defined by its commitment to preserve the unitary nature of the Sri Lankan state by resisting the Tamil nationalist argument for what was termed as 'national self-determination of the Tamil-speaking peoples.' The approach of the Tamil groups was to force the Sri Lankan government to accept the key premises of their militant nationalist project, which included the recognition of Sri Lankan Tamils as "a distinct nationality", the notion of "Tamil homeland" and the "right of self-determination of the Tamil nation".[9] These were by any logic of conflict settlement not negotiable positions. They were indeed maximalist political positions that only foreclosed any room for further negotiations. In contrast, the Sri Lankan government adopted a minimalist position of reiterating a framework of slightly improved District Development Councils. This was not an exciting attractive negotiation position either. Thus, the Thimpu talks could not plead to a breakthrough for compromise.

Although the Thimpu talks failed to produce a negotiated outcome, the subsequent developments demonstrated that the Indian government, which has been promoting the idea of a negotiated political settlement, had understood the centrality of state reform in any solution that could address Tamil grievances and demands. India's backdoor diplomacy with regard to Sri Lanka's conflict in this period seemed to have been shaped by the goal of persuading the Sri Lankan government and Tamil nationalists to accept a political compromise of a middle ground concerning the state.[10] The Indian conception of 'devolution' promoted in the early and mid 1980s envisaged a decisive shift from the maximalist as well as minimalist positions of the two

---

[9] Ketheshwaran Loganathan, Sri Lanka, Lost Opportunities: Past Attempts at Resolving Ethnic Conflict, (Colombo: University of Colombo, 1996), pp 104-105.

[10] For details of the Indian diplomatic engagement during this period, see Loganathan (1966), Dixit (1998), de Silva, (1998), Muni (1993)

sides to the Sri Lankan conflict. The system of Provincial Councils, established soon after the Indo-Lanka Accord of July 1987, encapsulated this middle ground concerning the state, as proposed by the Indian mediators. That middle ground called upon the Sri Lankan government to move away from its rigid adherence to the unitary state model and accept ethnicity-based power-sharing with the Tamil minority and regional autonomy as the principles to guide the reconstitution of the state. It also called upon the Tamil nationalists to abandon their goal of creating a separate ethnic state in Sri Lanka's Northern and Eastern provinces and accept a modified Sri Lankan state in which the Tamil ethnic minority could enjoy a certain measure of self-determination rights within a framework of regional autonomy. Devolution was the conceptual label attached to this middle ground. Provincial Councils were to be its institutional form. In fact, the Indo-Lanka Accord of July 1987, initiated by the Indian government, inaugurated a significant re-structuring of the post-colonial Sri Lankan state within a framework of quasi-federalism.[11] The 13th Amendment to Sri Lanka's 1978 Constitution legalized this new structural re-constitution of the Sri Lankan state.

The politics surrounding devolution in Sri Lanka shows in how the relationship between contesting perspectives on state power and the ethnic conflict has been intertwined in a fairly complex way. Five key points in this regard warrant mentioned here. Firstly, it was Indian government's coercive diplomacy that persuaded a section of Sri Lanka's United National Party (UNP) government that Sri Lanka's ethnic conflict required a political solution and that political solution called for altering Sri Lanka's unitary state in the direction of at least quasi-federalism. Sri Lanka's Sinhalese political elite would never have reached this position on its own, even if the conflict posed an immediate threat of disintegrating Sri Lanka's state. Secondly, not all Tamil nationalist groups accepted devolution as a credible alternative to the goal of secession. The LTTE, which soon emerged as the dominant Tamil rebel group, initially accepted the terms of the Indo-Lanka Accord only

---

[11] Shirani A Bandaranayake, "Devolution of Power and the Indo-Lanka Agreement of July 1987," pp 175-196, and Uyangoda, Jayadeva, 1989, "The Indo-Lanka Agreement of July 1987 and the State in Sri Lanka," in Shelton U. Kodikara (ed.), Indo-Sri Lanka Agreement of July 1987, Colombo, The International Relations Programme: University of Colombo, 71-88.

reluctantly, and even that only to re-launch its armed struggle for separation, within just three months of the Accord. Thirdly, the Accord, the 13th Amendment and the Provincial Councils were radically rejected by a sizeable section the Sinhalese political forces, including the main parliamentary opposition party, the Sri Lanka Freedom Party (SLFP). The Accord even created serious divisions within the ruling UNP. These developments indicated that political reform initiative of 1987 led to new ruptures within the Sri Lankan polity, ruptures that caused a severe political crisis. That crisis is the fourth point in the complexity surrounding the conflict resolution attempt made in 1987 by the Indian and Sri Lankan governments. The Sinhalese nationalist resistance to the Accord, the idea of a political solution to the conflict and the proposal to establish provincial councils immediately led to an anti-state rebellion in the Sinhalese society. The rebellion was organized and led by the JVP, which in 1971 launched its first anti-state insurgency. The new rebellion was supported by large sections of Sinhalese society in a context where Sinhalese nationalist politics took a radically new form, locating itself outside the mainstream political parties and appealing directly to the Sinhalese masses to rise up and capture state power. The rebellion lasted two years, and in 1988 and 1989, the crisis caused by the JVP's Sinhalese nationalist rebellion pushed the Sri Lankan state into a severe crisis. The UNP government could rescue the Sri Lankan state from that crisis only by entering into a tactical alliance with the LTTE, forcing the Indian peace keeping army out of the country by means of hostile diplomacy, and crushing the JVP rebellion by extreme military means. Fifthly, the Indian government which initiated the Accord, conceptualized and proposed the solution to the conflict, brokered the peace deal with the Sri Lankan government and the Tamil groups, volunteered to be the guarantor of the peace deal and acted as the enforcer of the terms of the peace agreement, became within two to three months of the Accord a party to the conflict and the war against the LTTE.

Despite this unusual complexity surrounding the state reform initiative of 1987, the idea of devolution and the system of provincial councils continue to be the centre of gravity in any subsequent thinking with regard to a political solution to Sri Lanka's ethnic conflict. For example, the argument for reviving the peace process emerged in the mid-1990s on the initiative of the People's Alliance (PA) government was based on the premise that the framework of the solution should be based on the exiting provincial councils, yet with enhanced autonomy and self-rule guaranteed to the Councils through constitutional reform. This argument also constituted the core of the notion 'thirteenth amendment plus' emerged in the mid-1990s and commanded support among a wide spectrum of Sinhalese, Tamil and Muslim political parties. Even then, the argument for a political solution through enhanced devolution/more state reform could not produce concrete political results, because of the fact that the PA government, which advanced this project of peace through greater political reforms, could not produce a broad political consensus required for such a substantial state reform agenda. A comparison of the of the PA government's failed initiative for greater devolution in the mid and late-1990s with the introduction of devolution by the UNP government in 1987-88 will provide some interesting insights into politics of ethnic conflict and state reform in Sri Lanka. In 1987, the UNP government of President J. R. Jayewardene was a reluctant agent for peace through political reforms. A powerful external actor – the Indian government – had used its political, military and diplomatic coercion to convince the Sri Lankan president the need to move in a reform direction. The Sri Lankan President signed the peace Accord with India having no democratic consultations within the ruling party, within the cabinet, let alone with other political parties. In short, it was a political reform measure initiated by an external actor and introduced from above. That indeed caused conditions for massive Sinhalese nationalist resistance to the reform measure itself. In contrast, the reform steps taken by the PA government in the mid-1990s were meant to be refined after a widest possible popular participation, public debates and consultations. The reforms were to be enacted through a democratic process of consensus building among political forces across the ethnic divide. However, the PA government failed to produce consensus among Sinhalese political parties, while failing to convince the Sinhalese nationalist forces that were committed to a military solution, of the efficacy of proposed reforms to resolve the conflict. The issue with the UNP, which had in fact initiated the devolution process in the late 1980s, was of a different dimension. For purely partisan and opportunistic reasons, the UNP did not extend its support to the PA government to secure a two-thirds majority in parliament in order to pass constitutional amendments necessary to institutionalize greater devolution and more self-rule authority to provincial councils.

The War and Its Consequences on the Conflict Resolution Process

The fact that Sri Lanka's civil war ended in may 2009 in total military defeat to the LTTE and unilateral military victory to the Sri Lankan state raises some key questions about why the parties to the conflict failed to find a joint, bi-lateral and political solution of compromise through its protracted period of two-and – half decades and despite five attempts at a negotiated settlement. The questions are of the following kind: Are negotiated compromises possible in militarized ethnic conflicts in which contestation is between an ethnic minority and the state controlled by the ethnic majority? When the question of state power is at the core of the conflict, defining its origins, spread, dynamics and trajectories, what actual possibilities are there for such a conflict to be terminated through a negotiated compromise? What is it that made the negotiated settlement to the question of state power impossible in Sri Lanka? Answers to these questions are not easy to formulate without revisiting the complex ways in which the conflict was not only originated at the outset, but also how the conflict was constantly re-produced by the processes of the conflict themselves. This observation leads the analysis to the 'conflict reproduction thesis.' In the following section, an attempt is made to outline the thesis of conflict re-production by highlighting some of the dynamics that made Sri Lanka's ethnic conflict protracted, intractable and beyond the pale of a negotiated political settlement.

There is a general tendency among scholars, journalists and even policy makers to explain social conflicts by referring to the original causes that led to the emergence of the conflict and then argue that if the root causes remain unaddressed, the resolution of the conflict would simply be impossible. Analysts of the Sri Lankan conflict have also used this 'root – causes thesis' for some good and valid reasons, and obviously the thesis enables us to historicize the origins and spread of the conflict. However, one can still argue that the root causes thesis may not tell us the entire story of a conflict, with its complexities, particularly when the conflict is or has been a protracted one. Here, the concept of 'conflict protraction' needs to be understood not merely in its temporal sense, in the sense that the conflict has spread over a fairly long period of time, say, for example, for two to three decades and even over. If we take a conflict to be a process of social and political life, such a conflict should also be understood by us as a dynamic process with specific conditions, moments, impetus and logic for its re-production as well. A conflict process is essentially a process of conflict re-production. At every stage of its re-production, a conflict may take a new life process as well.

The conflict reproduction thesis, as briefly outlined above, can be illustrated by looking at war and negotiations as intertwined aspects of the protracted conflict. In other words, negotiations during the war need to be seen not only as efforts to terminate the conflict, but also events that re-constituted the conflict structure and propelled the civil war forward. If we take the example of the Thimpu Talks of 1984, which we have already described in brief, the Indian-mediated negotiations between the Sri Lankan government and the Tamil groups enabled the two sides not to explore a mutually acceptable solution, but to explore how such a solution was even beyond their imagination. The Thimpu Talks can thus be seen as an initial key moment of the conflict that convinced the two sides, and even provided rationalization for, the necessity and inevitability of war as the dominant, if not sole, mode of working towards unilateral conflict outcomes.

The Indo-Lanka Accord of 1987 provided a different impetus for the continuation of war when it in a dialectical way did not bring the war to an end, but re-defined and re-intensified the conflict.[12] In fact, the Indo-Lanka Accord of 1987 can be seen as a major illustration of the hypothesis that peace agreements may not only bring a conflict to an end, but also re-define, re-invent and therefore re-produce the conflict leading to its protraction and making its intractability sharper. The Indo-Lanka Accord brought an external actor, the Indian government, to Sri Lanka's conflict not only as a mediator and peace broker and enforcer, but also a direct party to the war. The Indian involvement and intervention, while facilitating a policy shift in Sri Lanka towards political reforms, also sharpened the country's already intensified political contradictions and crisis which soon opened up political space for another anti-state rebellion. It in fact widened the scope of the Sri Lankan conflict, bringing the ethnic Tamil rebellion and radical

---

[12] There is a wide body of literature on India's engagement with Sri Lanka's ethnic conflict. Some notable examples are Kodikara (1989), Muni (1993), Loganathan (1996), Ganguly, (1998), Jayatilleke (1995), Krishna (1999).

Sinhalese rebellion together to oppose the state. One of its long-term outcomes is the erosion of legitimacy of India in particular and external actors in general as mediators in Sri Lanka's conflict. In brief, the Indian engagement in Sri Lanka in the 1980s, instead of mitigating the conflict, gave it a new fillip as well as a good reason for both Sinhalese and Tamil nationalists to continue with the conflict, resisting the devolution framework of settlement initiated by India.

The peace attempt of the United National Front (UNF) government in 2002 constitutes another link in the chain of conflict re-production in Sri Lanka in a context of negotiation failure under specific set of circumstances.[13] Unlike the previous peace attempts through negotiation, the 2002 peace initiative had conditions that showed greater capacity to produce an outcome leading to conflict termination. A new government elected on a platform of peace, launched the peace initiative with strong international backing. The LTTE too appeared to be keen on a negotiated settlement. The two sides signed a fairly comprehensive cease-fire agreement (CFA) in February 2002, which was facilitated by the Norwegian government. An international monitoring team called the Sri Lanka Monitoring Mission (SLMM) assisted the Sri Lankan government and the LTTE to implement the terms of the CFA. Direct peace negotiations between the two sides began in September 2002, under the auspices of the Norwegian government which represented the international community in its support for a negotiated peace in Sri Lanka. At the conclusion of the talks held in Oslo in February 2002, the two sides went so far as to agree on exploring a federal solution to the conflict. The LTTE's declared willingness to explore a federal solution was seen at the time as the most promising breakthrough ever occurred in the long and unpredictable history of peace negotiations in Sri Lanka. However, in March-April 2003, the LTTE suspended its participation in the negotiations making set of demands from the Sri Lankan government. The key demand which the LTTE made was for the government to propose a framework for an interim administration in the island's Northern and Eastern provinces, and those proposals to constitute the agenda of revived peace negotiations. When

---

[13] For extensive discussions on the progress as well as breakdown of the 2002 peace process, Uyangoda (2007), Uyangoda and Perera (2004), Goodhand and Clem (2005), Liyanage (2008), Stokke and Uyangoda (2011).

the UNF government presented two sets of proposal for an interim administration in June and July 2003, the LTTE rejected them as inadequate to be considered for its return to negotiations. Subsequently, in October 2003 the LTTE presented to the government its own proposals for an interim administrative authority. Called proposals for an Interim Self-Governing Authority (ISGA), the LTTE proposals sought an advanced form of federal administration to the Northern and Eastern provinces, and the proposals went beyond the limits of Sri Lanka's existing constitution. The extremely negative reactions to the LTTE's new proposals, despite the fact that this was the first time that the LTTE formulated in writing its own proposals for a political solution, indicated the ferocity with which the question of state power re-emerged in Sri Lanka's political debate on possible solutions to the ethnic conflict. The description of ISGA proposals by the SLFP as a 'blue print for separation' encapsulated the general reaction to them emerged at the time. LTTE's interim proposals envisaged a framework of sharing state power in a confederal framework, whereas the in the political debate in Sinhalese society, there was no consensus even on devolution, which was a minimalist form of power sharing. While the LTTE's vision for a political solution was to a large extent shaped by the logic of finding 'a credible alternative to a separate state,' the Sri Lankan government, which claimed to acknowledge the relevance of a federal solution, could envisage the political settlement essentially within a minimalist federal framework. Thus, at the core of the debate in 2003 was the question of the nature of Sri Lanka's post-civil war state. Two contending and irreconcilable perspectives on the nature of the post-civil war state clashed with each other, pushing the entire peace process into crisis. The way in which this crisis unfolded was quite symbolic of how political forces hostile to state reform option had returned to the centre stage of Sri Lankan politics during the 2002-2003 peace process. Soon after the LTTE submitted to the UNF government its ISGA proposals, President Chandrika Kumaratunga, who by this time had been backed by extreme Sinhalese nationalist groups, sacked the defence and foreign ministers of the UNF government and eventually sacked the entire government. President Kumaratunga's action was precipitated by political opportunism as well as the commitment to defending an unreformed Sri Lankan state.

The failure of the 2002-2003 peace attempts led to two consequences that were to shape the subsequent development of Sri Lanka's ethnic conflict on a path of its re-militarization which left no room whatsoever for a negotiated political settlement or political reforms. The first was the re-configuration of political forces, bringing the military solution perspective to the centre of political debate and irretrievably weakening the perspective for a political settlement. President Chandrika Kumaratunga's United People's Freedom Alliance (UPFA), which was formed in late 2003, provided the organizational and ideological unity to the newly emerged hard-line Sinhalese nationalist coalition. The UPFA's victory at the parliamentary elections held in April 2004 also saw the political defeat of the argument for peace through negotiations with the LTTE and political reforms. The new ideological position assiduously popularized by the UPFA government of 2004 and its hard-line Sinhalese nationalist coalition partners insisted that (a) only a military solution was possible to the ethnic conflict and that solution required a new phase of intense war against the LTTE, and (b) a political solution to the ethnic conflict would be possible only after a military outcome to the conflict, re-ensuring the capacity of the Sri Lankan state to define terms and scope of the political settlement. The second consequence was the LTTE's apparent decision to resume the war as a strategic option under conditions where the 2002-2003 peace process did not produce outcomes favourable to the LTTE's own goal of self-rule in the Northern and Eastern provinces. These two consequences produced from both sides to the conflict a strong argument with popular appeal to return to war as a new phase of the conflict. It appeared that both the LTTE and the UPFA government were keen to re-configure the balance of power between the two sides through a new and unilateral outcome in the battlefield. The slow build up to all out war that began in mid-2004 went on throughout the year until the Tsunami of December 26, 2004 compelled both sides to halt their offensive preparations.

Democracy, Governance and the Re-production of Ethnic Conflict

While the contestation for state power defined the core of Sri Lanka's ethnic conflict, its trajectories were affected by the country's forms of governance. The relationship between Sri Lanka's ethnic conflict and the forms of government can be discussed under two sub-themes, namely, (a) conflict trajectories under the parliamentary system of government and (b) conflict trajectories under the Presidential form of government.

The emergence of Sri Lanka's ethnic conflict within just a few years after a Westminster-styled parliamentary government was installed in 1947 and its spread under the same system of democratic government constitutes an excellent counter-point to any attempt at romanticising parliamentary democratic governance. The way in which a substantive question regarding a possible relationship between democracy and conflict should be raised is to formulate the question in the following manner: What kind of democracy has given rise to an ethnic conflict? What kind of democracy has failed to manage the ethnic conflict within the parameters of democracy, rule of law and human rights? The answer to both questions in relation to Sri Lanka, as already mentioned at the beginning of this chapter, is 'ethnic majoritarian democracy' which was paralleled with a process of 'communalizing' the post-colonial Sri Lankan state as well as struggles for sharing state power. Even in instances where minority parties were included in multi-ethnic coalition governments – for example in the first post independence government of 1947 under Prime Minister D. S. Senanayake and the seven-party coalition government of 1965 headed by Prime Minister Dudley Senanayake – ethnic minority parties could not influence government policies, because of the fact that even as partners in coalition governments they were kept in the periphery of political power by the dominant Sinhalese political elites. The minority ethnic elites remained subordinate political elites throughout the post-independence period, with no structural space available for them to shape public policy or the nature of the state. The powerlessness of minority parties to influence government policy took a qualitatively new turn when the SLFP-led United Front coalition, with its Sinhalese nationalist-socialist agenda, secured a two-thirds majority in parliament in July 1970. Earlier, Sinhalese parties needed the support of the Tamil parties to secure parliamentary majority. The electoral outcome of July 1970 altered this political arithmetic, rendering the role of Tamil parties in governance utterly insignificant.

When the Presidential system of government introduced by the UNP government came into operation in 1978, Sri Lanka's ethnic problem had reached a stage of maturity and the Sri Lankan state had already become unreformably communalistic. When the new Constitution introduced in 1978 under conditions of heightened ethnic conflict, the UNP government, with five-sixth majority in parliament, did nothing to change the nature of the Sri Lankan state in the direction of power sharing, even though the Tamil nationalist forces were threatening secession. What the framers of the 1978 Constitution did was to further entrench the unitary and centralized features of the Sri Lankan state. It needs to be noted that the transition from the Westminster-type parliamentary democracy to a Presidential system of government had nothing to do with Sri Lanka's ethnic conflict. This constitutional reform measure reflected the agenda of one faction of the Sinhalese political elites to secure control of state power in a framework of greater centralization of governmental powers and authority.

The relatively inflexible nature of the 1978 Constitution has also contributed to the rigidity of the unitarist state structure in Sri Lanka. One stumbling block which the PA government faced from 1995 to 2001 was the unitary clause of the constitution the alteration of which required both a two-thirds majority in parliament and people's approval at a referendum. The PA government's commitment to enhanced devolution to further empower the existing provincial council system required the alteration of the unitary clause of the constitution. However, the PA government had only one-vote simple majority in parliament, which fell radically far short of the required two-thirds majority for a constitutional amendment. The two-thirds majority could have been secured had the opposition UNP backed the PA government's conflict resolution initiative. However, the UNP, due to partisan political reasons, prevented the PA government from securing the necessary votes in parliament, thereby blocking and jeopardizing the entire peace initiative of the PA government.

The politics of the Presidential system of government once again played itself out in detriment to the conflict resolution process in Sri Lanka during the 2002-2003 peace initiative of the UNF government. The UNF government, which won the parliamentary election in December 2001 on a peace platform, became a victim of a constitutional anomaly produced by the peculiarities of the 1978 Constitution. When the UNF won the parliamentary elections in December 2001, Sri Lanka's Executive President had already been elected two years ago. With the UNF controlling the parliament and the President from the PA controlling the executive presidency, the structure of government came to be defined by the presence of two rival centres of state power, the executive, headed by the President and the legislature headed by the Prime Minister, thereby creating a 'fractured' form of government (Fernando: 2008).[14] This was not only a constitutional anomaly, but also a political anomaly that saw each branch of state power weakening and undermining the other, instead of evolving a framework of cohabitation. This context eventually led to the weakening of the peace process as well, since the President and her political allies threatened any possibility of constitutionalizing a peace agreement which the UNF government and the LTTE would have entered into. It is this political uncertainty caused by this anomaly in governance that partly led the LTTE to argue that any peace settlement with the UNF government would not be more than a piece of paper.[15]

Sri Lanka's Ethnic conflict: Beyond May 2009

One general question with regard to Sri Lanka's ethnic conflict can be formulated in the following manner: Despite (a) several attempts at a negotiated political settlement made by both the government and the LTTE and (b) pressure from the international actors on both sides to terminate the conflict through compromise, why did Sri Lanka's civil war end in the battlefield and in unilateral military victory to the state? This question warrants many answers. One answer that has been suggested in this chapter can be summarized as follows: Not all struggles waged on the question of state power end in negotiated peace, because state power is a question difficult to negotiate to produce joint outcomes. The non-negotiability of the question of state power in Sri Lanka was not an outcome of the root causes of the conflict, but rather the consequences of the conflict. Failure of negotiations can thus be seen as a fundamental failure to make the contestation for state power a negotiable object. That eventually created an inescapable logic towards the war as the only path to 'resolve' Sri Lanka's ethnic conflict, to resolve it militarily, and unilaterally.

---

[14] Austin Fernando, My Belly is White: Reminiscences of a Permanent Secretary of Defence, (Colombo: Vijitha Yapa Publications, 2008)

[15] For details of the politics of this constitutional anomaly and how it negatively impacted on the 2002 peace process, see Fernando (2008).

When the civil war came to an end in May 2009 with the total military defeat of the LTTE, the question of state reform emerged once again, under fresh circumstances. International actors who backed the Sri Lankan state in its military campaign against the LTTE in 2007-2009 began to raise the issue of a 'political solution to the ethnic conflict.' Their argument for re-opening the question of political solution was based on the premise that since the military defeat of the LTTE removed the 'main obstacle' to a negotiated settlement to the ethnic conflict in Sri Lanka, the government could even unilaterally implement a political solution in cooperation with the non-LTTE Tamil parties. The Sri Lankan government had also earlier indicated that a military defeat of the LTTE would make a political solution possible. However, the government has not taken steps in that direction.

Why is the Sri Lankan government refusing to implement a political solution to the ethnic conflict after the defeat of the LTTE? This question probably has a number of answers. The answer proposed in this chapter that the outcome of the war occurred in May 2009 – the LTTE's military defeat and the Sri Lankan state's military victory – has re-defined the ethnic conflict by altering conditions which defined the balance of power between the state and the ethnic minorities. Sri Lankan government appears to think that the concepts of a political solution, negotiated settlement and regional autonomy were valid only when the LTTE, with its military capacity, posed a threat to the Sri Lankan state. Once that threat is removed, and the parameters and conditions of the conflict radically altered in favour of the state, the question of negotiations or a political solution does not arise. According to this thinking, what matters most important in the post-civil war situation are consolidation of the unitary state, strengthening of national security, and achievement of rapid economic development in the war-torn areas. The government does not seem to acknowledge the traditional conceptualization of Sri Lanka's conflict as an ethnic conflict. Rather, it is a 'terrorist problem' which required a military solution. At the same time, the government does not seem to exclude the proposition that Sri Lankan Tamils do have problems. However, according to the government's argument, these problems do not arise from either 'ethnic' or political' grievances rather, they arise from the lack of economic development and due to protracted war as well as uneven regional development. Therefore, they require economic and developmental, and not political or devolution-based, solutions.

What does this thinking of the Sri Lankan government entail for Sri Lanka's ethnic conflict? It marks a key strategic shift in the way in which the nature of the conflict is understood and the conflict is managed. According to this policy shift, Sri Lanka's ethnic conflict is now over. Any future threat to the state can be and should be handled exclusively by military means, supported by developmentalist and co-optationist strategies. The developmentalist strategy calls for rapid infrastructure development in the North and East as well economic growth. The cooptationist strategy calls for the minority political elites to join with the coalition government of the UPFA so that they will benefit from the government's development agenda and be happy with the new and limitless opportunities for patronage and clientalist politics. In brief, national integration is seen essentially as a military-security, developmentalist and co-optationist project. It has no room for political reforms in the direction of regional autonomy or enhanced devolution.

10

ETHNIC CONFLICTS: BURMA

Lian H. Sakhong*

Introduction

The Union of Burma is one of the most ethnically diverse countries in Asia, which continues to suffer one of the longest internal ethnic armed conflicts in modern times. As a post-colonial modern nation-state, the Union of Burma was founded by pre-colonial independent peoples, namely the Chin, Kachin, Shan, and other peoples from what was termed Burma Proper, who in principle had the rights to regain their national independence from Great Britain separately and found their own respective nation-states. Instead, they all opted to form a Union together by signing the Panglong Agreement on 12 February 1947, based on the principles of voluntary association, political equality, and the right of self-government in their respective homelands through the right to *internal* self-determination, which they hoped to implement through a decentralized federal structure of the Union of Burma. In order to safeguard the above principles, the "right of secession" from the Union after ten years of independence was guaranteed to every State, i.e., all ethnic nationalities who formed member states of the Union, as it was enshrined in Chapter X, Articles 201-206 of the 1947 Constitution of the Union of Burma, and adopted as one of the founding principles of the Union.

Burma, however, did not become a federal union as it was envisaged in 1947 at the Panglong Conference. Instead, it became a quasi-federal union with a strong connotation of a unitary state where a single ethnic group called the Burman/Myanmar people controlled all state powers and

---

* Lian H. Sakhong, Research Director of Euro-Burma Office, Brussels, is also the Chairman of "Chin National Council" (CNC), and the Vice-Chairman of the "Ethnic Nationalities Council - Union of Burma" (ENC). He has published several books and numerous articles on Chin history, traditions and politics in Burma and was awarded the Martin Luther King Prize in January 2007.

governing systems of a multi-ethnic plural society of the Union of Burma. Closely related to this constitutional problem, which created the root cause of ethnic inequality and political grievances, another major problem that confronted Burma from the very beginning was what social scientists called "state formation conflict" which brought the country into civil war soon after independence. The "state formation conflict" broke up because the "made-up" of the Union was not inclusive.

Since the Panglong Agreement was signed by peoples from pre-colonial independent nations, i.e., the peoples who were conquered independently by the colonial power of Great Britain, not as part of the Burman or Myanmar Kingdom; three major ethnic nationalities from Burma Proper, namely, the Arakan, Karen, and Mon peoples were not invited officially to the Panglong Conference. They were represented by General Aung San as peoples from "Burma Proper", i.e., a pre-colonial Burman or Myanmar Kingdom. The futures of these peoples, especially the Karen who had already demanded a separate state, were not properly discussed at the Panglong Conference, which eventually triggered the first shot of ethnic armed conflicts in the form of a "state formation conflict" in 1949. Unfortunately, ethnic issues in Burma remain unsolved and as a result over sixty years of civil war continues today.

In addition to this state formation conflict, which is a conflict between the government and the identity-based, territorially focused, opposition of ethnic nationalities; another dimension of internal conflict in Burma, that arose out of independence, was the misconception of "nation-building" for "state-building", or what became the confusion between "nation" and "state", which resulted in the implementation of the "nation-building" process as a process of ethnic "forced-assimilation" by successive governments of the Union of Burma. The "nation-building" process with the notion of "one ethnicity, one language, one religion" indeed reflected the core values of Burman/Myanmar "nationalism", which originated in the anti-colonialists motto of "*Amyo, Batha, Thatana*", that is to say, the *Myanmar-lumyo* or Myanmar ethnicity, *Myanmar-batha-ska* or Myanmar language, and *Myanmar-thatana* of *Buddha-bata* or Buddhism, and it has become after independence the unwritten policies of "Myanmarization" and "Buddhistization", and a perceived legitimate practices of ethnic and religious "forced-assimilation" into *"Buddha-bata Mynamar-lumyo"* (that is, to say 'to be a Myanmar is to be a Buddhist'), in multi-ethnic, multi-religious plural society of the Union of Burma.

In the process of implementing the "nation-building" with the notion of "one religion, one language, one ethnicity", the successive governments of the Union of Burma, dominated and controlled by ethnic Myanmar, have been trying to build an ethnically homogenous unitary state of *Myanmar Naing-ngan*, in which the language of *Myanmar-batha-ska* will be the only official language and Buddhism will be the state religion; as the saying goes *'Buddha-batha Myanmar Lu-myo'*. When the "nation-building", not "state-building", process was implemented by using coercive forces for assimilation; the Arakan, Chin, Kachin, Karen, Karenni, Mon, Shan, and other ethnic nationalities, whose combined homelands cover sixty per cent of the territory of the Union of Burma and composed more than forty per cent of the country's population, were left to an either-or choice: either to accept forced-assimilation or resist by any means, including armed resistance. Fortunately or unfortunately, they all opted for the second option, resulting in over sixty years of civil war.

In this paper, I will analyse the dynamics of internal conflict that caused the conditions for over sixty years of civil war in Burma. In so doing, I will first investigate the root cause of ethnic armed conflict, and argue that the constitutional crisis and the implementation of the "nation-building" process with the notion of "one religion, one language, and one ethnicity" are the root cause of internal conflict and civil war in Burma. The political crisis in Burma, therefore, is not only ideological confrontation between democratic forces and the military regime but a constitutional crisis, compounded by the government's policy of ethnic "forced-assimilation" through the "nation-building" process, which resulted in militarization of the state, on the one hand, and "insurgency as a ways of life" in ethnic areas, on the other.

Nation-Building and the Problem of Ethnic Forced Assimilation

For newly independent countries like Burma in 1948, independence was not the end of the search for sovereignty but the beginning of a twin process of "nation-building" and "state-building". In a homogenous "state" or "nation-state" where the boundaries of the state or nation-state coincided with the extension of an ethnic population or a single language group, and where the total population of the nation-state share a single ethnic culture, "nation-building" and "state-building" are blended and even seen as a single same process. In such a situation, modern nation-state assumes the existence of "national identity" with the notion of "one ethnicity, one language, and one religion".[1]

In a modern nation-state, which receives its legitimacy from the people; a state requires some degree of identification from its citizens. Thus, in order to provide the citizens a feeling of community of statehood, especially in a homogenous nation-state, it is essential to build a "national identity", which is usually created by the state out of the national characteristics, such as history, culture and language. In a multi-ethnic, multi-religious and multi-cultural plural society, a modern nation-state also requires building a "state-identity", which is usually created out of the founding ideology and uniqueness of a particular "nation-state". While "nation-building" is a process of building a community of shared values through rites and rituals, culture and language, collective memories and historical experiences; "state-building" on the other is a process of constructing political institutions, establishing common economic and legal systems, promoting economic development, and protecting the security and well-being of its citizens.[2]

Since the emergence of the Westphalia model of "nation-state", which assumes a nation-state as a homogenous country where the boundaries of the "state" and "nation" coincided, it must be noted that religion plays an important role in the "nation-building" process. The ruler, according to the "Westphalia Agreement" of 1648, was entitled to enforce religious uniformity within his realm, as it was stated: *cuius regio, ejus religio*. In modern Burma, the Westphalia model of the "nation-state" reinforces the old notion of "*Buddha-bata Myanmar-lumyo*" (to be a Myanmar is to be a Buddhist), in which religion and ethnicity are not only blended but the kings were regarded as "the defenders of faith, the promoters of Buddhism, builders of

---

[1] Lian H Sakhong, "Federalism, Constitution Making and State Building in Burma: Finding Equilibrium between Nation-building for Self-rule and State-building for Share-rule in Federalism" in David Williams and Lian H. Sakhong (ed.al), Designing Federalism in Burma (Chiang Mai: UNLD Press, 2005), p 11-27

[2] Francis Fukuyama, State-Building (London: Profile Books, 2006), p 3

pagodas, and the patrons of the sangha.[3]

As the old saying of *Buddha-bata Myanmar-lumyo* so clearly put it, Buddhism, indeed, had been inseparably intertwined with the Myanmar national identity. Historically, Buddhism had played a most important role in binding together diverse ethnic groups such as the Burman, Mon, Shan and Rakhine (Arakanese).[4] Thus, it was quite reasonable for leaders like U Nu, the first Prime Minister of the Union of Burma, to believe that Buddhism could make a significant contribution to some aspects of national assimilation through the "nation-building" process.

However, although Buddhism had been a powerful integrative force in traditional Burman/Myanmar society, a multi-ethnic, multi-religious and multi-cultural modern nation-state of the Union of Burma is a very different country from that of the pre-colonial Myanmar Kingdom. The Chin, Kachin, Shan and other ethnic nationalities in the Union of Burma became member states of the Union in order to speed up their own search for "freedom", as it was stated in the Preamble of the Panglong Agreement. Thus, for them, the basic concept of independence was "independence without assimilation", that is, what political scientists used to term "coming together", or "together in difference", or "unity in diversity", which implies that nations come together in order to form a modern nation-state in the form of a Federal Union, or *Pyi-daung Suh* in Burmese.

Pyi-daung in Burmese means a "nation" or "country", and *Suh* means "together" or "combining". A combination of the two terms: *Pyi-daung Suh* means the nations coming together to build a state or a Union with the purpose of sharing and ruling the Union together; while maintaining the right of *internal* self-determination and the autonomous status of their respective nations and homelands with the purpose of self-rule. Thus, *Pyi-daung Suh* is a combination of "shared-rule" and "self-rule"; "shared-rule" for all ethnic

---

[3] Jerrold Schector, The New Face of Buddha: The Fusion of Religion and Politics in Contemporary Buddhism (London: Victor Gollance, 1967), p. 106.

[4] Burmese political history from the Pagan Dynasty (1044–1287) to the British conquest (1824–86) was characterized by endless struggle between the Burman, Mon, Rakhine (Arakan) and Shan. However, by adopting Buddhism from each other during their long struggles for power and domination, these four ethnic groups shared common values with regard to political systems, customary law and culture, stemming from their common religion of Buddhism.

nationalities who are the member of the Union, and internal "self-rule" for their respective homelands.

Within this concept of "coming together", it is important to differentiate between "nation" and "state"; and thereby between "nation-building" and "state-building" to understand what Hannah Arendt refers to as a "secret conflict between state and nation". According to Arendt:

> [The nation] presents the 'milieu' into which man is born, a closed society to which one belongs by the right of birth; and a people becomes a nation when it arrives at a historical consciousness of itself; as such it is attached to the soil which is the product of past labour and where history has left its traces. The state on the other hand is an open society, ruling over territory where its power protects and makes law. As a legal institution, the state knows only citizens no matter of what nationality; its legal order is open to all who happen to live on its territory.[5]

The state, far from being identical with the nation, is "the supreme protector of a law which guarantees man his rights as man, his rights as citizen and his rights as a national".[6] By signing the Panglong Agreement, the Chin, Kachin, and Shan co-founded a state or a nation-state or a Union, which is an administrative and legal unit, but they still wanted to keep their own "nation", a concept which according to Weber belongs to the sphere of values: culture, language, religion, ethnicity, homeland, shared memories and history, a specific sentiment of solidarity in the face of other groups or people.

A modern "nation-state" of the Union of Burma is a multi-ethnic, multi-religious, and multi-cultural country where many different ethnic groups who practice different cultures, adhere to different religious teaching, and speak different languages are "coming together" to form a new "nation-state" of the Union of Burma. Thus, the boundaries of the "state", which is the "nation-state" of the Union of Burma, and the boundaries of the "nations",

---

[5] Hannah Arent, "The Nation", cited by Ronald Beiner, "Arendt and Nationalism", in Dana Villa (ed.), The Cambridge Companion to Hannah Arendt (Cambridge University Press: 2000), pp. 44–56

[6] Ibid

which is the "homelands" of ethnic nationalities or "ethnic national states", do not coincide and the population of the Union of Burma cannot share a single ethnic culture, or a single language, or a single religious faith.

In multi-ethnic, multi-religious and multi-cultural countries where the boundaries of "state" and "nation" are not coincided, there is always a source of friction and conflict when the government implements a nation-building process based on the notion of "one religion, one language, and one ethnicity" through using coercive force for assimilation. The nation-building, as mentioned, belongs to "subjective values": values that cannot be shared objectively but differentiate one group of people from another. Thus, the very notion of nation-building is "hostile to multiculturalism and diversity".[7] Unfortunately, this conflict is exactly what has occurred in Burma during the past sixty years.

Since independence, the successive governments of the Union of Burma implemented "nation-building", not purely as "state-building", for the entire Union of Burma. Nation-building, for U Nu, Ne Win, Saw Maung and Than Shwe, was simply based on the notion of "one ethnicity, one language and one religion"—that is to say, the ethnicity of *Myanmar-lumyo*, the language of *Myanmar-batha-ska* and the state religion of Buddhism. Thus, what they wanted to achieve through the "nation-building" process was to create a homogeneous nation of *Myanmar Naing-ngan*, by drawing its political values from the cultural and religious values of *Mynamar-lumyo, Maynmar-batha-ska* and *Myanmar-thatana* of Buddhism. While U Nu (1948-1962) opted for cultural and religious assimilation as a means of a nation-building process by promulgating Buddhism as a state religion, General Ne Win (1962-1988) imposed the national language policy of *Myanmar-batha-ska* as a means of creating a homogeneous unitary state. Supplementing U Nu's policy of state religion and Ne Win's national language policy, the current military regime is opting for *ethnicity* as a means of national integration, by imposing ethnic assimilation into *Myanmar-lumyo*. They, thus, changed the country name from Burma to *Myanmar* in 1989.

---

[7] Cheryl Saunders, "Federalism, Decentralization and Conflict Management in Multicultural Societies" in Raoul Blindenbacher and Arnold Koller (ed.al), Federalism in a Changing World: Learning from Each Other (Montreal & Kingston. London. Ithaca: NcGill-Queen's University Press, 2003), p 198

Since all these ethnic nationalities in Burma could not find any other means of solving the political crisis, they have resorted to armed-struggle. Growing conflicts and over sixty years of civil war have crystallized a sense of ethnic identity in what was before often only a linguistic or ethno-religious category and still divided by religion and ethnic origin; it is this conflict with the state in which the Arakan, Chin, Kachin, Karen, Karenni, Mon, Shan and other ethnic nationalities are involved that have given the members of each ethnic group a wider self-awareness and a sense of their common history and destiny which strengthens their aspirations for a separate ethno-national identity in Burma.

The very different forms of ethno-national identities, created by the mobilization and transformation of formally passive *ethnicity* mainly through armed-struggle, have become rooted among ethnic communities in Burma. Through civil war and armed conflict, their ethno-nationalism has become the vehicle for a new national identity that draws many members of the community into new types of politicized vernacular culture and creates a different kind of participant society, or what Martin Smith called, "insurgency as a way of life." In today's Burma, while ethnic and political grievances have fuelled conflict in every governmental era, there have been "corollary factors underpinning the twin phenomena of insurgency as a way of life and the militarization of the state in post-colonial Burma".[8] I shall come back to the militarization of the state, but we shall first analyse the constitutional crisis which was the root cause of ethnic inequality and political grievances since independence.

U Nu's Policy of State Religion, Constitutional Crisis, and Ethnic Inequality

At the Panglong Conference in 1947, the Chin, Kachin, Shan and other non-Burman nationalities were promised, as Silverstein observes, the "right to exercise political authority of administrative, judiciary, and legislative powers in their own autonomous national states and to preserve and protect their language, culture, and religion in exchange for voluntarily joining the Burman in forming a political union and giving their loyalty to a new state".[9]

---

[8] Martin Smith, State of Strife: The Dynamics of Ethnic Conflict in Burma (Washington: East-West Center, 2007), p1

[9] Josef Silverstein, ("Minority Problems in Burma Since 1962", in Lehman (ed.,), Military Rule in Burma Since 1962 (Singapore, 1981), p. 51.

Unfortunately, Aung San, who persuaded the Chin, Kachin, Shan and other non-Burman nationalities to join Independent Burma as equal partners, was assassinated by U Saw on July 19, 1947. He was succeeded by U Nu as leader of the AFPFL. When U Nu became the leader of the AFPFL, Burman politics shifted in a retro-historical direction, backward toward the Old Kingdom of Myanmar or Burman. The new backward-looking policies did nothing to accommodate non-Myanmar/Burman nationalities who had agreed to join Independent Burma only for the sake of "speeding up freedom".

As a leader of the AFPFL, the first thing U Nu did was to give an order to U Chan Htun to re-draft Aung San's version of the Union Constitution, which had already been approved by the AFPFL Convention in May 1947. U Chan Htun's version of the Union Constitution was promulgated by the Constituent Assembly of the interim government of Burma in September 1947. Thus, the fate of the country and the people, especially the fate of the non-Burman/Myanmar nationalities, changed dramatically between July and September 1947. As a consequence, Burma did not become a genuine federal union, as U Chan Htun himself admitted to historian Hugh Tinker. He told Tinker, "Our country, though in theory federal, is in practice unitary".[10]

On the policy of religion, U Nu also reversed Aung San's policy after the latter was assassinated. Although Aung San, the hero of independence and the founder of the Union of Burma, had opted for a "secular state" with a strong emphasis on "pluralism" and the "policy of unity in diversity" in which all different religious and racial groups in the Union could live together peacefully and harmoniously, U Nu opted for a more confessional and exclusive policy on religion by applying cultural and religious assimilation as the core of the "nation-building" process. The revision of Aung San's version of the Union Constitution thus proved to be the end of his policy for a secular state and pluralism in Burma, which eventually led to the promulgation of Buddhism as the state religion of the Union of Burma in 1961.

For the Chin and other non-Burman nationalities, the promulgation of Buddhism as the "state religion of the Union of Burma" in 1961 was the

---

[10] Hugh Tinker, Union of Burma (London, Government Printing. 1957), p 13

greatest violation of the Panglong Agreement in which Aung San and the leaders of the non-Burman nationalities agreed to form a Union based on the principle of equality. They therefore viewed the passage of the state religion bill not only as religious issue, but also as a constitutional problem, in that this had been allowed to happen. In other words, they now viewed the Union Constitution as an instrument for imposing "a tyranny of majority", not as their protector. Thus, the promulgation of Buddhism as the state religion of Burma became not a pious deed, but a symbol of the tyranny of the majority under the semi-unitary system of the Union Constitution.

There were two different kinds of reaction to the state religion reforms from different non-Burman nationalities. The first reaction came from more radical groups who opted for an armed rebellion against the central government in order to gain their political autonomy and self-determination. The most serious armed rebellion as a direct result of the adoption of Buddhism as the state religion was that of the Kachin Independence Army, which emerged soon after the state religion of Buddhism bill was promulgated in 1961. The "Christian Kachin", as Graver observes, "saw the proposal for Buddhism to be the state religion as further evidence of the Burmanization [*Myanmarization*] of the country,"[11] which they had to prevent by any means, including an armed rebellion. The Chin rebellion, led by Hrang Nawl, was also related to the promulgation of Buddhism as the state religion, but the uprising was delayed until 1964 owing to tactical problems. Thus, the Chin rebellion was mostly seen as the result of the 1962 military coup, rather than the result of the promulgation of Buddhism as the state religion in 1961.

The second reaction came from more moderate groups, who opted for constitutional means of solving their problems, rather than an armed rebellion. The most outstanding leader among these moderate groups was Sao Shwe Thaike of Yawnghwe, a prominent Shan *Sawbwa,* who was elected as the first President of the Union of Burma. Although a devout Buddhist, he strongly opposed the state religion bill because he saw it as a violation of the Panglong Agreement. As a president of the Supreme Council of United Hills People

---

[11] Mikael Graver, Nationalism as Political Paranoia in Burma (Copenhagen: NIAS 1993), p. 56

(SCOUHP), formed during the Panglong Conference, he invited leaders of not only the Chin, Kachin and Shan, the original members of the SCOUHP, but also other non-Burman nationalities ⁻ the Karen, Kayah, Mon, and Rakhine (Arakan) ⁻ to Taunggyi, the capital of Shan State, to discuss constitutional problems. Unfortunately, these problems still remain unsolved. The conference was attended by 226 delegates and came to be known as the 1961 Taunggyi Conference, and the movement itself was known later as the Federal Movement.

At the Taunggyi Conference, all delegates, except three who belonged to U Nu's party,[12] agreed to amend the Union Constitution based on Aung San's draft, which the AFPFL convention had approved in May 1947. At the AFPFL convention, Aung San had asked, "Now when we build our new Burma shall we build it as a Union or as Unitary State? In my opinion, he answered, "it will not be feasible to set up a Unitary State". He strongly argues that "we must set up a Union with properly regulated provisions to safeguard the right of the national minorities".[13] According to Aung San's version of the constitution, the Union would be composed of ethnic national states, or what he called "Union States" such as the Chin, Kachin, Shan and Burman States and other ethnic national states such as Karen, Karenni (Kayah), Mon and Rakhine (Arakan) States. The "original idea", as Dr. Maung Maung observes, "was that the Union States should have their own separate constitutions, their own organs of state, *viz.* Parliament, Government and Judiciary". [14]

U Chan Htun had reversed all these principles of a Federal Union after Aung San was assassinated. According to U Chan Htun's version of the Union Constitution, Burma Proper or the ethnic Burman/Myanmar did not form their own separate ethnic national state; instead they combined the power of the Burman/Myanmar ethnic national state with sovereign authority of the whole Union of Burma. Thus, while one ethnic group, the Burman/ Myanmar, controlled the sovereign power of the Union, that is, legislative,

---

[12] Those three delegates who did not agree to the idea of a federal Union were Za Hre Lian (Chin), Aye Soe Myint (Karen), and Sama Duwa Sinwanaung (Kachin).

[13] Aung San, Burma's Challenge (Rangoon, 1947), reprinted in Josef Silverstein, The Political Legacy of Aung San, (New York: Cornell University Press, 1993)

[14] Maung Maung , Burma's Constitution (The Hague, 1959), p. 170.

judiciary, and administrative powers of the Union of Burma; the rest of the ethnic nationalities who formed their own respective ethnic national states became almost like "vassal states" of the ethnic Burman or Myanmar. This constitutional arrangement was totally unacceptable to the Chin, Kachin and Shan who had signed the Panglong Agreement on the principle of equality, a view that was shared by the other nationalities.

They therefore demanded at the 1961 Taunggyi Conference the amendment of the Union Constitution and the formation of a genuine Federal Union composed of ethnic national states, with the full rights of political autonomy, i.e., legislative, judiciary and administrative powers within their own ethnic national states, and self-determination including the right of secession. They also demanded separation between the political power of the ethnic Burman/Myanmar national state and the sovereign power of the Union, i.e., the creation of a Burman or Myanmar ethnic national state within the Union.[15]

The second point they wanted to amend on the Union Constitution was the structure of the Chamber of Nationalities. The original idea of the creation of the Chamber of Nationalities was that it was not only to safeguard the rights of non-Burman nationalities but also the symbolic and real equality envisaged at the Panglong Conference. Thus, what they wanted was that each ethnic national state should have the right to send equal representatives to the Chamber of Nationalities, no matter how big or small their ethnic national state might be. In other words, they wanted a kind of Upper House similar to the American Senate.

But what had happened, based on U Chan Htun's Union Constitution, was that while all the non-Burman nationalities had to send their tribal or local chiefs and princes to the Chamber of Nationalities; it allowed Burma Proper to elect representatives to the Chamber of Nationalities based on population. Thus, the Burman or Myanmar from Burma Proper, who composed the majority in terms of population, was given domination of the Union Assembly.

---

[15] See Documents of Taunggyi Conference, 1961 (Rangoon: Published by the SCOUP, 1961) in Burmese.

In this way, the Union Assembly, according to U Chan Htun's version of the Union Constitution, was completely under the control of the Burman or Myanmar ethnic nationality. Not only did the powerful Chamber of Deputies have the power to thwart aspirations and the interests of non-Burman nationalities, but the Burmans also dominated the Chamber of Nationalities. That was the reason why the total votes of non-Burman nationalities could not block the state religion bill even at the Chamber of Nationalities. Thus, all the non-Burman nationalities now viewed the Union Constitution itself as an instrument for imposing "a tyranny of majority" and not as their protector. They therefore demanded a change from such constitutional injustice at the 1961 Taunggyi Conference.[16] Therefore, the Federal Movement and the Taunggyi Conference can be viewed, as noted by Shan scholar Chao Tzang Yawnghwe, as "a collective non-Burman effort to correct serious imbalances inherent in the constitution" of 1947. [17]

In response to the demand of the 1961 Taungyi Conference, U Nu had no choice but to invite all the political leaders and legal experts from both Burman and non-Burman nationalities to what became known as the "Federal Seminar" at which "the issues of federalism and the problems of minorities would be discussed with a view to finding a peaceful solution".[18] The meeting opened on 24 February 1962 in Rangoon while parliament was meeting in regular session. But before the seminar was concluded and just before U Nu was scheduled to speak, the military led by General Ne Win seized state power in the name of the Revolutionary Council. In the early morning of 2 March 1962, he arrested all the non-Burman participants of the Federal Seminar and legally elected cabinet members, including U Nu himself, dissolved parliament, suspended the constitution and thus ended all debate on federal issues.

In this way, U Nu's great hope of a Buddhist state religion as the unifying identity of the Union of Burma proved to be one of the decisive dividing factors that led to his own defeat and the end of the parliamentary

---

[16] See Documents of Taunggyi Conference, 1961 (in Burmese).

[17] Yawnghwe, Chao Tzang, "The Burman Military", in Josef Silverstein (ed.), Independent Burma at Forty Years: Six Assessments (Cornell University, 1989), pp. 81-101.

[18] Silverstein, Josef (1981) "Minority Problems in Burma Since 1962", in Lehman (ed.,), Military Rule in Burma Since 1962 (Singapore, 1981), p. 51.

experiment in Burma. Buddhism, which used to be a vital source of political legitimacy for traditional Burmese kingship, could no longer provide the values needed to create a modern Burmese national identity in the multi-ethnic, multi-religious and multi-cultural plural society of the Union of Burma.

Ne Win's National Language Policy, Scorched Earth Campaign, and Militarization of the State

Since the independence movement, "nationalism" had been an enduring element of the Burmese concept of political legitimacy, the "*sine qua non* of political life*", as Steinberg so aptly puts it. As we have seen, U Nu apparently mixed nationalism with Buddhism in his attempt to legitimize his government. General Ne Win, on the other hand, mixed nationalism with socialism, and he also used military leadership as a means to introduce socialism into the country.

Nationalism, for both U Nu and Ne Win, was simply based on the notion of "one ethnicity, one language, one religion", that is., the *Myanmar-lumyo* or Myanmar ethnicity, *Myanmar-batha-ska* or Myanmar language, and the *Myanmar-thatana* of Buddhism. Although their approaches to ethnic and religious "forced-assimilation" were different, U Nu and Ne Win both had the same goal of creating a homogeneous people in the country. While U Nu opted for cultural and religious assimilation into Buddhism as a means of "forced-assimilation", Ne Win removed the rights of the country's religious and cultural minorities, especially minority's language right, as a means of creating a homogeneous unitary state, under the motto of "one voice, one blood, and one nation", and adopted the "national language policy" as a means of ethnic "forced assimilation". U Nu and Ne Win thus complemented each other, although their approaches in depriving cultural and religious minorities of their rights were different in nature.

The elimination process of ethnic rights began with the promulgations of the 1962 Printers and Publishers Registration Law and the 1965 Censor Law. As these two laws made stumbling blocks for the publications of ethnic languages, including the curriculums and teaching materials for both secular schools and Sunday Schools, the Chin and other ethnic nationalities in Burma were unable to promote their language under the military dictatorship. Since the basic rights to promote the non-Burman/Myanmar languages, cultures and belief systems were severely curtailed, the incentive for preserving, protecting and promoting through teaching, learning, writing, circulating, practicing and propagating of their own languages, cultures and religions has become a life and death matter for the Chin and other ethnic communities in Burma. This is a life and death matter because the survival of ethnic nationalities in Burma as distinctive peoples who practice different cultures, speak different languages, and worship different religions, depends so much on whether they are able to preserve, protect and promote their ways of life as fundamental rights.

Accumulation from the 1962 Printers and Publishers Registration Law, the 1965 Censor Law, and the 1966 Revolutionary Council's decree, which declared the *Myanmar-batha-ska* or *Maynmar-sa* as the medium of instruction at all levels of schools, colleges and universities; General Ne Win's national language policy finally reached its peak when the 1974 Constitution was promulgated, which adopted the *Myanmar-batha-ska* as the *official language* of the Union of Burma. Although, ethnic languages were allowed to use for the communication purpose between the central government and ethnic states, as stated in Article 198, no mechanisms or institutions were provided to preserve, protect and promote ethnic languages. Since the highest law of the land allowed the existence of the *Myanmar-batha-ska* as the only "official language", the rest of the ethnic languages, including the Chin and its various dialects, were legally "unofficial" and therefore could be discriminated against "legitimately" in various means by using all kind of state mechanisms and existing laws.

General Ne Win, in fact, deployed the *Tatmadaw* to implement his "national language policy" as part of the military campaign against ethnic minority groups in the country under the "four-cut" strategy, which was implemented within the framework of "people's war doctrine" with the motto of "one voice, one blood, and one nation". Although he adopted the "national language policy" as a means of ethnic "forced-assimilation", Gen Ne Win thinly disguised this policy under the programme known as the "Burmese Way to Socialism" (BWS) as its "nation-building" process. In order to implement his BWS programme, General Ne Win established the "Burma Socialist Program Party" (BSPP), and used the armed forces, known as Tatmadaw, as the nucleus of "nation-building" not only by building the

Tatmadaw as a national institution and a state mechanism, but also by promoting members of the armed forces as the "the guardian of the people and protectors of the Union". As part of his ambitious to build an army state under the disguise of the need for a strong army that would prevent the Union from its collapsed, General Ne Win adopted the "people's war doctrine" as the military doctrine of the Tatmadaw in 1965, and formed hundreds of militia organizations all over the country, known as *Kar-Kwe-Ye* (KKY) in Burmese, and applied the "four-cut" strategy against ethnic armed groups.

The "four-cut" strategy was first practiced in 1966 but officially adopted as the Tatmadaw military's doctrine in 1968, which aims at "to cut food supply to the insurgents; to cut protection money from villagers to the insurgents; to cut contacts (information and intelligence) between people and the insurgents; and to make the people cut off the insurgent's head, that means, involving the people in fighting, particularly the encirclement of insurgents".[19]

The third aspect of the "four-cuts strategy" is directly linked with the "national language policy" of campaigning against ethnic nationalities; for this strategy is about to cut off people to people contact, information, and intelligence. I have argued elsewhere about the link between the "national language policy" and "four-cut strategy" as follows:

In order to cut "information" off in ethnic areas, successive military regimes in Burma have prohibited the publication of any information in ethnic languages. So, there is no independent newspaper, no independent radio station and no printing house for any ethnic language. This strategy is implemented hand in hand with the government policy of "national language": through which ethnic languages are systematically eliminated. While ethnic languages are systematically eliminated and even destroyed, the national language of *Myanmar-batha-ska*, the dominant Myanmar language, is protected and promoted by using state mechanisms. The regime as also forced the non-Myanmar or non-Burman ethnic nationalities to speak the

---

[19] Maung Aung Myoe (2009), Building the Tatmadaw: Myanmar Armed Forces (Singapore: Singapore Institute of Asian Studies, 2009), p 26

Myanmar-batha-ska at all the government's official functions and forced them to learn the *Myanmar-sa*, which is the only official language in the country.[20]

The national language policy was thus implemented hand in hand with the military campaign of the "four-cut strategy", which was also known as a "scorched earth" military campaign, in ethnic areas. While the "scorched earth" campaign was designed as a short-term strategy against ethnic nationalities in the country, the "national language policy" was adopted as a long-term strategy to build a "homogenous" country through a so called "nation-building" process.

In 1974, when the new constitution was promulgated, General Ne Win was able to fulfil his vision of building the army state, and the divisions between the state, the army, and the party (BSPP) ceased to exist. The army and the party were not only the supporting mechanisms and institutions of the state but part and parcel of the state because the state was meant to exist for the army and the party, and vice-versa. In this way, General Ne Win used the army (Tatmadaw) and the party (the BSPP) not only as a mechanism of building the army state with the notion of "one voice, one blood, one nation", but also as a means of building ethnically homogenous unitary state with the notion of "one religion, one language, one ethnicity". In the process of building ethnically homogenous army state, the fundamental rights of all citizens, political equality of ethnic nationalities, and internal self-determination for all member states of the Union are all eliminated. By eliminating cultural, religious and language rights of ethnic nationalities through the laws made by the BSPP in the name of the state, the notion of "unity in diversity" as "political values" ceased to exist in Burma.

The Ethnic Nationalities' Response to Constitutional Dictatorship and the 1988 Popular Uprising for Democracy

By the time the new constitution was promulgated in 1974, and General Ne Win became U Ne Win, the President of the Socialist Republic of the Union of Burma, all the ethnic nationalities in Burma had insurgent groups. Most

---

[20] Lian H Sakhong, In Defence of Identity: Ethnic Nationalities' Struggle for Democracy, Human Rights and Federalism in Burma (Bangkok: Orchid Press, 2010), p 193

notable of these were the Karen National Union (KNU), the Kachin Independent Organization (KIO), the Shan State Army (SSA), the New Mon State Party (NMSP), the Karenni National Progressive Party (KNPP), the Arakan Liberation Party (ALP) and the Chin Democracy Party (CDP). The Chin Democracy Party was founded by John Mang Tling, a former parliamentary secretary of the Union of Burma, who went underground and joined U Nu, who also went underground and formed the Parliamentary Democracy Party (PDP), and took up arms to overthrow General Ne Win's military regime in 1969.

The most effective reaction from the various ethnic nationalities to the promulgation of a new constitution in 1974 was undoubtedly the formation of the "Federal National Democratic Front" in 1975, which was eventually transformed into "the National Democratic Front" (NDF) in May 1976. The significance of the NDF was that it was formed exclusively by the non-Burman ethnic nationalities, with the aims and objectives of "the establishment of a genuine federal union, based on the principles of national self-determination, political equality and progress of all nationalities", declared its intention "to abolish national chauvinism, military bureaucratic dictatorship and the unitary system", and expressly ruled out a "one-party state".[21]

Despite the success of the "four-cut" campaign against communist insurgency led by the Communist Party of Burma (CPB) in the Delta and Pegu Yomas, the NDF members of ethnic nationalities, most notably, the KNU, KIO, and SSA were capable of controlling a vast areas in the respective regions as "liberated areas", as Martin Smith observes, and "they were well armed and trained and capable of out-fighting the *Tatmadaw* in conventional and guerrilla warfare", and "each could put several hundred troops into battle, if occasion demanded, before they retreating back into safe mountain strongholds". He continues:

> Buoyed by the booming black market and anti-government disaffection, many ethnic forces grew markedly in strength. Armed opposition controlled virtually the entire eastern borders of Burma, from the Tenasserim division in the south to the Kachin state in

---

[21] Khiang Soe Naing Aung , A Brief History of National Democratic Movement of Ethnic Nationalities (National Democratic Front, 2000), pp. 78–79.

the north. The three strongest ethnic forces, the KNU, KIO, and SSA, each maintained over 5,000 troops in the field and, and like the CPB's People's Army, were capable of fighting the Tatmadaw in the fixed positions of conventional war, which was vital for the defence of border strongholds and trading posts (Smith, 2007: 36).[22]

The black market taxation, one of the main financial sources for ethnic armed groups, ironically was sustained and prolonged by Ne Win's regime. Because of mismanagement, nationalization, centralized socialist economic policy, and isolationism, Burma was economically unable to sustain but relied on the black markets for its consumer goods that came from neighbouring countries crossing the borders that were controlled by ethnic armed groups: the Karen, Karenni, Mon, and Shan from the eastern borders of Thailand and China; the Kachin from northern borders of China, and Chin from the north-western borders of India, and Arakan from western borders of Bangladesh. Viewing that ethnic armed groups had controlled all the black markets, which in turn influenced the financial markets, Ne Win's once again applied the "four-cut" strategy, this time "to cut off the financial resources" to ethnic armed groups. He thus announced the demonetization of the country's three highest denominations of banknotes: Kyats 25, 50 and 100, on 5 September 1987. The government openly admitted that the demonetization was aimed at "insurgents and black marketers".[23]

The regime's four-cut strategy missed its target this time. The ethnic armed groups, who never trusted the regime in Rangoon, were "chiefly based in border areas and kept most of their funds in Thai or Chinese [or Indian] currency".[24] The black marketers might have suffered temporarily but they were able to make up for the loss after a few more trade deals. The ones who suffered the most were the ordinary people, who lost their saving. It was estimated that "sixty to eighty per cent of all the money in circulation in Burma had become worthless, in one sweep".[25] The announcement came at a time when the final exams were approaching for

[22] Martin Smith, State of Strife: The Dynamics of Ethnic Conflict in Burma, p.36
[23] Bertil Lintner, Burma in Revolt, (Chiang Mai: Silkworm Books,1999), p 338
[24] Ibid
[25] Ibid

the students at Rangoon University and Rangoon Institute of Technology, and "there was a spontaneous outburst of violence minutes after the announcement had been made".[26] The student demonstrations spread to several campuses but the government responded swiftly by closing all the universities and colleges in the country.

The schools were reopened a month later but closed again in March 1988, when a brawl in a tea shop, which led to the death of a student at the hands of the Police, resulted in violent campus wide disturbances. The government responded once again by closing all the universities and in an attempt to calm the situation promised an inquiry. Believing the environment to be more stable, universities were reopened in June. However, violence once more broke out at the failure of the government to bring to justice those responsible for the student's death. Unrest soon spread nationwide and martial law was declared. A general strike on the 8th of August 1988 was bloodily suppressed with thousands of demonstrators and students gunned down in the streets. On the 18th September student led demonstrations were once again brutally crushed and soon gave way to an army staged coup, but it was only after Ne Win resigned from his combined-post as the head of the state and the Chairman of the Burma Socialist Program Party (BSPP).

In final analysis, Ne Win's policy of imposing ethnic "forced-assimilation" through the "nation-building" process with the notion of "one religion, one language, and one ethnicity", especially when his "national language policy" was combined with the "scorched earth" campaign against ethnic nationalities, proved to be one of the main factors that brought him down after 27 years in power.

The New Regime's Policy of Forced-Assimilation, Myanmarization, and Militarization

In 1989, the new military regime, known as the 'State Law and Order Restoration Council' (SLORC), under the leadership of General Saw Maung, announced that the country's name be changed from "Burma" to "Myanmar". The change of the country name from "Burma" to "Myanmar" indeed was the highest level of enforcing ethnic forced-assimilation through the "nation-

---

[26] Ibid

building" process with the unitary version of "one religion, one language, and one ethnicity".

The term "Myanmar", indeed, refers exclusively to one particular ethnic group in the country, while the term "Burma" refers to a post-colonial multi-ethnic, multi-religious, and multi-culture plural nation-state of the Union of Burma. Ever since the first Myanmar Kingdom of the Pagan dynasty was founded by King Annawrattha in 1044, the term "Myanmar" has been used to denote the ethnicity of Myanmar, which is in turn inseparably intertwined with Buddhism, as the saying goes: *Buddabata Myanmar Lu-myo* (broadly, the implication is that to be "Myanmar" is to be Buddhist). The Myanmar Kingdom from the beginning of Pagan Dynasty in 1044 to the end of Kungbaung Dynasty in 1885 was nothing to do with the Chin and other ethnic groups, who joined together in a union, the Union of Burma, in 1947 on the principle of equality. The term Myanmar, therefore, does not include the Chin, Kachin, Shan, and other nationalities who became the members of the Union only after signing the Panglong Agreement.[27]

The regime's political objective is clear: the implementation of ethnic forced assimilation through the "nation-building" process, and the establishment of a homogeneous country of *Myanmar Ngaing-ngan,* with the notion of one ethnicity of *Myanmar-lumyo*, one language of *Myanmar-batha-ska*, and one religion of *Buddha-bata* or a state religion of Buddhism. They argue, however, that the Tatmadaw is the only patriotic institution that is capable of implementing the "nation-building" process, or what Sr. General Than Shwe called "national reconsolidation". As stated as one of its main objectives of the national convention, the armed forces will "participate in the national political leadership role of the state", meaning: no government in Burma would be formed without the participation of and the leading role taken by the Tatmadaw.

Soon after its came to power, the SLORC abolished the 1974 Constitution, together with the Pyitthu Hluttaw, but promised a new election which was eventually held in May 1990. To participate in the election the

---

[27] It might in parenthesis be noted that there is controversy over the use of the terms Myanmar, Bama, Burman, and Burmese, revolving around the question about whether the terms are inclusive (referring to all citizens of the Union) or exclusive (referring only to the Burmese-speakers).

BSPP changed its name to the "National Unity Party" (NUP) and also began to canvass. However, it soon became evident that the NUP was losing to the "National League for Democracy" (NLD), especially due to the popularity of Daw Aung San Suu Kyi. After slanderous attacks on her in the media had failed, the government had both Aung San Suu Kyi and U Tin Oo arrested on the 19th July 1989. Despite the fact that two of its main leaders were under house arrest and disqualified, the National League for Democracy was still able to win 392 (80%) of the 485 seats. The military-backed party, the National Unity Party (NUP), won only 10 seats (2%). The balance of power was held by the ethnic parties, the United Nationalities League for Democracy (UNLD) – 67 seats (16%) and 10 independents (2%).

Despite the party's clear victory, the SLORC refused to hand over power to the NLD claiming that a constitution needed to be drafted first. The NLD and the newly formed United Nationalities League for Democracy (UNLD), an umbrella group of ethnic party representatives, issued a joint statement calling on the State Law and Order Restoration Council (SLORC) to convene the Pyithu Hluttaw in September, 1990. Despite such calls the SLORC refused to honour the election result and instead sought to hold on to power claiming that a National Convention would need to be convened to write a new constitution. After two years of political impasse, and with members of the NLD still in jail or under house arrest, the SLORC announced, on the 23rd of April 1992, that it would hold a National Convention, which was eventually convened in 1993.

After 14 years of deliberation and several sessions, constant suspensions and reopening, the National Convention was concluded on the 3rd of September 2007. On the 9th of February 2008, the SPDC stated that a National Referendum to adopt the constitution would be held in May 2008. In spite of the fact that Cyclone Nargis struck the country on the 2nd and 3rd of May 2008 causing widespread devastation, the regime insisted on continuing with its plan to hold the referendum, except for a few townships where the destruction occurred most, on the 10th of May 2008. The regime announced that the draft Constitution had been overwhelmingly approved by 92.4 per cent of the 22 million eligible voters, stating that there had been a turnout of more than 99 per cent.

In order to build a homogeneous nation-state of *Myanmar Ngain-ngan*, in which the military will take the leading role in national politics, the 2008 Constitution was designed in such a way that the armed forces would remain above the law and be independent from the government, and, therefore, would dominate and control the three branches of political power. To control the legislative power at both the Union and State and Regional Assemblies, the 2008 Constitution reserves 25 percent of the seats in all legislative chambers for the military personnel's. In this way, according to the 2008 Constitution, a total of 386 military personnel will be appointed as lawmakers; (110 out of 440 seats for lower house; 56 out of 224 seats for upper house; and 220 out of 883 seats for 7 states, 7 regions and 3 autonomous regions).

The executive power of the state, according to the 2008 Constitution, will be totally under the control of the armed forces. The President and two Vice-presidents, who are the head of the state and represent the country, will be elected not by the public but by the Presidential Electoral College, consisting of three groups of parliamentarians: upper house, lower house and military appointed lawmakers. Each group will nominate one candidate for the presidency. Members of the Electoral College will then vote for one of the three to become president. The candidate with the most votes takes the top job and the unsuccessful candidates will become vice-presidents. All will serve five year terms. In this way, the military constitution has by-passed the public in presidential election process, but guaranteed the armed forces, as decision makers, participation in the highest level of national politics. In addition to the 386 military personnel already appointed as lawmakers, the Commander-in-Chief of the Defense Service will appoint three generals as ministers of defense, the interior and border affairs. The president can also select military officers to head other ministries. Armed forces members serving in government, parliamentary or civil service roles accused of a crime will be tried by a military court martial court rather than a judicial one.

The 2008 Constitution creates a powerful body, the "National Defense and Security Council", consisting of 11- member committee tasked with making key decisions. While the president will serve as the Chairman, military personnel will occupy five of the 11 places on the National Defense and Security Council. In this way, the armed forces will control the decision making process at a political body which is granted the right to declare "state of emergency". The "state of emergency" in the 2008 Constitution, unlike a democratic constitution, is a mechanism created for the armed forces to control the state. Through the right to declare "state of emergency" the highest law of the land granted the chief of armed forces the right to take over the state power, or the constitutional right of a military coup. With presidential approval, the armed forces chief can assume sovereign power and declare a state of emergency, with full legislative, executive and judicial power. In this way, the armed forces will remain above the laws and control the state.

After making sure that the domination of the military in the new government was properly designed in the new constitution, which was eventually approved by using all available state mechanisms and military might through the national referendum in 2008, new general elections were held in November 2010, and installed a new military-dominant-civilian-government in March 2011.

Concluding Remarks

As the military regime had accelerated its seven-step roadmap since 2004, tensions between ethnic armed groups and the Burma Army, Tatmadaw, have intensified. As the tension has increased, ethnic armed groups from both ceasefire and non-ceasefire groups have discussed joint cooperation should the SPDC launch an offensive against them. In May 2010, the first meeting between the two sides of ethnic armed groups, ceasefire and non-ceasefire, was held. At the second meeting in September 2010, they jointly formed a committee, the "Committee for the Emergence of a Federal Union" (CEFU), comprising three ceasefire groups: KIO, NMSP, and SSA-N (Shan State Army-North), and three non-ceasefire groups: KNU, KNPP (Karenni National Progressive Party), and CNF (Chin National Front).

In February 2011, CEFU was transformed into the "United Nationalities' Federal Council" (UNFC). As the "committee" is transformed to the "council" its members increased, from 6 to 12 armed groups with approximately 20,000 troops; and supported its formation process by the Ethnic Nationalities Council (ENC), which is a political alliance of all ethnic nationalities from seven ethnic states. The ENC and UNFC are committed to collaboration on political and military matters with the final objective of achieving a genuine federal union of Burma. This has been a solid work in progress over the last decade. The UNFC issued a statement soon after it was formed, and urged the international community "to force the Burma Army to negotiate with the ethnic nationalities in order to find a political solution". They also declared in the statement that "we will wage unconventional warfare until the Burma Army negotiates."[28]

The formation of the UNFC, similar to the formation of the NDF in 1976, indicates that so long as the government practices the policy of ethnic forced-assimilation in the name of "nation-building" process, there will always be strong reactions from ethnic armed groups, as Nai Han Tha, General Secretary of UNFC, recently said, "we can continue our struggle for another sixty years" (Radio Free Asia, 11 Sept 2011). Sixty years of ethnic armed conflicts and civil war have proved that the policy of ethnic forced-assimilation through the "nation-building" process with the notion of "one religion, one language, and one ethnicity" is unsuitable for multi-ethnic, multi-religious, and multi-cultural countries like the Union of Burma. The Myanmar ethno-nationalism with the motto of *"Amyo, Batha, Thatana"*, which serves as the foundation for enforcing the policy of ethnic forced-assimilation into *Buddha-bata Myanmar-lumyo*, has always been confronted by strong reactions from the Arakan, Chin, Kachin, Karen, Kerenni, Mon, Shan and other ethnic nationalities.

Unfortunately, both the government's policy of ethnic forced-assimilation and the ethnic nationalities reactions of holding arms are not the solution for Burma. Such practices and reactions have resulted only in the militarization of the country, on the one hand, and "insurgency as a ways of life" in ethnic areas, on the other. What the Union of Burma as a multi-cultural plural society needs is not "nation-building" but "state-building", not a centralized unitary state but a decentralized federal union, not an army state but an open society where many different ethnic groups who speak different languages, practice different cultures, and follow different religious teachings can live peacefully together.

---

[28] UNFC's Statement, on 17 February 2011.

Contributors

Dr Geeta Madhavan is an Attorney with specialisation in International Law and a consultant to academic departments that feature International Relations programmes. She is Visiting Faculty of Tamil Nadu Dr. Ambedkar Law University. She holds a PhD with doctoral thesis on Terrorism and International law. Her areas of interest include international security and terrorism and has published several articles on issues of strategic security matters. She is a Founder Member of Centre for Security Analysis.

Mr B G Verghese is a columnist, author and currently Visiting Professor at the Centre for Policy Research, New Delhi. He is Chairman of the Commonwealth Human Rights Initiative and Fellow, Administrative Staff College of India, Hyderabad. He received the Magsaysay Award for Journalism in 1975. He has served on a number of official and non-official commissions, committees and boards and is a member of the Track II Indo-Pakistan Neemrana Initiative. He has authored several books on issues relating to water resources, the Northeast, Asian geo-politics and the media.

Dr Rekha Chowdhary is Dean, Academic Research, University of Jammu. Her area of interest is Politics and Society of Jammu and Kashmir. She has been specifically focusing on varied dimensions of conflict analysis particularly ethnicity, religion, models of nation building and political economy.

Dr Nani Gopal Mahanta is an Associate Professor, Department of Political Science and Coordinator, Peace and Conflict Studies, Guwahati University. His areas of interest are Peace and Conflict in South Asia and Human Rights. He has extensively written on conflicts in Northeast India.

Dr Samir Kumar Das is a Professor of Political Science, University of Calcutta and Research Coordinator, Calcutta Research Group (CRG). He specializes in and writes on issues of ethnicity, security, migration, rights and justice.

Mr Uddhab Pyakurel is a lecturer in Kathmandu University and political analyst. He writes on the conflict related issues of Nepal.

Mr Chiran J Thapa holds Masters Degree in International Affairs (MIA) with a specialization in international security policy, UN studies and conflict resolution from Columbia University, New York and Bachelors Degree in International Relations from State University, New York. His research interests include national security, civil-military relations, security sector reform including Disarmament, Demobilization and Reintegration.

Prof K Tudor Silva is a Professor of Sociology at the University of Peradeniya, Sri Lanka. He has more than 30 years of experience in teaching and research in Sri Lanka and abroad. His field of expertise include Development Sociology, Poverty Analysis, Social Mobilisation, Conflict Analysis, Relief, Rehabilitation and Resettlement. He has several publications to his credit.

Prof Jayadeva Uyangoda is prominent political scientist and constitutional expert in Sri Lanka. He is presently Head of the Department of Political Science and Public Policy at the University of Colombo and Founder-Director of the Centre for Policy Research and Analysis, Colombo. He has written extensively on Sri Lanka's conflict and peace processes. Active in civil society movements, he has been a leading advocate of a negotiated settlement to the ethnic conflict and federalist state reforms in Sri Lanka.

Dr Lian Sakhong Research Director of Euro-Burma Office, Brussels, is also the Chairman of "Chin National Council" (CNC), and the Vice-Chairman of the "Ethnic Nationalities Council - Union of Burma" (ENC). He has published several books and numerous articles on Chin history, traditions and politics in Burma and was awarded the Martin Luther King Prize in January 2007.

CSA Publications

Books

Conflict Resolution and Peace Building

1. Conflict Resolution and Peace Building in Sri Lanka

2. Federalism and Conflict Resolution in Sri Lanka

3. Peace Process in Sri Lanka: Challenges & Opportunities

4. Conflict over Fisheries in the Palk Bay Region

5. Conflict in Sri Lanka: The Road Ahead

6. Peace and Conflict Resolution: Emerging Ideas

7. From Winning the War to Winning Peace: Post War Rebuilding of the Society in Sri Lanka

8. Internal Conflicts in Myanmar: Transnational Consequences

9. Internal Conflicts in Nepal: Transnational Consequences

10. The Naxal Threat: Causes, State Responses and Consequences

11. Conflict in Sri Lanka: Internal and External Consequences

12. Conflicts in North-East: Internal and External Effects

13. Conflict in Jammu and Kashmir: Impact on Polity, Society and Economy

14. Post Conflict Sri Lanka- Rebuilding of the Society

15. Internal Conflicts: Military Perspectives

Security Studies

16. US and the Rising Powers: India and China

17. Maritime Security in the Indian Ocean Region: Critical Issues in Debate

18. Public Perceptions of Security in India: Results of a National Survey

19. Essential Components of National Security

20. Economic Growth and National Security

21. Security Dimensions of India and Southeast Asia

22. India & ASEAN: Non-Traditional Security Threats

23. Emerging Challenges to Energy Security in the Asia Pacific

24. Security Dimensions of Peninsular India

25. Socio-Economic Security of Peninsular India

Civil Society and Governance

26. Civil Society and Governance in Modern India

27. Civil Society in Conflict Situations

28. Civil Society and Human Security: South & Southeast Asian Experiences

Bulletins

1. Nuclear Terrorism and Counter Proliferation: Issues and Concerns; After the Afghanistan and Iraq Wars: Perspectives from the US; Indo-Pak Relation: Limited War to Limited Peace?

2. Unconventional Weapons and Threats of Accidents and Terrorism; The Stability- Instability Paradox: South Asia and the Nuclear Future; Post 9/11: New Research Agenda?; The US and India: Divergent and Convergent Interests

3. Conflict Prevention and Peace Building

4. Indo-Japan Relations; Independent Police Complaints Commission; Brief on the Seminar on Security Dimensions of Peninsular India

5. Proceedings of the Seminar on Proliferation Security Initiative

6. Proceedings of the Seminar on Women and Legal Security

7. Political Islam: Image and Reality; UK and India on the World Stage

8. Proceedings of the Seminar on Women and Comprehensive Security

9. Global Nuclear Weapon Prospects; India-Pakistan Peace Process Dividends

10. Security Perspectives from Pakistan; Indo-US Relations: Changing Perceptions

11. Sri Lankan Peace Process: Current Status; Sri Lanka Today: Policy Challenges and Dilemmas

12. Religion, Civil Society & Governance

13. Politics of the Nuclear Deal and the US-India Relations

14. India –US Relations; Japan India Partnership in the New Asian Strategic Dynamism

15. Environmental Security; National and International Security in the Context of Globalization and Economic Prosperity; India, East and Southeast Asia: Security Dimensions

16. India-EU Relations

17. India-Japan Strategic Partnership; India-UK Economic and Business Partnership.

18. Right to Information

19. A Sustainable Future: India and Britain Working Together; India and Africa: Issues of Globalization and Development

20. New Initiatives in Nuclear Disarmament; Preventing Nuclear Proliferation and Nuclear Terrorism;Nuclear Fuel SupplyAssurances

21. The Economic Cost of the War in Sri Lanka; Peace Process in Sri Lanka; The Sri Lankan Diaspora: The Way Forward

22. Nuclear Deterrence and Disarmament

23. Naxalism: Threat to Internal Security; Ethno-Political Situation in India's Northeast.

24. Japan and Asian Security; India as a Superpower.

25. India's Water Relations with her Neighbours